Rabbi Joseph B. Soloveitchik

Man of Halacha, Man of Faith

Rabbi Joseph B. Soloveitchik

Man of Halacha, Man of Faith

edited by

Menachem D. Genack

Ktav Publishing House

Library of Congress Cataloging-in-Publication Data

Rabbi Joseph B. Soloveitchik: man of Halacha, man of faith / edited by Menachem D. Genack.

p. cm.

Includes bibliographical references.

ISBN 0-88125-612-9

1. Soloveitchik, Joseph Dov. 2. Rabbis—United States—Biography. 3. Jewish scholars—United States—Biography. 4. Orthodox Judaism. I. Genaḳ, Menaḥem Dov ben Ḥayim Yitsḥak.

BM755.S6144R33 1998
296.8'32'092—dc21 98-11558
[B] CIP

Manufactured in the United States of America
Ktav Publishing House
527 Empire Blvd. Brooklyn, NY 11225
www.ktav.com | orders@ktav.com
(718) 972-5449

Contents

Dedication

IT IS THE EVENING OF THE THIRD OF *SHEVAT*, the *yahrtseit of* the Rav's father, Rav Moshe, *zt"l*, and we are in Lamport Auditorium at Yeshiva University awaiting the arrival of the Rav to deliver his annual *Yahrtseit Shiur.* Some of us have been sitting for a few hours, having come early to obtain seats as close as possible to the Rav. The auditorium is now packed and overflowing. Suddenly, as if an electric current has run through the room, the entire audience, as one, rises: the Rav has arrived!

Sitting in front, we do not immediately see the Rav, for he enters from the rear, and must traverse the entire length of the auditorium to reach us. Everyone is standing, blocking our view; yet the feeling of his presence pervades the room. Finally, the Rav emerges from the crowd, walking briskly, manuscript in hand, steps onto the stage and sits down behind an empty table to begin the *shiur.*

Then the journey starts. The Rav, usually focusing on one or more *halakhot* of the *Rambam,* ticks off one question after another that reflect obvious difficulties in the *halakha*—at least they are obvious after the Rav sets them out in his clear, lucid and inimitable manner of exposition. Then, after developing each of his questions—superlative pedagogue that he is—he reviews in summary form all of them, to assure that we understand what the problems are that will now be clarified.

That phase of the *shiur* concluded, the Rav goes on to develop a concept—the *hiddush* of the *shiur*—traversing a plethora of passages in the *Talmud,* commentaries (mostly *Rishonim*), *Midrashim,* and others. We watch, listen, and many of us avidly write notes, trying to keep up with the Rav's rapid-fire delivery as he lays out the *hiddush,* brick by brick by brick, reconciling all the varied and seemingly contradictory texts.

Now that the foundation has been set and the text reconciliation completed, the Rav returns to the original series of questions. Each is repeated, and then almost summarily disposed of through application of the *hiddush,* one after the other, after the other. It is more than two hours later and the circuit has been completed; the first portion of the *shiur* is concluded.

The Rav now turns to the *agaddic* portion of the *shiur,* usually with a prefatory, albeit rhetorical, question—*"Ir vilt nach?* (Do you want more?)" The audience responds with a resounding "yes" as the Rav embarks on another two-hour *tour de force,* in his beautiful poetic Yiddish. We sit there entranced, swallowing every word. It is much more difficult now to take notes. In this portion of the *shiur,* we are overwhelmed, not only by the ideas and concepts being presented, but also by the beauty of the language, the choice and combination of words and phrases, the sheer poetry of the presentation, the masterful delivery and, of course, of course, the absolute brilliance of the speaker. We sit entranced; the *shiur* is entering the fifth hour. Finally, it is over. It takes us a while to return to reality, but, *perforce,* we return.

It was an unforgettable experience, one that we will carry with us the rest of our lives. We will relate this special privilege we lived through to our children and grandchildren, but we must acknowledge how ill-equipped we are to convey the feeling, the mood—indeed, the exhilaration—we felt at the time.

And all that is now history!

There are various customs surrounding the timing of setting up and unveiling the monument over a grave. In Jerusalem, the custom is to set the monument immediately after *shiva;* in many other places, the custom is to wait until after the first *yahrtseit.*

Rav Akiva Eiger explained the latter custom by pointing out that there is a generally accepted psychological phenomenon that the memory of a departed one fades after twelve months, so the monument is not needed as a remembrance until that point in time.

From time to time, the Rav would point out during the annual *Yahrtseit Shiur* that, contrary to this psychological principle, as the years had gone by, his longing for his father had not diminished; indeed, it had increased. What he would have given to have fifteen more minutes with his father to discuss some of the critical issues facing him!

What we would give to have fifteen minutes with the Rav, *moreinu verabbeinu, zt"l*! But all we have now are our memories. In dedicating this volume to him, we hope to hold on to those memories a bit longer, sharing them with those who were not privileged to learn with him directly, reminding those of us whose lives were directly shaped by him of our debt and gratitude.

Yehei zikhro barukh.

Julius Berman

Introduction

THE *ARON*, THE HOLY ARK, HAD TWO POLES, *badim* with which it was to be carried. Surprisingly, despite the divine design of the Temple, when the Ark was placed in the Holy of Holies, these two poles, which were never to be removed, were not completely contained within the cubits of the sacred chamber and therefore protruded into the curtain, the *parokhet* which separated the Holy from the Holy of Holies.

The Ark containing the Torah was cloistered in the secluded Holy of Holies, where no one, save the High Priest on *Yom Kippur,* may enter. This represents the pristine, unadulterated quality of the Torah. Above the Ark were the *keruvim,* the cherubs, with their childlike faces, representing the innocence and purity of Torah. Yet while the Torah must remain pure, undiluted and unchanging as the day when it was plucked from its heavenly abode to be given to man, it must leave the Sanctum Sanctorum to animate all of life outside the protected environment of the Holy of Holies. The *badim* represent the portability of Torah and its significance in all times, circumstances, places and areas of human endeavor. From its protected sacred quarters, the immutable Torah radiates sanctity and meaning to our ever changing lives. From its secluded private realm, which must be guarded and sheltered, the Torah bursts forth to the hurly-burly of the marketplace and public domain.

The Rav, Rabbi Joseph B. Soloveitchik, *zt"l*, represented in his life's work this dimension of the *Aron*. He protected the integrity of our traditions, both intellectual and practical, from all illicit incursions into the Holy of Holies. But he was not satisfied to live in an ivory tower, isolated from the contemporary scene, for that would have limited the impact, message, and thereby, the grandeur of Torah. He made Torah portable, relevant and alive even in the modern environment, far from the protected existence he had known as a child.

Our Rabbis (*B. Yoma* 54a) interpret the verse, "My beloved is unto me as a bag of myrrh, that lieth betwixt my breasts" (*Song of Songs* 1:13) as an allusion to the protrusion of the *badim* into the parochet. This represents the eternal, life-giving nourishment which the Torah grants us. So too, were we nourished by the richness of the Rav's personality and erudition, "as a nursing-father carrieth the suckling child unto the land which thou didst swear unto their father" (*Num.* 11:12).

When Rabbi Yehuda haNasi died, the bitter news was communicated with the metaphor that the Ark had been captured. Rabbi Yehuda, the author of the *Mishna* who saved Torah in a time of great transition, personified the Torah, the *Aron haKodesh*. Our own rebbe's brilliant life of commitment and devotion in times of great challenge is also personified by the *Aron*—the *Aron* with the *badim*.

This new volume is dedicated to the Rav's memory, and is, in small measure, reflective of the Rav's vast range. These articles are reprinted from *Tradition*, almost all from the special issue in memory of the Rav which I edited.

I want to thank the Rabbinical Council of America and TRADITION's editors, for affording me the opportunity of serving as editor of this volume. Special thanks to Dr. Joel B. Wolowelsky, without whose sage advice on many editorial and technical matters, this volume would not have been possible.

MENACHEM GENACK

The Rov

YITZCHAK TWERSKY

A PROFILE OF THE ROV *ZEKHER TSADDIK LIVROKHA* should include comments on his persona, his teaching and his influence. This would have been the appropriate way to introduce him, with love and reverence, during his lifetime and remains appropriate for a retrospective presentation. What follows is such a three-tiered introduction; ואם אשגה, ה' הטוב יכפר בעדי.

1.

To understand fully who this great man was and what he represented, it is necessary to recall that he was, first of all, a worthy heir of the *beit ha-Rav* (בית הרב), that most remarkable institution of modern Jewish life—vibrant, fascinating, invigorating, ennobling. The *beit ha-Rav*, sometimes referred to as *beit ha-malkhut*, (בית המלכות) was a focus of Jewish creativity and rabbinic leadership in Lithuania, and eventually in all Eastern Europe. *Beit ha-Rav* became synonymous with intensive, trail-blazing Torah scholarship, exemplary piety, and dedicated leadership. We know of many uninterrupted spiritually-aristocratic traditions in the last two or three centuries of Jewish history; it is fair to say that the *beit ha-Rav* in Lithuania is in many respects probably *sui generis*, really in a class

Rabbi Twersky, the Talner Rebbe זצ"ל*, was Nathan Littauer Professor of Hebrew Literature and Philosophy at Harvard University.*

by itself, the cradle of so much of Jewish life and learning in modern times. Rabbis of the *beit ha-Rav* were trusted mentors to countless members of the Jewish communities in Europe. People, learned and unlearned, rabbis and laymen, would refer to *beit ha-Rav "mit a tzitter"*, with deep reverence and great affection.

He was, I must add, *not only* a worthy, luminous heir of the illustrious *beit ha-Rav*, to which he frequently referred in his lectures and shiurim, for to this should be added the special individuating characteristics of Brisk, a simple place name that has been transformed into a complex of values, associations and ideals, a network of great achievements and lofty aspirations. Brisk became a code-word for conceptual precision and rigor in Torah study, laser-type analysis of and commentary on baffling passages or difficult themes, economy of expression and clarity of exposition, intellectual honesty together with intellectual boldness, strenuous discipline and disciplined sensitivity—all this as well as a pervasive tradition of *hesed*. *Rav hesed ve-emet*, abundant in goodness and truth, was an uplifting, enticing ideal and a remarkable, irresistible reality. Reb Hayyim's acts of *hesed* are legendary; the Rov's *hesed* was bountiful.

2.

The Rov was all this and more, because his glorious heritage was filtered through his unique personality, through the original constructs of his mind and heart, through that new entity formed by his majestic Torah learning together with his all-encompassing philosophic, scientific and humanistic education. We need to be precise: even his sovereign mastery of the traditional sources of halakah together with his creative control of aggadah, kabbalah, Jewish philosophy, Biblical exegesis, and the literature of hasidism would make his learning unique—how much more so with the catalytic addition of the other ingredients. To be sure, comprehensiveness, impressively wide-ranging learning, was always the lodestar of *gedole Yisrael*—it was assumed that rabbinic authorities had mastered the vast corpus of Torah teachings; however, his knowledge and range of associations in the universe of Torah and *hokhmah,* his erudition and creativity, his powers of analysis and interpretation, his insight and intuition represent a *special* kind of comprehensiveness. This needs to be recognized and underscored, for even apparently devoted students are not able to acknowledge the true dimensions of his uniqueness. As we shall note, it is easier—yet unpardonable—to reduce the extraordinary to the ordinary; this is the case even if the ordinary refers to recognized standards of intellectual-piritual greatness. There are differences even among the great and we need to free ourselves from routinized thinking in order to perceive and appreciate these differences. The Rambam already taught us that among the "causes of disagreement" is the fact that "man has in his nature a love of, and an inclination for, that to which he is habituated. For this reason also man is blind to the apprehension of the true realities. . . ."[1] It takes special effort and honest concentration to transcend conventions of perception and expression, to recognize something new and beautiful and authentic—something beautiful in its original mode and authentic force.

As for comprehensiveness, the Rov always taught that for Torah to be rich and repercussive, charming and challenging, timely and timeless, it must be comprehensive and commodious and dare not be compartmentalized or fragmented, shallow or routine. In *Kiddushin* 30a, our rabbis interpret *ve-shinnantam le-vanekha* (Deut. 6:7) rather strikingly: "Do not read *ve-shinnantam* but rather *ve-shilashtam.* A person should always divide his study time into three parts: a third should be devoted to Scripture (*Mikra*), a third to Mishnah and a third to Talmud." How are we to understand the transition from *ve-shinnantam* to *ve-shilashtam*? This is certainly not to be seen as just another application of the well-known *al-tikrei* principle, which is based upon a different vocalization of the same letters (e.g., *banayikh-bonayikh*); phonetics and semantics are intertwined in cases of *al-tikrei* in order to focus our attention on a new insight or novel inference. It appears that we have here a new conceptualization, a dynamic interpretation which underscores a basic principle and essential feature of Torah study. *Ve-shinnantam* means to have a clear, unobstructed grasp of the subject matter (*Torah*) in its entirety which may then be transmitted without hesitation, with zeal and accuracy, charm and authoritativeness. ושננתם (לבניך): שיהו דברי תורה .מחודדין בפיך. שאם ישאל לך אדם דבר, אל תגמגם ותאמר לו אלא אמור לו מיד ["You shall teach them . . .": that the words of the Torah should be 'sharp' in your mouth, so that if someone asks you something, do not stumble and then tell him, instead, tell him immediately.]*

This mode of teaching and transmission is attainable only if one has comprehensive scope and the ability to systematize; that is the thrust of *ve-shilashtam* as setting the groundwork for *ve-shinnantam*—study methodically so as to include everything (Mikra, Mishnah, Talmud [in which, according to the Rambam, philosophy is included]) and then you will be in a position to transmit Torah precisely and unfalteringly. Fragmentation often results in distortion.

At the beginning of *Hilkot Talmud Torah*, Rambam cites *ve-Shinnantam* when emphasizing the obligation to teach Torah to everyone—all students are perceived as sons—whereas he could have cited the verse ולמדתם אותם את בניכם. ["And you shall teach them to your sons."] He says: ולא בנו ובן בנו בלבד אלא מצוה על כל חכם וחכם מישראל ללמד את כל התלמידים אע״פ שאינן בניו. שנאמר ושננתם לבניך. בניך אלו תלמידיך. [Not just his son and grandson, but every sage of Israel is commanded to teach all students, although they are not his sons, as it says, "You shall teach them to your children": "Your children"—these are the students.] We must be attentive to the significance of this formulation.

It appears that there are in fact two levels of teaching: *limud*, teaching everyone something, on many different levels—a task which everyone is able to perform in one way or another; *shinun,*—teaching which requires finely-honed interpretive-expository skills

*The bracketed translations were provided by the editors.

and extensive knowledge, which only the sages have acquired. This explains the Maimonidean formulation which shifts from the commandment to teach one's children and grandchildren to the obligation incumbent upon every scholar to teach all the disciples even though they are not his children. In sum, *ve-shinnantam*, interpreted also as *ve-shilashtam*, underscores the lesson that the ideal fulfillment of the mitsvah of Talmud Torah (to study and to teach) hinges on lucid, systematic knowledge which is all-inclusive. Seen from this perspective, it is clear why Talmud Torah is a special, open-ended mitsvah which is fulfilled with different degrees of intensity and creativity by different people.[2]

The Rov's virtuosic-versatile teaching is a vigorous, persuasive illustration of the truth of this interpretation. His Torah is comprehensive and therefore sharp; it is systematic and therefore effusive; his fulfillment of the mitzvah reflects his individuality. He occupies a position in Torah teaching which is his and his alone.

3.

What needs to be emphasized repeatedly, and unequivocally, is his uniqueness. His extraordinary Torah erudition together with his wide-ranging general knowledge, his dazzling brilliance, lucid, compelling analysis, phenomenal originality (which did not tolerate the shallow or the commonplace), astonishing intuition, almost legendary preoccupation with Torah (even when drinking a cup of tea or crossing the street—as was pointed out by my son Reb Mosheh), uncompromising honesty, unfailing eloquence, deep-seated sensitivity and lyricism, carefully-crafted philosophy (or *hashkafah*), and overpowering charisma—all combined to shape a remarkable Torah personality, unlike others whom we knew. This is the concept and reality of "לא כן עבדי משה Not so my servant Moses" (Numbers 12:7). It is a cardinal principle that Mosaic prophecy is not only of a higher order but is intrinsically different, unique, generically and qualitatively incomparable. Failure to recognize that Moses was not just another prophet was, in the opinion of

Rambam, the error and sin of Miriam; she did not malign or slander her brother Moses but she, who was "older than he and had nurtured him on her knees and had put herself in jeopardy to save him," did not acknowledge his unique status and stature. She thought that he was like the other prophets. והיא לא דברה בגנותו אלא טעתה שהשותו לשאר הנביאים. [She did not speak of him disparagingly, she only erred in equating him with the other prophets.] Failure to discern precisely and acknowledge properly the true greatness of a person is part of "raillery and slander" (ליצנות ולשון הרע) according to Rambam. 3

Many years ago, the Rov mentioned to me with words of high praise an article on Rav Hayyim Brisker by Rav Meir Berlin in which the latter used the expressive, repercussive phrase לא כן עבדי משה to characterize Reb Hayyim vis a vis his contemporaries—indeed truly preeminent *gedole Yisrael,* whose light never dims. The point was that Reb Hayyim was unquestionably different even in this galaxy of great sages; routine praise, even if sincere, misses the mark.

The Rov subsequently used this same highly-charged phrase to portray his uncle the Brisker Rov and we may properly, with a full measure of intellectual rigor and accountability, honesty and discipline, apply it to the Rov. Let us listen to his words and learn from them:

> ובכל זאת, לא כן עבדי משה . . . הרב מבריסק הלא היה מופרד ומופרש מהם; שונה בדרכיו וארחותיו. התואר גדול הדור אינו הולמו ואינו מבטא את האופייני לו. היחיד שבדור או בחיר הדור היה. עולמו המחשבתי, השקפתו, חסידותו, מידותיו ופעולותיו אינם נתפסים במטבעות שטבעו הספדנים. ההספדים שנאמרו אחרי מיתתו והמאמרים שנכתבו עליו קיצצו כמיטת סדום את מקוריותו וייחודו של האיש הזה. במקום להביע את אשר היה האיש, נהיה הוא את אשר רצו הספדנים לומר עליו בכליהם הלשונים שכבר העלו חלודה.

> [Nevertheless, 'Not so My servant, Moses' . . . the Brisker Rov was separate and distinct from them; different in his ways and paths [of behavior]. The appellation, 'gadol ha-dor' (sage of the generation), does not suit him and does not express what was

unique about him. He was *sui generis* or 'the choicest of the generation.' His world of thought, *weltanschauung*, piety, character, and endeavors are not captured by the formulae employed by the eulogizers. The eulogies delivered after his passing, the articles written about him artificially and thoughtlessly truncated his originality and uniqueness. Instead of expressing what the man was, he became what the eulogizers wanted to say about him with their rusted linguistic tools.]

What could be more appropriate for us as we continue to think about the Rov and confront the challenging and daunting task of portraying him as he was and not as stereotyped phraseology or conventional plaudits would depict him, not as he would appear as the result of self-mirroring. We all know that language, imperfect to begin with, is debased; we find everywhere inflated rhetoric, meaningless hyperbole, sweeping generalization, unbalanced comparison, insipid stereotype, perfunctory praise. The leveling process casts its net even on truly great *hakhme Yisroel*; they are presented as if they were all alike—same youthful precocity, same Torah expertise, same piety, same kind of communal leadership. In this scheme there is no room for individuating characteristics. As for us,there is no fear of contradiction in saying simply and forthrightly—without any trace of posthumous flattery or eulogistic license—that the Rov was different: different in his teaching, different in his outlook, different in his style, different in his behavior, different in his charisma. Indeed, לא כן עבדי משה.[4]

The truth is that it is not really possible for anyone to say, without proper qualification, that the Rov was identical with his father and grandfather—great tribute that it is, this would be an example of a kind of oversimplification which impoverishes our spiritual-religious history. Of course, there were basic similarities and common features but equally evident is the fact that there were essential differences and individuating features. Juxtaposing the semikah given him by the Kovner Rav, Rabbi Avraham Shapiro, and the letter written about him by his father in 1935 is a good way of balancing and integrating judicious comparison to his ancestors with candid recognition of his own persona. The Kovner Rav underscored with passionate elegance the intellectual similarities between grandfather and grandson:

> נחה עליו רוח זקנו הארי החי הגדול שבחבורה... כמוהו מושל בים התלמוד עד עמקי תהומותיו, וכל רז לא אניס לי׳. מעלה נסתרות ומפענח נעלמות ובוקע נתיב אורה בהלכות העמומות.
>
> [The spirit of his grandfather, the greatest of his age, whose teachings are immortal, rests upon him . . . like him, he rules over the sea of Talmud to its uttermost depths, and no secret is hidden from him. He raises the hidden, deciphers the concealed, and illuminates obscure *halakhot*.]

His father readily and emphatically acknowledged the unique endowment of his son—his unique talents together with his unique training, his erudition coupled with his analytical skills, his mastery of halakhah and of Jewish thought, his great creativity in the study of Torah and philosophy. The father introduces the son, whom he describes as having been a youthful prodigy and a distinguished philosophy student, in a way that allows his radiant persona to shine forth; he focuses on the fact that the diverse resources converge to emphasize the Rov's preeminence in knowledge and understanding of Torah.

After emphasizing his son's fame (תורתו וחכמתו הלכה לפניו והכריזה עליו) [His Torah and wisdom have preceded and heralded him.] and highlighting the fact that he is really *sui generis* (הוא מין בפ״ע שצריך התכוננות מיוחדה, תכשיט לעם הישראלי) [He is in a class of his own, who requires special preparation [in order to be appreciated], a jewel for the Jewish nation.], he writes as follows concerning the Rov's unique achievement:

> בדורות הקודמים ד׳מו שא׳ אפשר במציאות להיות תורה ושארי חכמות משולבים יחד. אמנם בדור זה כבר פוגשים תורה וחכמה מחוברים. אבל באופן הזה גדול הדור בתורה באופן מבהיל.

> כאחד מגדולי הדור בדורות הקודמים, ואם בשארי חכמות באופן גדול הנו היחיד ומיוחד. אין ספק, כי הוא כעת יחיד הדור בהבנת התורה. הבנתו היא המשקולת ודעתו היא המכרעת בכל דיני התורה, קלות וחומרות.

> [In previous generations they believed that it was impossible in practice for Torah and the other branches of wisdom to be combined. Indeed, in this generation we already encountered Torah and [secular] wisdom together. But in this manner! The *gadol ha-dor* in Torah to an astounding degree, like one of the *gedolei ha-dor* in the earlier generations. And with regard to other branches of wisdom, he is preeminent and unmatched. There is no doubt that he is now unique in the generation in understanding the Torah. His understanding provides the true measure of Torah, his opinion is decisive in all of Torah law, in light and heavy matters.]

In a subsequent paragraph he refers explicitly to his son's general education and distinguished achievement in philosophy:

> הי׳ עילוי וגאון בילדותו ועתה כבר כל התורה חקוקה על לבו . . . והלא אינו בעל מלאכה אחת. רכש במידה מרובה גם הפרפראות לחכמה, המעטירים אותו ונותנים לו לוית חן ויופי. השיג את תאר ד״ר פילוסופי׳ באפן הכי מצוין בהאוניברסיטה דברלין, והפרופסורים דשם היו בהתפעלות מגודל כשרונותיו ורוחב הבנתו העמוקה שלא ראו כזאת. ומחדש גם בחכמה זו כגאון הדור.

> [He was a prodigy and *ga'on* in his youth, and by now all of the Torah is engraved on his heart . . . and yet he is not monolithic in his knowledge. He has acquired to a great degree the auxiliary branches of wisdom, which adorn him and give him charm and beauty. He earned the doctoral degree in philosophy in the most outstanding manner at the University of Berlin, and the professors there were deeply impressed by his abilities and the breadth of his deep understanding, the likes of which they had never seen before. He is creative in this discipline as well, like the *ga'on* of the generation.]

The conclusion is powerful and succinct:

ואך הוא הגברא דכולי' בי', גדול התורה בתורה, אב וגאון בשארי חכמות, אחד המיוחדים בכשרונות בין עם ישראל.[5]

[But.he is the man in whom everything is found: singularly great in Torah, a master and ga'on in the other branches of wisdom, one of the unique ones among *Am Yisrael* in his abilities.]

4.

This uniqueness also underlies the abundance, the bountifulness, what almost seems to be the ubiquitousness of his teaching—a fulfillment and manifestation of (ולהורות נתן בלבו), (He has put in his heart that he may teach" (*Exodus* 35:34)[6]; the extraordinary ability to communicate ideas and insights is a special gift, a special dimension of genius, for not every person, even one possessed of great learning, is blessed with ולהורות נתן בלבו. The Rov had it and his inspired, disciplined teaching was like a spring flowing with undiminished, ever-increasing strength.

This extraordinary ability was felicitously coupled with his unfailing readiness to teach. I am inclined to suggest that his real greatness lay not in the majesty of his erudition, the force of his originality or the brilliance of his intuition. (People always admired the sheer pageantry of his learning and were enchanted by the elegance of its various manifestations and formulations). His greatness—intellectual and moral—lay in his extraordinary ability and amazing readiness to teach and converse effectively, vigorously and intelligibly *on all* levels; moreover, he did so sympathetically and graciously in a way that simultaneously satisfied and stimulated the listener. In order for the Rov to give a shiur, a derashah or a lecture, he had to engage in an act of צמצום, contraction; he had to restrict and restrain a mighty intellect and channel it, to select prudently from an awesome erudition and a vast reservoir of original insights in a carefully controlled way. The profundities of his learning and the subtleties of his thinking had to be unfolded slowly and methodically. Otherwise, students and listeners would have been overwhelmed, would have drowned in the sea of his Torah. His teaching would not have been intelligible—it would rather become a source of frustration and restlessness. He knew that teaching, no matter how profound, must be pleasant and palatable.

> דבש וחלב תחת לשונך. כל שאומר דברי תורה ברבים ואינם ערבים לשומעיהם כדבש וחלב המעורבים זה בזה, נוח לו שלא אמרן. (שיר השירים רבה ד:כב).
>
> ["Honey and milk are under your tongue": One who says words of Torah in public, and they are not sweet to their audience like honey and milk mixed together, it would have been better for him not to say them (*Shir haShirim Rabba* 4:22).]

Every shiur, every speech, was crafted with consummate artistry. This is not only an expression of his literary-conceptual perfectionism but of his realization that if he was to teach effectively, he had to contain his immense learning and unbounded creativity. Style and exposition required sustained attention; hasty writing like shabby thinking was intolerable.[7] He had to find the best way to combine felicitous generalization and lucid, compelling interpretation of detail, while interjecting a sprightly parenthetical remark, an anecdotal reference or a lyrical note. Otherwise we would not have been able to learn from him. He, therefore, happily fused apparently limitless erudition with enthralling elegance and immense pedagogic skills. When he repeated an idea or interpretation—and the repetition was always eloquent—his intention must have been to guarantee that the presentation was properly textured and fully-nuanced, that one theme had been adequately developed and the transition to the next one was crystal clear. Ever mindful of his audience and the goals of his presentation, he used as much learning—*lomdus*, midrash, philosophy, history, literature—as was necessary and no more.

When I think of and see him, before my eyes, preparing and delivering a shiur, I am reminded of the following: The Gemara

(*Sukkah*, 28a) says, in referring to the fact that Hillel had eighty disciples, that "the greatest of them was Jonathan ben Uzziel and the smallest was Rabban Johanan ben Zakhai." The text then continues to depict graphically the greatness of the smallest, least distinguished disciple: he is described as knowing everything.

> אמרו עליו על רבן יוחנן בן זכאי שלא הניח מקרא ומשנה גמרא הלכות ואגדות דקדוקי תורה ודקדוקי סופרים קלים וחמורים... דבר גדול ודבר קטן דבר גדול מעשה מרכבה, דבר קטן הוויות דאביי ורבא.
>
> [They said about Rabban Yohanan ben Zakkai that he did not omit [any aspect of] Scripture, Mishna, Gemara, *halakhot, aggadot, dikdukei Torah* and *dikdukei soferim,* light and heavy laws . . . any great topic, any small topic; "any great topic"—the workings of the Divine chariot; "any small topic"—the disputes of Abayei and Rava.]

The stage is set for the Gemara to ask a crucial question: וכי מאחר *שקטן שבכולם כך, גדול שבכולן על אחת כמה וכמה.*" If the smallest of them was so great, how much more so the greatest." However, we are eager to know what remains to be said in laudatory characterization of the greatest; what is the extra dimension that may be identified and attributed to the most distinguished of the disciples. This is the answer: They said of Jonathan ben Uzziel that when he used to sit and occupy himself with the study of Torah, every bird that flew overhead was immediately burnt, כל עוף שפורח עליו מיד נשרף.[8]

In studying this remarkable passage and pondering its significance, the yeshiva student focuses on a legal issue to be decided in accord with the *Hoshen Mishpat* or *Hilkhot Hovel u-Mazik*: who has to pay, who is liable for the damage and the loss. The Kotzker hasid, conscious of and questing for ecstasy, marvels: if this is how the student is portrayed and celebrated, what is left to describe the teacher וואס איז שוין ביים רבין? What unusual resourcefulness does he possess?

To paraphrase the Talmudic sentence, וכי מאחר שהתלמיד כך הרב על

אחת כמה וכמה. We seem to have exhausted everything; every factual assessment, every metaphor, every category of praise has been used. Our armamentarium is depleted. The answer of Kotzk was: ביים רבין ווערט נישט פארברנט.* The master has sovereign control over his mighty resources and uses them with laser-like precision. He creatively summons forth from his reservoir of knowledge and skills only that which is necessary for the task at hand. While revealing one thing, he conceals many things. Nothing is squandered; no available resources are used needlessly or mindlessly. There is no exhibitionism, no ostentatious parade of erudition, no ornamental accumulation of source references. The rebbe produces much light and just enough heat—nothing is burnt and the Torah teaching shines luminously.

The Rov always dispensed his Torah learning in a measured way. He shared his learning graciously and benignly in order to make it possible for others to be partners or participants in the intellectual process. His thorough, meticulous preparation as well as masterful, deliberate presentation were expressions of this. He always prepared very carefully, regardless of the level of his presentation. I recall vividly how he would write out his remarks for the boys and girls of Maimonides School when he came to address them on *Erev Yom Ha-Kippurim*—remarks about the beauty and sanctity of *Yom Ha-Kippurim*, about *taharah*, about the role of the Kohen Gadol, about the exaltedness of prayer, about *teshuvah* and *kapparah*, about the inseparability of mitsvot between man and man and those between man and God, about the striving for moral perfection, about the multiple meanings of לפני ה׳. Everything was carefully crafted even—or especially—for young boys and girls who needed to be reassured and aroused in the quest for understanding and insight, piety and spirituality.

The great master-teacher is described as follows:

*CF., however, *Hidushei ha-Ritva* ad loc.

ויותר שהיה קהלת חכם, עוד למד דעת את העם, ואזן וחקר ותקן משלים הרבה.

["And besides being wise, Kohelet also imparted knowledge to the people; he listened, sought out, and arranged many proverbs" (*Ecclesiastes* 12:9).]

His learning enables him to teach and disseminate knowledge among the people, among all the people; for this purpose of effective, inspiring teaching, he devises multiple techniques of clarification and exposition and various strategies of explanation—*meshalim harbeh*. The wise man pays a price for his teaching, which is *torat hesed*.[9] For a sage to transmit knowledge and wisdom to the people, not to a pre-selected elite, is to be deflected from his own study and writing, his attainments and advance. Nevertheless he persists and teaches in a stimulating way. This was the Rov: the rabbi's scholar, the layman's rebbe, the child's guide—all luminous facets of his untiring teaching—ולהורות נתן בלבו.

5.

This remarkable achievement was the consummate expression of combined intellectual and moral prowess—of magnanimity, generosity and graciousness. The statement in *Nedarim* 38a comes to mind:

לא ניתנה תורה אלא למשה ולזרעו . . . משה נהג בה טובת עין ונתנה לישראל ועליו הכתוב אמר: טוב עין הוא יבורך (משלי כב:ט).

[The Torah was given exclusively to Moses and his descendants . . . (but) Moses behaved generously and gave it to Israel. Concerning him Scripture says: "He who has a bountiful eye will be blessed" (Prov. 22:9).]

The Rov had a very bountiful eye; he was a great טוב עין. He shared his wisdom and learning with everyone—rabbis and students, various groups of baale batim, young and old, large gatherings and small assemblies. Whether he was interpreting a difficult passage in Tosafos, explicating a particularly recalcitrant formulation by Rambam, interpreting a comment of Rashi or Ramban on the Torah, he was always the master-teacher—happily and skillfully making his rich learning available to all.

In addition, he felt—and compellingly expressed the idea—that wisdom, like prophecy, was not to be seen as the private possession of an individual אין הנבואה וגם החכמה קנין היחיד. שייכות הנה לכל. The halakah obligating a prophet to communicate his prophecy—נביא הכובש נבואתו חייב מיתה בידי שמים[10] should govern the behavior and attitude of the wise man, even if a high price is paid. Noblesse oblige; the sage is driven to share his learning. The Rov illustrated untiringly the lesson implicit in the opening halakhot of Rambam, *Hilkot Talmud Torah*,[11] that studying and teaching constitute one unified mitsvah, one fully integrated performance. As we shall subsequently note, his magnanimity—making his great mind and soul available to those who thirsted for "the word of God"—together with the charm and cogency, pedagogic refinement and rhetorical force of his teaching resulted in an extraordinarily widespread impact which literally made him the רבן של ישראל.

6.

These comments on magnanimity and bountifulness lead to one more comment on the Rov's personality. This great man, whose unique scholarship was admired far and wide and whose wise counsel was sought throughout the world, was totally unpretentious, free of all pompousness and officiousness. He deserved and received the greatest respect but never wanted this to be tinged with artificiality. He opened the door, answered the telephone, conducted all his correspondence—without secretaries, without an office staff, without any bureaucracy. His resistance to and antipathy for mechanization, institutionalization, stodginess, perfunctoriness—above all artificiality and pretense—carried over to his personal behavior. Just as he was far from banality and platitudinousness in thought or style, so he had no use for the artificial, which is also superficial, in behavior and human relations. The Rov's greatness was thus expressed also in his individuality, personal authenticity and naturalness in everything he did.

7.

As for his method of Torah teaching—the celebrated Brisker mode of analysis, interpretation and exposition—let me, in the interests of brevity, mention two salient components.

(1) This method necessitates treating Rambam's *Mishneh Torah* not only as a code of halakhah (as the influential precursor of the *Shulkhan Arukh*), but as a commentary on the Talmud; it recognizes that Rambam the authoritative codifier is eo ipso a versatile, original commentator. This premise yields great exegetical-interpretive freedom in reconstructing the implicit commentary. The characterization of a statement as a "difficult Rambam" usually presumes a conventional explanation of the Talmud text or a common form of reconciliation of several texts;[12] when this conventional interpretation fails to illumine the Maimonidean formulation, we are left with a "difficult Rambam." It is self-evident that a curt, normative formulation, an halakhah pesukah, in the *Mishneh Torah*, reflects Rambam's latent explanation of Talmudic texts and halakhic concepts—an explanation that often differs from the standard commentators. Consequently, a major task of the rabbinic scholar is to unfold or reconstruct Rambam's unarticulated interpretive processes—in other words, to compose, by means of fastidious reasoning and disciplined hypothesis, the kind of commentary that Rambam would have written on the Talmud.

The testimony of Rav Menahem ha-Meiri (introduction to *Bet ha-Behirah*) concerning the mode of study followed in his school is particularly informative and enlightening. Having completed the study of a Talmudic passage and arrived at what seemed to be the "true explanation" of the passage, he would consult the Mishneh Torah in order to find the practical codificatory summation and frequently the latter, in its Maimonidean formulation, convinced him that his explanation of the passage was defective or imprecise. The attempt to align the *pesak* with the *sugya* necessitates intensive intellectual exertion and relies on great ingenuity and resourcefulness. Failure to do this will often leave one with an inadequate understanding.

> וכלל אמר לך, ומחסדך אל תבוז אליו, והוא שכל מי שלא יחוש לידיעת פסק הענין לא יעלה בידו בהרבה מקומות אמתת הפירוש וגם הוא לא יתעמל בזה. וחי השם, הרבה פעמים קרה על סוגית ההלכה והייתי חושב שכונתי בה לביאור אמתי, וכשהייתי מחפש לידיעת הפסק בספרי המחברים הקדמונים בפסקיהם ויותר בספרי הרב ז״ל אשר היו לי מכוש אחרון וסוף הוראה לכל החבורים המחברים דרך פסק הייתי מרגיש בעצמי שלא היה ביאור הסוגיא עולה בידי כהוגן.

> [I will tell you a rule, and in your kindness, please do not disparage it: one who is not mindful of knowing the practical halakhic conclusion in many instances will not arrive at the correct interpretation nor will he exert himself to accomplish this. By the life of God, it happened many times that I thought I arrived at a truthful explanation of a halakhic discussion in the Talmud and then when I would search for the halakhic decision in the codes of earlier authorities and especially in the code of Maimonides which is the final word and ultimate authority amongst all codes, I would realize that my interpretation was incorrect.]

It is especially interesting, in light of this, to read the Rov's description of how his father was accustomed to study.

> אבא מרי דיבר תמיד על אודות הרמב״ם, וכך היה עושה: היה פותח את הגמרא; קורא את הסוגיא. אחר כך היה אומר כדברים האלה: זהו פירושו של הר״י ובעלי–התוספות; עכשיו נעיין נא ברמב״ם ונראה איך פירש הוא. תמיד היה אבא מוצא כי הרמב״ם לא פירש כמותם ונטה מן הדרך הפשטה.[13]

> [My father, my master, spoke always of the Rambam, and so would he do: he would open the *gemara*, read the *sugya*, and then say as follows: "This is the explanation of the Ri and the Tosafists. Let us now analyze the text of the Rambam and see how he explained." Father would always find that the Ram-

bam had not explained as the others did, and had veered from the simple path.]

Hence the biggest challenge and the delightful opportunity provided by the Rambam—is the invitation to disciplined yet imaginative interpretive hypothesis, to a hermeneutic which fuses textual precision with conceptual insight.

I emphasize "disciplined yet imaginative" because that is the key to understanding what is colloquially referred to as a *hiddush.*

8.

A *hiddush* is not something contrived or extraneous or completely autonomous, but an age-old time-less truth waiting to be brought to the surface. It is an inspiring, edifying, insight not hitherto perceived, a novel interpretation based upon previously unnoticed associations or connotations, an elegant clarification which resolves hard-core difficulties. A *hiddush* is present in Torah, but temporarily invisible. The resourceful, erudite interpreter, using penetrating logic and creative powers of association and differentiation, brings this new-old truth to everyone's attention. This is really what the Ramban is telling us in the introduction to his *Milhamot ha-shem*: החיוב המוטל עלינו לחפש בעניני התורה והמצוות ולהוציא לאור תעלומות מצפונים. [It is incumbent upon us to probe the subject matter of Torah and *mitsvot* to bring the hidden to light.] The highest praise in Brisk was to react to an idea or insight, to a beautiful compelling *hiddush,* with the rhapsodic exclamation: אמתה של תורה i.e., the *hiddush* reveals the truth which has not previously been grasped. In the letter which we have already mentioned, the Rov's father says of him: הוא יחיד הדור בחידוש התורה לאמתה.

It is well known that the Talmud (*Sukkah* 28a) characterizes R. Eleazar as never having transmitted a teaching which he did not hear from his teachers—indeed, he himself proclaimed ולא אמרתי דבר שלא שמעתי מפי רבי מעולם. Yet, elsewhere (in אבות דרבי נתן), our Rabbis emphasize that he was the master of doctrines which nobody ever heard prior to his teaching them: שלא שמעתן אוזן אדם מעולם. Many have correctly suggested that these two descriptions are not contradictory. R. Eleazar's grasp of the *masorah* was so comprehensive, his knowledge so fastidious, his understanding so profound, his intuition so keen, that his שמועה, his tradition, included themes and motifs, premises, conclusions and insights unknown to others. He elaborated them and they, in turn, became components of the *masorah*.

There are in the Rambam's *Mishneh Torah* hundreds and hundreds of *hiddushim*—in addition to those explicitly signaled by the phrase "it seems to me" (יראה לי)—which the commentators acknowledge by noting that they are original Maimonidean formulations: דברי רבנו ראויים אליו; סברא דנפשיה וראויים הדברים לאומרם ["The words of our master are appropriate to him," "This is his own reasoning, and the words are appropriate to the one who said them."] and similar phrases. They do not strain to find an explicit source; rather they highlight the novelty, are stimulated by its profundity, savor the felicity of style, power of compression, wealth of allusions while they experience time and again the delicacy and dynamism of the innumerable original explanations and conclusions; in a word, they confront, admire and are stimulated by the multi-splendored originality.

The *masorah* is being deepened and expanded by a great *hakham ha-masorah* who succeeds in discovering inherent, authentic ideas which have not received any attention or have not been given the primacy and prominence which they deserve and, concomitantly, the opportunity to influence our thinking and behavior.

The Rov, at the beginning of his essay *Ra'ayonot 'al ha-Tefillah*, had occasion to comment on this phenomenon, this process of *hiddush* (intuitive, authentic interpretation and expansion) as follows:

> הכל זקוקים לגאולה ולפדיון: הציבור ההיסטורי, גם היחיד. לפעמים נשארת אידיאה גלמודה ואלמונית במערכות המחשבה, עד שבא גואלה הקרוב לה ומוציא אותה מבדידותה ומשממותה לחרות ולמרכזיות.

[All are in need of redemption: the historical community as well as the individual. Sometimes and idea remains forlorn and unidentified in the systems of thought, until its redeemer, its 'close relative,' comes along and extricates it from its isolation and desolation into freedom and centrality.]

ישנה גאולה גם במחשבה ההלכתית. ישנן סברות שנידונו לזמן רב או קצר לגלות וחתרו לגאולה במשך דורות עד שבא הגואל וגאל. הגואל הוא אחד מחכמי ישראל שאותו בחרה ההשגחה להוציא את השיטה או הסברה מבדידותה למרכזיות המחשבה ההלכתית.

[There is redemption also in halakhic thought. There are some lines of reasoning which were condemned, for a long or short time, to exile and they strove for redemption through the generations until their redeemer came and redeemed. The redeemer is one of the sages of Israel, chosen by Providence to extricate that opinion or line of reasoning from its loneliness and grant it centrality in halakhic thought.]

It is self-evident that not everyone is qualified or licensed to submit novellae and not every *hiddush* will be absorbed into the mainstream of our *masorah*. When we read the Talmudic statement that כל מה שתלמיד ותיק עתיד לחדש was included in the original revelation of Torah, the adjective *vatik* resonates in a special way: only a trusted, thoughtful transmitter, one who carries the *masorah* and contributes to it with dedication, authenticity and creative understanding, joins the august company of *hakhme ha-masorah*. Originality and innovativeness are outgrowths of being saturated with traditional categories and concepts. There is a weighty inducement to novelty but it is accompanied by a deep sense of responsibility and accountability.

9.

It should be noted that mighty historical challenges—conditions of adversity, tendencies to decline, symptoms of erosion—elicit especially creative responses from these great sages who are the guardians and interpreters of the *masorah*. My son Reb Mayer called attention to the complementary terminology used by Rambam to describe the *hakhme ha-masorah*: they are מעתיקי השמועה and מגידיה (*Mishneh* Torah, introduction and *Hilkot Teshuvah*, III, 8), transmitters of tradition and its interpreters. Actually the Rov commented on the significance of the phrase מכחיש מגידיה in *Hilkot Teshuvah III*, 8 in his famous shiur on *kiddush ha-kodesh* (now reprinted in *Kovets Hiddushe Torah*, p.61.) They counter the challenge, which ordinarily produces pessimism and demoralization, with intellectual creativity and spiritual virtuosity which can only result in optimism and revitalization. These wise men, teachers par excellence, inexhaustible sources of inspiration and commitment, sustain and advance the authoritative *masorah*.[14]

10.

(2) The second component in his method of teaching is the following: the primary mode of interpretation used in this process is abstract conceptualization—i.e., to find or extrapolate the unarticulated idea, the unperceived association, the unifying or differentiating characteristic which informs the plethora of details; to identify and analyze the concept which undergirds the many apparently disparate facts. This often involved the imaginative translation of facts into ideas; "pots and pans" become abstract concepts. The method probes into the inner strata of Talmudic logic and formulates the disparities as well as similarities between various passages in the light of conceptual analysis. Complex concepts, discussed fragmentarily in numerous sections of the Talmud or unrelated contexts of the Maimonidean code, are defined with vigor and precision, with dialectical insight and acuity.

11.

This entire method which, at the risk of oversimplification, I have reduced to its most essential features, lends dignity to Torah, enhances כבוד התורה. Original and profound, elegant and enthralling, such novel interpretations combining massive erudition with great intuition speak not only to one's religious consciousness but fully engage the mind as well. They powerfully rebut the platitudinous Haskalah indictment of Talmud study as intellectually insipid and spiritually stultifying. There is not only technical proficiency and extensive knowledge but intellectual-aesthetic delight in the process of learning. By his mastery and repercussive application of this method, as a result of readily discernible, extraordinary sophistication and generally admired unfailing originality, the Rov enhanced *kevod ha-torah*. His teaching was intellectually exciting and religiously uplifting.

There is a story that when the Rov's great-grandfather, the *Beit Halevi*, met Reb Yisroel Salanter, he would repeat to him some *hiddushim* of his son Reb Hayyim, the most forceful protagonist, if not the originator, of this approach in modern times. Reb Yisroel Salanter, who was very much attuned to contemporary nineteenth century developments coming in the wake of emancipation and enlightenment, and who agonized over the negative phenomena which he observed, responded as follows: "The next generation will study Torah that way and we shall overcome the haskalah." What are we to make of this remarkable statement? What is the connection between the two parts of his statement?

Reb Yisroel Salanter meant to say that in addition to the religious-metaphysical commitment which must be nurtured and sustained, young people need intellectual challenge and intellectual satisfaction. He knew well that many thought—mistakenly—that *haskalah* provided this kind of intellectual excitement; that is why an analytic-conceptual method, equal to any in its rigor and profundity, in its vigorous discipline and its invigorating results, would rehabilitate halakah while repudiating haskalah.

The Rov does not tell this story, as far I know, but I found one sentence in his eulogy on his uncle the Brisker Rov which makes the same point very poignantly. In that remarkable-revelatory essay, which contains a spirited characterization of Reb Hayyim's method (שיטת ר׳ חיים איש בריסק), more sharply delineated than what is described in *Ish Ha-Halakhah*—the Rov asks about his grandfather's decisive impact: במה היה כחו יפה. שאילמלא הוא היתה משתכחת תורה מישראל ולא היינו יכולים להרביץ אותה בתקופה זו.

What was the secret of his genius; if not for his trail-blazing, stimulating, widely repercussive achievement, we would not be able to teach and disseminate Torah.

The Rov, who frequently emphasized the importance of enhancing כבוד תורה, who saw this as the assignment given us in this age by Divine Providence, was privileged to do this more than anyone else. He was the teacher who disseminated Torah in this age with verve and zeal, emphasizing the nobility of the intellectual process, the exhilaration of learning, the beauty of Torah study [15].

The same statement that he made about his grandfather is applicable to him, ...במה היה כחו יפה

We should note that the Rov's early חידושי תורה deal with themes of זרעים and קדשים; they are markedly original and completely classical in theme and format. He has appropriated Reb Hayyim's approach and individualized it by his erudition, clarity of insight and mode of exposition. His innovations and acuity—using a method characterized by innovation—are salient. Subsequently, he chose to concentrate on themes of prayer, benedictions, Torah reading, festivals and fast days—these are, of course, the topics of his celebrated Yahrzeit Shiurim. He sought themes that had not been studied in this way; dichotomies between technical-theoretical and popular-practical were not real. Topics considered to be popular, well-known and accessible were transformed by his profoundly original and repercussive analysis.

12.

The other major area of his teaching, which is conventionally described as his philosophy, is, in my opinion, best seen—to use traditional religious categories—as his incessant, inspired preoccupation with פנימיות התורה or נשמת התורה. One utilizes contemporary philosophic terminology and phenomenology—that is a stylistic, conceptual requirement basic to the very enterprise—but one's goal is the same as that of the great thinkers of previous generations: to penetrate to the inner core of Torah, to expound its essential beliefs, to explain what is contained in *mitsvot*, to unfold their teleology (which is sometimes explicit and sometimes allusive), to understand the dynamics of Torah *shebe'al peh* and its axiology and hence to deepen one's comprehension and intensify one's experience. This endeavor is not extraneous to Torah, not independent of halakah, but is an integral, indispensable part of it; as the Ramban put it: לימוד אמונת התורה הוא לימוד בתורה. It is not merely an intellectual indulgence or a concession to the attraction of philosophic study but the fulfillment of a basic religious duty. Use of philosophic language and conceptualization is integral—indeed it may provide the stimulus for an analysis which yields new insights in the realm of פנימיות התורה.

The Rov illustrated vividly and powerfully the meaning and majesty of the Rambam's formulation (*Hilkot Teshuvah*, X, 6) concerning the instrumental relationship between wide-ranging philosophic knowledge and the ultimate religious attainment.

> אינו אוהב הקב״ה אלא בדעת שידעהו, ועל פי הדעה תהיה האהבה, אם מעט מעט ואם הרבה הרבה. לפיכך צריך האדם ליחד עצמו להבין ולהשכיל בחכמות ותבונות המודיעים לו את קונו כפי כח שיש באדם להבין ולהשיג.
>
> [One can love God only with the knowledge one has of Him; according to the degree of knowledge is the degree of love, if little, then little, if much, then much. Therefore, a person must dedicate himself to understanding and comprehending the branches of wisdom and knowledge which afford him knowledge of his Creator to the degree that a human can understand and grasp.]

This resonant formulation highlights the inexorable link between knowledge of God and love of God; it provides a double spiritualistic teleology for a comprehensive and rigorous intellectualism. Wide ranging philosophic knowledge leads to knowledge of God which in turn is a prerequisite for love of God. Indeed, no attempt is made, here or elsewhere, to camouflage or gloss over the robust intellectualism—only to emphasize its true spiritual purpose.

We may say that the Rov disproved the assumption of practically all religious philosophers since William James that "primary experience and conceptual articulation are always at odds with each other", that there is a difference between "philosophy of religion as dialectic of ideas and living religion in its "pristine form".[16] His point of departure—his method, his objective—was not formal scholastic philosophy of religion, which he knew well in all its guises, but rather a glorious masorah of *Ahavat Hashem, De'ot*, and *Talmud Torah*, of *Zohar* and *Sha'are Orah*, of *Reshit Hokhmah* and *Likkute Torah*; a *masorah* in which the dialectic of ideas provides a natural, nurturing framework for the primary religious experience—for the primary experience and for the open-ended, ongoing religious quest. He is in the tradition of the *Hovot Ha-Levavot* (e.g., introduction, book one, book five) and of that ever-fascinating Chapter 51 of the third part of the *Moreh Nevukhim* which insisted that profound knowledge of God is necessary for the true service of God. This is intellectualism, to be sure, but not a self-contained or self-sufficient intellectualism. It is intellectualism with a higher purpose which thus bridges what seems to be a yawning chasm between dialectical analysis and philosophical discourse on one side and subjective experience and normative religious action on the other.

13.

I want to clarify a bit more the role of philosophy. There is, in my opinion, no justification for debate or equivocation concerning the Rov's relation to general culture—philosophy, science, literature—but it is necessary to put this in a proper perspective. The facts are unmistakable. He achieved sovereign mastery of these fields and used his knowledge selectively, creatively and imaginatively, with great philosophic acumen and originality. He often reminisced with me about his student years and his unquenchable thirst for knowledge, which, he said, was characteristic of many of his contemporaries. He recalled that straitened material circumstances never dampened his enthusiasm for study. The impact of those years on him was great and lasting; his quest for wide-ranging scientific-humanistic knowledge was successful. The record of his dedicated quest for and ongoing use of this knowledge is clear and unambiguous.

The following may be a useful way of approaching this topic. If you knew nothing about the Rambam's programmatic statements concerning the religious value of the process of intellectualization, his ideological conviction concerning the indispensability of philosophy for Torah, his passionate commitment to demonstrating the inseparability and complementarity of two apparently discordant but intriniscally harmonious disciplines (referred to as *Torah* and *gufey Torah*); if you were not acquainted with these forcefully articulated positions and merely studied the *Commentary on the Mishnah*—the most popular of his writings—you would be struck by the multiple contexts in which philosophy, philosophers, and philosophic ideas appear. Indeed, you need read only the *Shemonah Perakim* and the commentary on *Pirke Avot* and you will encounter directly his extensive use of philosophy, repeated references to philosophers and incisive analysis of philosophic problems. There is no need for any apriori statement of intention or a methodological—ideological prologue. His actions, his words, the message which he communicates to his readers, by the scope, style and subtlety of his writing, tell the entire story. The ready, abundant references and forceful disquisitions buttress his reputation as an enthusiastic propagator of philosophy and a creative religious philosopher.

Similarly, if you knew nothing about the Rov's biography and merely studied the *Ish Ha-Halakah* (published in 1944) you would confront a massive, strategic reliance on the history of philosophy and science. The first two pages introduce you to Hegel, Kierkegaard, Rudolph Otto and Karl Barth, Eduard Spranger and Ferdinand Lasalle, Rousseau, Nietzsche, Bergson, Spengler and Heidegger—a breathtaking list. A page later you meet Plato and Aristotle, Galileo and Newton and soon thereafter Husserl, Scheler, Berkeley and Hermann Cohen. If you persisted and made your way to the end of this remarkable philosophical-spiritual meditation, the very last note refocuses your attention on a cast of influential figures: Kant and Hermann Cohen, Kierkegaard, Ibsen, Scheler and Heidegger together with the Rambam and ibn Gabriol and then once again, after a passing reference to Duns Scotus, on to Schopenhauer and Nietzsche. These references reflect not only great erudition and precision in the history of philosophy but also a philosophic temper, a philosophic mode of thinking, a subtle, analytical mind.

In addition, we may note certain propositions, affirmations or generalizations which stand out. For example, the following sentence summarizing the views of many thinkers concerning "religious consciousness" (*toda'ah datit*), (perhaps the major motif in the Rav's writings) in the opening paragraph of the *Ish Ha-Halakah*, is enthralling:

> יש הרבה מן האמת במשנתם הדיאלקטית של הירקליט והגל בנוגע לתהליך ההוויה בכלל, ובהשקפתם של קירקגור, קרל ברט ורודולף אושו ביחס אל התודעה הדתית והתגלמות הוויתו של איש הדת בפרט, שכוח יוצר נטוע באנטיתיזה.
>
> [There is much truth in the dialectical philosophies of Heraclitus and Hegel with regard to the process of existence in general and in the views of Kierkegaard, Karl Barth, and Rudolf Otto with regard to the religious consciousness and its embodiment in the experience of *homo religiosus* in particular, namely, that there is a creative *elan* embedded within antithesis.]

The halakic master invites the reader to ponder carefully certain philosophical and theological classics which illumine the antithetical structure of religious experience and creativity—the theme which enthralled him.

Similarly, the following sweeping generalization concerning Christian theology, in *Kol Dodi Dofek*—the great manifesto of religious Zionism—also arrests your attention by virtue of its authoritativeness and comprehensiveness:

> יש צורך בידיעה מקיפה בספרות התיאלוגית, מאז ימי יוסטין מרטיר עד התיאלוגים החדשים בימינו, כדי להבין את הפלא הגדול הזה, שעל ידו נהפכה ההנחה המרכזית בתיאלוגיה הנוצרית.
>
> [It is necessary to have a sweeping knowledge of the theological literature, from the days of Justin the Martyr to the new theologians of our day, in order to understand this great wonder, through which the central assumption of Christian theology was overturned.]

In the evocative eulogy of his uncle, the Brisker Rov, the Rov finds it useful and appropriate to characterize the innovative aspects of R. Hayyim Brisker's method by positioning it in the framework of the conceptualization and mathematization of nature developed by the founders of classical and modern physics from Galileo and Newton until our own time. He then suggests, a bit further in the same essay, that there is a basic analogy between Kant's declaration concerning the independence of pure reason and Reb Hayyim's insistence upon the autonomy of the reason of halakah:

> קאנט בשעתו הכריז על עצמאותה של התבונה הטהורה של ההכרה המדעית-מתימאטית. ר' חיים נלחם את מלחמת השחרור של תבונת ההלכה ותבע לה אוטונומיה שלמה.
>
> [Kant, in his day, declared the independence of the pure reason of scientific-mathematical understanding. Reb Hayyim fought the war of independence of the logic of the halakha and demanded complete autonomy for it.]

The clarity and naturalness of the comparisons underscore that this mode of reference, and of perception (using universal concepts and moving from the general to the particular), is integral to his way of thinking and exposition. That is the way to clarify, to conceptualize, or to put in perspective; that way of conceptualization and exposition provides the infrastructure of all his writing.

Particularly striking in this context are the citations from belles-lettres: e.g., Tolstoy's *Death of Ivan Ilitch*; Ibsen; Stefan Zweig's article on Tolstoy (which is introduced for purposes of comparison with Reb Hayyim) Y. L. Peretz's *Bonze Shweig*, or *Reise Bilder*; or the theory of literature (Aristotle's *Poetics*). I note parenthetically that the Rov liked literature and appreciated good literary criticism; he could easily have been a literary critic—erudite and insightful.

All this is a given—crystal clear, absolutely incontestable, very meaningful.

14.

What is distinctive is the fact that the Rov does not preach or cajole, persuade or brainwash; he does not present an elaborate rationale for the study of philosophy. The latter simply appears as part of his intellectual capital; he uses it freely and wisely and effectively in his various expositions and explorations of Jewish thought. The Rov's philosophic and homiletical corpus has *no apologetics;* there is no attempt to argue and demonstrate the importance of general learning as an abstract proposition just as there is no attempt to defend or glorify western culture. Similarly, there is no attempt to demonstrate that traditional Judaism is completely congruent with philosophy (or any part of it). This truly noteworthy feature is a result of the fact that for the Rov there was nothing essentially problematic about the *masorah*; he did not feel compelled to prove that Torah and philosophy or science are compatible. Neither Kant nor Kierkegaard, Hegel or Husserl are a source of authoritative norms or principles to which Judaism *must* conform. Rather Kant and Kierkegaard, Bergson and James and many other figures from classical to contemporary thought provide a reservoir of ideas and insights, concepts and categories to be used critically and constructively in the analysis and clarification of aspects of the *masorah*—indeed, in the attempt to portray and explain the traditional, often-maligned Talmudist or to enhance one's appreciation for the unique religious significance of halakhah. The cliches of the history of Jewish thought—synthesis, symbiosis, harmony, reconciliation—are missing from his vocabulary and are not applicable to his teaching. His all-encompassing philosophic, scientific and humanistic knowledge served him for his own purposes, for creative, enthralling exposition, for urbane, intelligent discourse, for subtle, sophisticated commentary on Torah ideas.

Indeed, I think that what the Rov reports in the name of Reb Hayyim Brisker concerning the proper understanding of the famous midrash on the *akedah* is emblematic of his intellectual position. The midrash says that only *after* the angel told Abraham not to harm the young Isaac (אל תשלח ידך אל הנער) did he inquire of God about the apparent contradiction in His statements to him: אתמול אמרת לי כי ביצחק יקרא לך זרע. ואתמול אמרת לי קח את בנך את יחידך והעלהו שם לעולה.

On the one hand you told me yesterday that "it is through Isaac that offspring shall be continued for you" and then, on the other hand, you said to me "take your only son and offer him as a sacrifice." The drama of the *akedah* is not only in binding Isaac on the altar but also in the inner struggle of Abraham to avoid positing even for a moment that God's words are contradictory: שלא תפס את דברי ה' כאילו, חס ושלום, הכחישו אהדדי.

His faith had to remain consistent and unfragmented. When the angel's appearance resolved the apparent contradiction, the apparent absurdity and self-negation of two such antithetical statements, only then was Abraham free to ask. The Rov quotes his grandfather's interpretation: כל זמן שהכתוב השלישי המכריע לא בא, לא היה אברהם רשאי לשאל ולפיכך התאפק עד סוף המחזה. [As long as the "third decisive verse" had not come, Avraham was not allowed to ask, and therefore he restrained himself until the end of the drama.] and then adds his peroration: התודעה של איש האלקים וכוח הבלגתו הענקי והנורא בוקעים כאן באור בהיר וזך. [The consciousness of the man of God and his tremendous, awesome capacity for self-restraint break forth here in a clear and pure light.]

We recognize the significance and forcefulness of this statement, for descriptions of the religious consciousness—the self-awareness, turbulence and steadfast commitment of the homo religiosus—are among the salient, recurrent themes of the Rov's writing. This formulation reflects a man of perfect faith who does not feel a need to look for external justification or adventitious vindication. Faith, the motive force and defining norm in the behavior and thought of the *homo religiosus*, needs to be understood, to be analyzed and internalized; its demands may be challenging but its essence is restraint, discipline and commitment.

The Rov's teaching is not cast as an apology for traditional Judaism or as an attempt to harmonize it with some general school of thought. The *masorah* is not subordinated to any extraneous system nor does it need to be validated by aligning it with Kant or Hegel. It needs to be appropriated and explicated, to be analyzed and conceptualized. The Rov's teaching—drawing freely from Torah and hokhmah—fascinates us for its compelling interpretive insights and uncanny intuitions, its theological subtleties, philosophical perceptions and moral nuances, its beauty and profundity. We are never told to be defensive or apologetic. The Rov's message is the following: When you know your way—your point of departure and goals—then use philosophy, science and the humanities to illumine your exposition, sharpen your categories, probe the profundities and subtleties of the *masorah* and reveal its charm and majesty; in so doing, you should be able to command respect from the alienated and communicate with some who might otherwise be hostile or indifferent to your teaching as well as to increase the sensitivity and spirituality of the committed.

The discussion of the *akedah* is completely congruent with the

Rov's finely-honed comments on the significance of the cosmological and ontological proofs for the existence of God—an axial theme in the history of philosophy. The Rov emphasizes with great passion that these proofs should *not* be seen as logical, objective, epistemologically valid but as expressions of man's natural yearning for God. אין אנו זקוקים למופתים אלה לשם הוכחה. כי הלא חווית האלוקים היא יסוד הוודאיות. [We do not need these demonstrations to serve as proofs [for the existence of God], for is not the experience of God the foundation of certainty?]

Direct religious experience guarantees absolute certitude; logical inferences from the finite to the infinite, from the temporal to the Eternal are insignificant and pale in comparison. Proofs should be seen as functions of direct religious experiences, not based on the process of logical deduction, not making scientific-epistemological claims. אין התודעה הדתית חותכת מופתים. אין היא מקישה ולא מסיקה. "מרגישה" היא וחיה את הא-לוה בתוך תוכה של התודעה האונטולוגית. [The religious consciousness does not formulate proofs, nor does it draw analogies and conclusions. It experiences and lives God in the deepest recesses of its ontological consciousness.]

Again we return to the nature of "religious consciousness" which makes the experience of the living God part of the ontological awareness. The religious consciousness is not to be subservient to or derivative from any philosophic impetus; indeed, it is powerful and plays a leadership role in philosophical reflection. This is the thrust of R. Hayyim's statement about "two passages which contradict one another," שני כתובים המכחישים זה את זה. This is the upshot of the Rov's statement concerning proofs of the existence of God. The context is different, the vocabulary is different, the religious-intellectual position is the same.

Such a perspective highlights the uniqueness of the Rov's teaching, both in comparison with modern Jewish thinkers and with the *rishonim* as well. Unlike R. Azriel Hildesheimer who devoted his immense learning to showing, inter alia, that there was no conflict between the philological-historical methods of modern scholarship and traditional views and assumptions; unlike R. Samson R. Hirsch or Rav Reines or Rav Kook who, with varying degrees of success or consistency, elaborated philosophic, meta-historical conceptualizations explaining the importance of western culture; unlike those nineteenth and twentieth century thinkers who believed that Judaism had to be vindicated and verified in terms of contemporary European philosophy; the Rov made no sophisticated arguments in behalf of philosophy and did not engage in intricate apologetics. There is no confrontation with philosophy. Synthesis was not the driving force of his system. He mastered philosophy—it was a valuable part of his intellectual endowment. He then selected from his magisterial erudition what was useful and constructive, insightful and enhancing—e.g., Kant on the noumenon-phenomenon, Bergson on epistemological pluralism, Otto on the nature of the holy, Kierkegaard on the existentialist critique of Hegelianism, Barth on the role of dialectics and antithetical categories; he selected and used ideas strategically and effectively. Of course, he did the same—mutatis mutandis—with the *Moreh Nevukhim* and the *Tanya*. His blessed combination of massive knowledge and great originality enabled him to formulate and express axial religious ideas in a universal philosophic language as well as a particularly Jewish idiom—a special kind of לישנא דרבנן.

This is the secret of his extraordinary creative philosophic writing; he was not artifically constrained by any one school.[17] He did not have to conform in a rigid-scholastic way to any system. His works reflect the same structural pattern: abstract analytical-dialectical philosophical writing laced with lyrical flashes, autobiographical reminiscences and touching scenes based on familial lore or related generally to *hakhme ha-masorah*. While the philosophic exposition is erudite and enlightening, the impetus and the objective of his writings are distinctly religious; generically they belong to the great religious literature of all times.

Hence, to look for apparent contradictions and inconsistencies in his various works, to quibble whether his premises and arguments are medieval or modern, rationalistic or pietistic, to argue whether his thought should be described as existentialist or dialectical, Kierkegaardian or neo-Kantian, is not very edifying. He was neither Kantian nor Kierkegaardian and he could be both; while he had the intellectual ability and resourcefulness to expound their ideas vigorously and critically, what he chose to do was to use them carefully and selectively for his constructive-expository purposes. The apparent contradictions reflect his dialectical style of writing, his effective use of typologies in which opposite phenomena and antithetical attitudes are elucidated. In addition, it has been frequently noted that style is a mixture of self-expression and self control, of exposition and concealment; in our idiom we would describe this dialectic as יותר ממה שקריתי לפניכם כתוב כאן or דברי תורה עניים במקומן ועשירים במקום אחר. Therefore, it is only natural, quite predictable and fully understandable that the degree of expression and control will vary, that different modes of self will be selectively expressed, that we will find varying exposures, different modalities and successive moods—all of which, taken together, produce a complete, polychromatic picture. We must avoid fragmentization of his literary corpus, be wary of extrapolating one theme or one segment and analyzing it in isolation. The archimedean points of his teaching always need to be identified.[18]

15.

The *hakhme ha-Masorah* who are chosen to affect the destiny of the Jewish people *often* appear at a critical juncture in history—at a time of fatigue and frustration, social despair and intellectual gloom, when Torah study seems to be in irreversible decline and its very continuity threatened as a result of historical vicissitudes and inexorable, apparently insurmountable pressures. I emphasize "often" because obviously there is an unbroken chain of *hakhme ha-Masorah*, of *ma'atike ha-shemu'ah* (מעתיקי השמועה)—but times of crisis bring forth especially creative sages, driven by a mission and a vision, whose role is crucial and whose influence is profound and re-invigorating. The powerful words of Rambam, simultaneously frightening and energizing, resonate in our minds: ובזמן הזה תקפו הצרות יתירות ודחקה השעה את הכל. ואבדה חכמת חכמינו ובינת נבונינו נסתרה.

"In our days," Maimonides writes in the introduction to the Mishneh Torah, "all feel the pressure of hard times. The wisdom of our wise men has disappeared, the understanding of our prudent men is hidden;" this motif from Isaiah (29:14), the disappearance of the wisdom of our wise men, becomes a standard slogan describing the worrisome decline in scholarship, as evidenced by its use in the introduction to the *Tur* and the *Shulhan Aruk*. At such a time of intellectual-spiritual eclipse, Rambam felt that he had to act boldly and heroically: "I, Moses the son of Maimon the Sefardi, bestirred myself . . . to compose a work from which the entire Oral Law might become systematically known to all . . . so that all the rules shall be accessible to young and old עד שתהא תורה שבעל פה כולה סדורה בפי הכל. עד שיהיו כל הדינין גלויין לקטן ולגדול. His response to a critical situation characterized by diminishing knowledge of Torah was to compose a comprehensive, systematic work that could be studied by great and small, learned and unlearned. This was a novel, daring enterprise—an act of intellectual and religious courage.

It is noteworthy that a similar sense of crisis, of challenge and response, underlies his description of the period of R. Yehudah ha-Nasi and his momentous redaction of the Mishnah. "And why did our holy master act thus [to reduce the oral tradition to writing] and not leave the matter as it was? Because he saw that the disciples were becoming few, and new troubles were coming upon them." ולמה עשה רבינו הקדוש כך . . . . ולא הניח הדבר כמות שהיה? לפי שראה שתלמידים מתמעטין והולכין, והצרות מתחדשות ובאות . . .

The chaotic and unsettled conditions of the country, the widespread demographic-social instability, the crushing confrontation with destructive historical forces, brought in their wake a serious impoverishment of the people's spiritual-intellectual forces. R.

Yehudah ha-Nasi was stationed on the crest of a great wave of learning and, before his contemporaries and successors fell into the troughs, he had to act decisively. The redaction of the Mishnah, like the Mishneh Torah many centuries later, was a novel, daring achievement. R. Yehudah ha-Nasi and, consciously following him, R. Mosheh Ben Maimon were *hakhme ha-masorah* who acted creatively, courageously, and decisively to safeguard the *masorah*.

Recent sages, fully aware of the nexus between crisis and creativity in the history of our *masorah*, reflected upon the aetiology and teleology of this phenomenon. Let us note two beautiful, resonant examples. The illustrious founder of Gerer hasidism, known as the *Hidushe Ha-Rim*—a spiritual-intellectual giant of formidable resources who guided Polish Jewry during the first half of the nineteenth century and whose influence remains widespread—provides insight into this phenomenon by commenting on R. Akiva and his troubled, turbulent, traumatic times. The terse comment of the *Hidushe Ha-Rim*[19] contains an entire philosophy of Jewish history, a religious conceptualization of the development of Torah study focusing especially on why there are periods of strikingly intense creativity and overwhelming originality.

וזה עצמו מ״ש בגמ׳ כל יקר כו . . . דברים שלא נגלו למשה נגלו לר״ע וחבריו. שר״ע הי׳ בזמן החורבן הי׳ מהצורך להאיר אור תורה ביתר שאת כל שכן דורות אחרונים שאבדנו הכל בעוה״ר, ואין לנו שיור רק התורה הזאת כמ״ש לולי תורתך כו . . . מהצורך לקיום שלנו שיאירו פירושי התורה . . . לזאת מאירים לפעמים בדורות אלו דברי תורה בעמקות יותר, כדי שאולי ע״ז נזכה להשות לבבנו להש״ת.

[This is the meaning of the talmudic passage . . . matters which were not revealed to Moses were revealed to Rabbi Akiva and his colleagues. Since Rabbi Akiva lived in the time of the destruction [of the Temple] it was necessary for the light of Torah to shine more profoundly. How much more so in later generations, when we have lost everything because of our many sins and have nothing left but the Torah, as it says, "Were it not for the Torah . . .", it is necessary for our continued existence that the interpretations of the Torah shine. For this reason, in these generations, the words of the Torah sometimes shine with greater brilliance so that through this we may perhaps merit to turn our hearts to God.]

Because R. Akiva lived during a particularly turbulent and pessimistic period—the aftermath of the destruction of the beit ha-Mikdash and the tragically abortive uprising of Bar Kochba—the light of Torah had to shine more radiantly and more powerfully than ever. Precious perspectives on Torah (כל יקר ראתה עינו), unperceived even by Moshe Rabbenu, were made visible. Intense preoccupation with and discernible enhancement of Torah was the only effective response to the historical challenge—and this describes R. Akiva and his mission as a *hakham ha-masorah*. The first Gerer Rebbe adds that this dynamic feature accounts for the fact that sometimes, in these generations, words of Torah are illuminated with greater profundity. This burst of creative energy is a historic-providential need.

In the second half of the nineteenth century the remarkable Rabbenu Zadok ha-Cohen of Lublin—another charter member of the academy of unique *hakhme ha-masorah*—also comments on the dialectic which characterizes the relation between adversity of dispersion and glory of creativity.

ויהי בנסוע הארון מרמז על הגלות והטירדא, כי הנסיעה הוא טירדא. וזהו דייקא היסוד להרבות ולהבנות ע״ז בחי׳ תושבע״פ, וכאמרם ז״ל פעמים שביטולה של תורה זהו יסודה. וכמו שהי׳ מיד בגלות בבל שנתייסדה שם התושבע״פ ע׳ החרש והמסגר. וכדאי׳ בתנחומא (פ׳ נח) על העם ההולכים בחושך ראו אור גדול, אלו בעלי תלמוד. וכמו שנאמר כי ברוב חכמה רוב כעס, שע״י הרוב כעס בא התרבות החכמה של תושבע״פ.

["*Va-yhi bi-nso'a ha-aron*" hints at exile and burdens because travel is a burden. The principle is to increase [study] and thereby become rebuilt. As [our Sages] of blessed memory have said, "At times the neglect of Torah [ultimately] strengthens

Torah," as happened immediately in the exile of Babylon, where the Oral Torah was strengthened by the Torah sages, as the *Tanhuma* says (*Parashat No'ah*), "The nation which walked in darkness saw great light": these are the authors of the Talmud. And as it says, "For in much wisdom there is much anger", the "much anger" leads to an increase in the wisdom of the Oral Torah.]

The verse from *Kohelet* (I:18) "for in much wisdom is much anger" is interpreted to mean that the increase of anger (*ka'as*), despondency, and irritation brings in its wake an increase in wisdom (*hokmah*) knowledge and understanding of *Torah shebe'al peh*. This paradoxical principle was already discernible during the Babylonian exile, for then the *Torah shebe'al peh* was established. The people walking in darkness saw a great light—profound knowledge of Torah. In a time of exile, of demographic and spiritual dislocation, there is paradoxically a quantum leap in Torah study and creativity. The *hakhme ha-masorah* must adopt heroic measures which not only preserve but exponentially increase—deepen and expand—the tradition and reveal its luminousness.[20]

In light of this dialectical principle, we may turn our attention to a remarkable, provocative passage in Masseket Gittin (88a), מאי דכתיב וישקוד ה׳ על הרעה, ויביאה עלינו, כי צדיק ה׳ אלוקינו.

God was zealous with regard to the evil and brought it upon us, for the Lord our God is righteous. משום דצדיק ה׳ אלוקינו, וישקוד ה׳ על הרעה ויביאה עלינו. This almost sounds like a cruel joke, a perverse, cynical statement made tongue in cheek. If God accelerates the pace so that good events happen quickly, we understand and appreciate that as an expression of His compassion and benevolence. However, zeal with regard to evil—how is that perceived and justified as divine righteousness? (כי צדיק ה׳ אלוקינו): The Gemora clarifies:

> צדקה עשה הקב״ה עם ישראל שהגלה גלות צדקיהו ועדיין גלות יכניה קיימת דכתיב ביה בגלות יכניה, החרש והמסגר אלוף (מלכים ב, כד) ׳חרש׳ שבשעה שפותחין נעשו הכל כחרשין. ׳מסגר׳ כיון שסוגרין שב אינן פותחין, וכמה אלף.

> [God acted charitably with Am Yisrael when He exiled the exile of Tsidkiyyahu while the exile of Yekhonya still existed, as is written regarding the exile of Yekhonya, "And the *harash* and the masger a thousand": *"harash"* (mute)—when they began (their Torah discourses) all became (silent as) as mutes; *"masger"* (one who closes)—when they concluded (their Torah discourses), no one could begin again. And how many? A thousand.]

The answer is based on interpreting החרש והמסגר in the verse from the Book of Kings as metaphors for the great *hakhme ha-masorah.* The divine righteousness is manifest in the fact that the last exiles (*galut Zidkiyahu*) from the Land of Israel arrived while the authoritative, universally respected transmitters and interpreters of Torah were still alive and able to secure the *masorah* among the exiles. Had more time elapsed between *galut Yechonya* and *galut Zidkiyahu,* the influential transmitters of Torah would no longer have been on the scene: the exiles would have been doomed to spiritual impoverishment and gradual estrangement from the *masorah*—they would have been caught in the assimilation syndrome.

In American Jewish history, the pattern of immigration was the reverse. *Galut Zidkiyahu*—large numbers of exiles from Europe—reached the shores of the United States and there was spiritual confusion and desolation. There was little Torah leadership and the situation of the *masorah* was precarious—it looked as if the ominous possibility of Torah being forgotten (תורה שתשתכח) might be realized. People lacked learning and dignity and pride—and the anxiety about the future was deep. In my opinion it is clear that dispassionate and non-partisan chroniclers of American Jewry in the twentieth century (and, by extension, of the fate of traditional Jewry everywhere) will underscore the arrival of the Rov over sixty years ago (at the end of 1932) as a turning point in the spiritual destiny of American Jewry, as the beginning of the arrival and flourishing of *galut Yechonya,* the saving of the battered *galut Zidkiyahu* as a result of the new vitality, remarkable resilience and enhanced confidence generated by the *hakhme ha-masorah* of *galut Yechonya*. The Rov, basing himself on his father Reb Mosheh, and then the Lubavitcher Rebbe R. Yosef Yitzhak Schneerson and R. Aaron Kotler—and many other Torah leaders—were responsible for the spiritual change, the beginning of Torah renaissance—and he probably more than anyone. He emerged as the *hakham ha-masorah* par excellence. As was the case with previous *hakhme ha-masorah* who appeared at critical moments when people were engulfed by despondency and a sense of futility, the Rov, whose reputation as a youthful prodigy was widespread, emerged on the stage of history and was destined to bring brilliant, beautiful Torah to the twentieth century from his base in Boston and New York. We should not underestimate the impact of one great *hakham*; one towering scholar, whose grasp of the *masorah* is majestic and magisterial, whose teaching is original and insightful, whose influence is profound and pervasive, is indeed able to change the entire landscape.[21] The Rov was such a *hakham ha-masorah*. His decisive contribution was quantitative and qualitative: he disseminated Torah and enhanced *kevod ha-Torah*. His tireless, vigorous, imaginative teaching, on so many different levels, suffused the *masorah* with new charm and fascination, revealed its profundities and thereby buoyed the confidence of so many individuals who were demoralized and pessimistic. He energetically and modestly combined the methods of R. Hanina and R. Hiyya as reported in the Gemara.[22]

The circumstances surrounding the establishment of Maimonides School in Boston and the energies expended subsequently for its maintenance are reminiscent of R. Hiyya; the outpouring of shiurim and lectures gives substance to the claim of R. Hanina. The combination of the methods and characteristics of R. Hiyya and R. Hanina is truly amazing—a very special fusion of the vita activa and vita contemplativa: a great teacher and tireless fundraiser for his school, a formulator of enthralling *hiddushim* and beautiful categories of thought as well as a communal rabbi who manifested great *hesed* whether by generous charity, wise counsel, astute guidance or, indeed by being available to people who needed to talk with him as well as assuming national leadership roles.

Indeed, the Rov took his place among the *hakhme ha-masorah* and the *ma'atike ha-shemu'ah*.

NOTES

1. *Moreh Nevukhim*, Part I, ch. 31, See also *Perush ha-Mishnah, Sanhedrin, perek Helek*, ed. J. Kapah, pp. 203-04.
2. Mishneh Torah, *Talmud Torah* I, 1-3 and the beautiful comments of *Or Sameah*.
3. Mishneh Torah, *Tumeat Tsara'at*, XVI, 10. Note *Divre Hagut ve-Ha'arakhah*, p. 65 ff. See also *Yesode Ha-Torah*, VII, 2.
4. The eulogy for the Brisker Rov is included in *Divrei Hagut ve-Ha'arakhah*.
   Our rabbis affirm (*Moed Katan*, 25a) that חכם כבודו בהספדו. What meaningful link is there between a eulogy and honor to the sage? A wise man does not need praise during his lifetime and certainly not posthumously. Apparently, our rabbis teach that a *hesped*, honest and sensitive, allusive and revealing, honors the departed sage by sharply delineating the magnitude of our indebtedness to him and the scope of his influence. Any posthumous evaluation should enrich our lives by helping us appropriate the teachings of the *hakham*; it must, therefore, be true and disciplined. This is how we honor the *hakham*,—by engaging in a meditation and reflection galvanized by a spiritual-intellectual teleology. In this way, the sage remains a source and a model, a stimulus and a catalyst, a challenge and a guide. We are obligated to recognize the unique characteristics and achievements of the *hakham*.
5. The letter of the Kovner Rav is reprinted as the foreword to זכרון הרב. Reb Moshe Soloveitchik's letter (dated 19 Elul, 1935) is found at the end of volume one of ספר יובל להגרי"ד סולוביציק (Jerusalem, 1984).
   Allow me to recreate the following experience. The Kovner Rav, R. Avraham Shapiro is known for his classic three-volume collection of responsa דבר אברהם. I remember my excitement when I received a posthumously published copy of a volume of דבר אברהם subtitled חלק הדרוש (N.Y. 1949). On p. 115 the following note caught my attention:

   ראוי להתעורר על חסרון גדול, שמן ספר העקרים להרי" אלבו ז"ל, לא נתחבר כמעט שום ספר כמתכונתו העוסק באופן שיטתי והתעמקות בעניני הדת ועיקרה, בהשתמשות עם הספרים והידיעות הנחוצות, כמו שעשו הראשונים ז"ל, בעוד שהשעה צריכה מאד לכך . . . אמנם ידעתי כי לא מלאכה קלה היא ואין לנו אנשים רבים מוכשרים ומומחים לזה ע"פ חינוכם והכשרתם . . .

As I read these insightful words, I immediately assumed that he was thinking of the Rov.

6. See Perush ha-Torah of ibn Ezra *ad. loc.* כי יש חכם גם חרש לא יוכל להורות היטב.
7. Long before the famous epigram that the style is the man was formulated, the Talmud underscored the importance of style: סגנון אחד עולה לכמה נביאים ואין שני נביאים מתנבאים בסגנון אחד (סנהדרין, פט:). Rambam emphasized (in *Moreh Nebukim*, II, 29): ודע כי לכל נביא, דבר אחד מיוחד בו, כאילו הוא לשון האיש ההוא.

   Marcel Proust might have cited these references when he said: "Style is in no way a decoration, as some people believe; it is not even a matter of technique; it is—as color is with painters—a quality of vision" [see Peter Gay, *Style in History*, New York 1974, p. 5, n. 1.]—The Rov's style is, as all acknowledge, quite unique.
8. *Sukkah*, 28a and see Tosafos *ad. loc.* Cf. Ramhal, *Derek Ha-Shem*, part IV, ch. 2, end.
9. See *Sukkah*, 49b. Cf. Hasam Sofer, *Teshuvot*, *Yoreh Deah*, introduction (פתוחי חותם).

   Actually, the *hakham ha-masorah*, whose grasp of the tradition is total, is obligated to relate to the totality of the *masorah* community. Everyone has a share in the *masorah* and, therefore, none should be excluded from the process of transmission and enhancement which we have been discussing; no one should be denied the opportunity to benefit from inspired-inspiring teaching, Already Rambam underscored the fact that his monumental codification, the *Mishneh Torah*—a distillation of the entire corpus of Torah literature, broadly conceived—was intended to provide a creative systematization of the Torah and make its contents known to all: עד שתהא כולה סדורה בפי הכל. With greater emphasis he added: לקטן ולגדול.

   Everybody will find meaning and insight, guidance and edification. A halakic formulation that will seem simple and straightforward to an unscholarly or insensitive reader will appear original, provocative and multifaceted to a scholarly and sensitive reader ואפשר שידעם הכל קטן וגדול, איש ואישה, בעל לב רחב ובעל לב קצר. (יסודי התורה, פרק ד, הלכה יג)

   The *hakham ha-masorah* uses his knowledge and pedagogic skill to write and teach in such a way that two distinct voices may be heard therein; for the small and for the great. He has to achieve the right fusion of popular and sophisticated components, exoteric and esoteric elements. Indeed, Rambam succeeded in this regard—he remains a teacher of great and small; the echoes and reverberations of Rambam's great work were heard in different ways by varied members of the community through the ages. It is noteworthy that even the *Moreh Nevukhim* was conceived in such a way that it had something even for beginners. In the introduction Rambam writes: "I know that, among men generally, *every beginner* will derive benefit from some of the chapters of this treatise, though he lacks even an inkling of what is involved in speculation; a perfect man, on the other hand, devoted to Law and, as I have mentioned, perplexed, will benefit from all its chapters."

R. Joseph Karo also affirms that his *Shulhan 'Aruk* was intended to serve beginning students as well as advanced scholars, to increase Torah knowledge among the small and the great "ומבטח אני בחסד עליון כי על ידי ספר זה תמלא הארץ דעת את ה׳, הקטנים עם הגדולים. תלמיד עם מבין חכם חרשים ונבון לחש."

The model for this teaching and transmission is none other than the Almighty "who teaches Torah to His people Israel." On the verse (Deut 32:2) יערף כמטר לקחי תזל כטל אמרתי R. Ovadiah Siforno comments:

> הנה תורתי היא תערוף ותבא בשטף כמטר למבינים המוכנים לקבל מבוע מקור חכמה. וניתנה ג״כ כפי הנגלה ממנה איזו ידיעה להדיוטות, שעם היותה מועטת היא טובה מאד כטל. באפן שהיא כשעירים עלי דשא, שהמשכילים יבינו נפלאות ממנה. וכרביבים עלי עשב שגם ההדיוטות יקנו בה איזה מדה להכיר בו בראם באפן מה.
>
> The great teacher is walking in the ways of God—fulfilling the mandate of imitatio dei—when he takes pains to make his teaching accessible to great and small. Religious-moral imperatives and didactic-pedagogic purposes merge.

We may add, furthermore, that the great teacher knows that his own knowledge and insight are ultimately refined and enhanced by the ability to address "small and great" (קטן וגדול), for the reactions of each contribute to full understanding, mature formulation and judicious interpretation. As Rambam summed it up: וכשם שעץ קטן מדליק את הגדול כך תלמיד קטן מחדד הרב עד שיוציא ממנו בשאלותיו חכמה מפוארה (הלכות תלמוד תורה, פרק ה, הלכה יג).

Let us note the Rov's explicit awareness of this moral-pedagogic feature:

> איש ההלכה הוא פדגוג נפלא, בעל הסברה מצוינת, מזדקק לקטנים ולגדולים.
>
> (מה דודך מדוד, p. 85)

He himself performed this act of *imitatio dei* with zeal and dedication so that heterogenous audiences were enthralled by his teaching.

See also *Uvikashtem Misham*, p.233 and note *Pesahim* 109a, *Kiddushin* 30a.

10. Sanhedrin, 89a.
11. Talmud Torah, I, 1-7 and see *Sefer ha Mitsvot.*
12. See Netziv, introduction to his commentary on the *Sheiltot.*
13. Ha-Meiri, Bet ha-Behirah, Berakhot, introduction, *Uvikashtem Misham* in Ish Ha-Halakah, Galuy ve Nistar, p. 230.
14. See the concluding section of this article.
15. *Divre Hagut ve-Ha'arakhah*, p. 70. See the reference (above, n. 8) to Ramhal, *Derekh Ha-Shem.*
16. See the introduction by John E. Smith to the new edition of W. James, *The Varieties of Religious Experience* (Cambridge, 1985).
17. He once commented to me that the Ramban may have been conceptually more creative than the Rambam for this very reason. The Rambam was

subject to Aristotelian constraints and operated within a clearly defined philosophic framework. The Ramban was unfettered. Note that Julius Guttman (Philosophies of Judaism, N.Y. 1964, p. 153) said the same thing with regard to the Rambam: "But there is also such a thing as originality of creative synthesis. . . ."

I think that something I wrote many years ago about the Ramban is applicable to the Rov: "He had profound all-embracing conceptions of God, Israel, history and the world, and his total anschauung needs to be meticulously reconstructed. He defies facile categorization, as evidenced for example by his agile critique of philosophy and deft use of philosophic materials and ideas. . . ." See *Rabbi Moses Nahmanides (Ramban): Explorations in His Religious and Literary Virtuosity*, p. 7. It is worth mentioning here that the Rov was drawn to the halakic analysis found in the *Milhamot* and *Hiddushe ha-Ramban* and frequently pointed out similarities in modes of reasoning between the Ramban and R. Hayyim Brisker. As is known, the Rov contributed significantly to the revival of the study of the Ramban's *Perush al ha-Torah*; he certainly agreed with the saying of the Hasam Sofer:

ספרי הרמב"ן מצויים אלא שעוסקיו אינם מצויים.

18. Note *Teshuvot ha-Rambam*, ed. J. Blau, n. 436:

וכל המניח דברים שביארנו שהם בנויים על יסודי עולם והולך ומחפש בהגדה מן ההגדות או במדרש מן המדרשים או מדברי אחד הגאונים ז"ל עד שימצא מלה אחת ישיב בה על דברינו שהם דברי דעת ותבונה, אינו אלא מאבד עצמו לדעת.

אלא כך ראוי למי שהוא מבין ולבו נכון לטול דרך האמת שישים ענין זה המפורש בתורה עיקר ויסוד שלא יהרוס בנין ויתד התקועה אשר לא תמוט.

19. *Hiddushe ha-Rim 'al ha-Torah, Hukkat*.

Note that this resonant statement serves to justify an original explanation of the sin of Moses. Novel explanations are thus part of the texture of Torah shebe'al peh.

20. Rabbenu Zadok, *Peri ha-Zaddik, Beha'alotka*.
21. Gittin 6a עשינו עצמינו בבבל כארץ ישראל, מכי אתא רב לבבל.

Note the divergent explanations in Rashi and Tosafot. The Rov wrote as follows about the idea of individual mission and vocation:

את העובדה שמישהו חי בזמן מסוים, בתקופה מיוחדת ובמקום מוגדר, ולא נולד בתקופה אחרת ובנסיבות אחרות, נוכל להבין אך ורק אם נקבל את עצם הרעיון בדבר שליחותו של האדם. ההשגחה יודעת היכן וכיצד יכול הפרט – היחיד על חסרונותיו וכוחות הנפש האצורים בו, לקיים את שליחותו, באילו נסיבות ותנאים ובאיזו חברה יהא זה בכוחו של האדם למלא את שליחותו . . . משום כך נברא היחיד בתקופה ובמקום שבהם יוכל לקיים את פעולתו לשם קיום שליחותו.

See *Yeme Zikkaron*, (Jerusalem, 1989) p. 11.

22. Ketubot, 103b, Bava Mezi'a, 85b.

The Rav at Jubilee: An Appreciation

AHARON LICHTENSTEIN

ANY ACCOUNT, TESTIMONIAL OR CRITICAL, of the significance of a major spiritual figure must refer to two intersecting axes: the vertical and the horizontal. On the one hand, he is to be perceived within his own field, as a laborer in its vineyards—relating in part to current peers, but as a link in a historical chain, to be measured primarily against predecessors and successors. On the other hand, he is to be regarded within the ambience of his broader contemporary milieu, with which he interacts and upon which he presumably impacts.

This point is particularly salient with respect to *moreinu ve-rabbeinu*, the Rav *z.t.l.*, inasmuch as this dichotomy dovetails with a second distinction, pertinent to the Rav generally, and to his first major work, *Ish haHalakha*, particularly. The Rav always had, of course, a penchant for positing antitheses and antinomies; and one of these—classically rooted in *Hazal* and *rishonim*, and constituting a major crux of general religious thought—was the relation of *talmud* and *ma'ase*. Throughout *Ish haHalakha*, a dual—at times, even an ambivalent—attitude obtains with respect to the issue. At one juncture, we read:

Rabbi Aharon Lichtenstein is Rosh Yeshiva, Yeshivat Har Etzion.

> And when many halakhic concepts do not correspond with the phenomena of the real world, halakhic man is not at all distressed. His deepest desire is not the realization of the Halakhah but rather the ideal construction which was given to him from Sinai, and this ideal construction exists forever.

Indeed, disengagement is idealized even with reference to Torah activity proper, so that abstinence from *pesak* is not just reluctantly countenanced but virtually celebrated:

> The foundation of foundations and the pillar of halakhic thought is not the practical ruling but the determination of the theoretical Halakhah. Therefore, many of the greatest halakhic men avoided and still avoid serving in rabbinical posts. They rather join themselves to the group of those who are reluctant to render practical decisions . . . The theoretical Halakhah, not the practical decision, the ideal creation, not the empirical one, represent the longing of halakhic man.[1]

This formulation is fully consistent with the Volozhin tradition's emphasis upon *Torah li-shma*, on the one hand, and with an ardent interest in the abstruse abstractions of neo-Kantian metaphysics and epistemology, on the other. Yet, elsewhere, a very different chord is struck. At one point, *talmud* and *ma'ase* are defined, objectively, as twin coordinates of halakhic existence:

> If a Jew lives in accordance with the Halakhah (and a life in accordance with the Halakhah means, first, the comprehension of the Halakhah per se, and, second, correlating the ideal Halakhah and the real world—the act of realization of the Halakhah), then he shall find redemption.[2]

Indeed, at one point, realization seems to be regarded as the ultimate telos, to which instrumental study is possibly subordinate:

> Halakhic man does not long for a transcendent world, for "supernal" levels of a pure, pristine existence, for was not the ideal world—halakhic man's deepest desire, his darling child—created only for the purpose of being actualized in our real world?[3]

At the subjective plane, similarly, practical implementation is described as a desideratum of Halakhic man—perhaps, as *the* desideratum: "Halakhic man implements the Torah without any compromises or concessions, for precisely such implementation, such actualization is his ultimate desire, his fondest dream."[4]

This antithesis—ultimately, I believe, unresolved in the essay—is reflected in the Rav's life as well. As he and his father *z.t.l.* spent days and long winter nights by the hearth of the Khaslavitch *bet ha-midrash*, poring over the niceties of *hatfasa bi-shvua* or of *holakhat ha-ketoret beYom haKippurim*, could any flight of the imagination have led either to envision him as battling, in later years, for the welfare of as yet ununionized *shohetim*, scraping to meet weekly Maimonides School salary deadlines, or regularly addressing RCA or Mizrachi conventions? Yet, both aspects, the contemplative and the active, engaged the Rav throughout; and each, as well as their interaction, must be discussed in any survey of his achievement.

Between the distinctions I have posited, there is, to be sure, no correspondence. There is, however, a measure of correlation—the world of *ma'ase* being viewed primarily with reference to the contemporary, while that of *talmud* looks before and after. Beginning, then, with the vertical axis, we focus initially upon the Rav's place within the historical continuum of *hakhmei ha-mesora*. His role in this capacity is itself dual, spanning the realms of halakha and *mahshava* respectively. I believe that his position with respect to both differs markedly, however. Any objective description of the Rav as a *gadol* in the world of "learning" begins perforce by referring to his place within the Brisker tradition—begins, that is, by positing that in this sphere, he has not so much innovated a course as pursued one. The element of *hiddush*—as measured, say, against the achievement of the Rav's grandfather, Reb Haym, or of a Rabbeinu Tam—is, therefore, in a meaningful sense, constricted.

This is, of course, stated without the slightest trace of deprecation. By definition, genuine methodological innovation in any field is unusual—all the more so in the Torah world, so oriented to *mesora;* and it would be singularly rare for a person reared, like the Rav, in a highly self-conscious and articulate tradition, at a stage at which one could yet meet its founder. Moreover, excessively frequent sharp methodological shifts are, from an overall perspective, not only unlikely but undesirable, the value of novelty being very much a function of its historical context. Surely, however, such radical originality is not the litmus test of intellectual greatness—within the Torah world, or elsewhere. Does anyone challenge the credentials of Rash of Sens or Rashba simply because they trod in the footsteps of Ri or Ramban, respectively?

If the Rav did not found a tradition, he certainly proved himself, within the parameters of the Brisker mode in which he was reared, a remarkable *me-haddesh.* Over the years, the Rav's creative powers awed *talmidim* repeatedly and, more than any other factor, charged the atmosphere of so many *shiurim.* The fusion of imagination and precision, of energized sweep and rigorous discipline, continually resolved cruces and informed insights. At its most electric, however, it enlarged the bound of halakhic empire by enriching its lexicon with fresh concepts. Ideas such as the *safek* of *tarti de-satri*—doubt resulting from unresolved tension of conflicting elements rather than lack of knowledge—or of *mitsvot* whose *kiyyum* is inwardly experiential, although their implementation entails a normatively mandated physical act, may perhaps be retrospectively traced to some inchoate precedents. Unquestionably, however, as developed concepts, they bear the Rav's stamp, and it was he who implanted them within the Torah world.

Moreover, his creative energies ranged far afield. He was instrumental in significantly extending the scope of *lomdut*, particularly with respect to many areas of *Orah Hayyim*. What the Rav said of Reb Haym—that he had transmuted the *siddur* from the preserve of *shamashim* and *ba'alei batim* into the domain of *talmidei hakhamim*—was even truer of himself.

And yet, at bottom, the Rav's achievement in the realm of halakha, remarkable as it was, bore fruit within a familiar field, one Reb Haym had tilled and sown; and he acknowledged this readily and gratefully. The situation is quite different with respect to the sphere of *mahshava*. The areas of experience explored, the mode and level of inquiry, the resources employed, the problems formulated, above all, the ideas and emotions expressed—these indeed, constitute, conjunctively, a new departure. As regards halakha, the Rav's achievement had, at least, analogues within the panoply of his peers—especially among those who moved within a common orbit and, hence, paralleled some of his *hiddushim*. None, however, even remotely approached the range and depth, the subtlety and complexity, of his *mahshava*. And it was truly his—neither an extension nor an expansion of an existing defined tradition, but genuine innovation. After one has peeled away some of the homiletic component, for which there was ample precedent, so much of his work—and, particularly, the entire constellation—remains remarkably original, as regards both form and substance. Raw material he, of course, mined from many sources; but he was, in no sense, eclectic, and the product bore the imprint of his innermost thought and being. If there have been recent significantly comparable antecedents in the Torah world, I am unaware of them. Only Rav Kook, with whose views the Rav agreed in certain areas but from which he diverged sharply in others, provides any basis for comparison; and both his primary concerns and his philosophic focus were very different. With regard to some aspects of the Rav's work, there were, of course, analogues in general culture, and this is obviously of interest to students of his thought or to intellectual historians at large. However, for *benei Torah*, in quest of spiritual direction, this fact does little to alter our perception of the uniqueness of the Rav's total *hashkafa* and experience.

His contribution was particularly significant at the interface of his two primary interests—in his attempt to formulate and enunciate a philosophy of halakha. The attempt is not, of course, novel; but its undertaking by a *gadol* of the first rank, endowed with a rigorous philosophic training, is—at least, in the modern period—most striking. In approaching the issue, the Rav evidenced traces of both rationalism and fideism—and yet, in the spirit of *na'ase venishma,* transcended both. While seeking, in a sense, to interpret halakha in terms of general categories, he had little propensity for *ta'amei ha-mitsvot* in the tradition of, say, the *Sefer haHinukh* or Rav Samson Raphael Hirsch. For one thing, he eschewed the recourse to utilitarian considerations, if not the outright apologetics, which often typify this tradition. Rather, he persistently stressed that while the halakhic regimen is, as the Torah describes it, ultimately, *le-tov lakh,* its short- and intermediate-term message is that of demand and sacrifice. Beyond this, however, he had no predilection for explaining—much less, explaining away—the nitty-gritty of minutiae, and manifested no sense of responsibility to do so. He preferred, instead, broader vistas—addressing himself to overarching concerns, delineating underlying assumptions and ultimate goals, positing values and direction, defining the nature and thrust of halakha as a normative order. In doing so, he sought—in the spirit of a much-cherished analogy to modern science—to focus upon the "what" rather than the "why." He insisted upon rigorous analysis of a halakha, in its own legal terms, as a prerequisite to philosophizing about it; and he differentiated, radically, between rationale as extraneous to a mitsvah and that which may be of its woof and warp.

The enterpise is, admittedly, at times, delicately balanced. The Rav was vehement in rejecting the intrusion of subjective pseudo-philosophic explanations as an instrument of interpreting objective halakhic material. And yet, with respect to mitsvot whose halakhic essence itself bears moral or theological import—*tefilla* is a prime example—the Rav's own *hiddushim* clearly reflect his philosophic orientation. He insisted, vigorously, upon the autonomy of halakha, regarding as quasi-heretical attempts to ascribe its content to historical, sociological, or psychological factors. And yet, the very notion of a "philosophy of halakha" entails, by definition, viewing—although not, of course, judging—*devar Hashem* through the prism of universal categories. Moreover, the use of detail—to which recourse may be had to buttress a thesis but which can be neutralized, fideistically, as technical and inscrutable when inconsonant with it—opens up the charge of selectivity.

These issues are legitimate concerns, and certainly need to be addressed in any serious analysis of the Rav's work. And yet, delicate or not, balance there is. The fundamental difference between a philosophic orientation which is grounded upon halakha and that which is imposed upon it, is clear. Even if, as applied to borderline cases, the distinction is nice, it is, nevertheless, conceptually sharp. Fine though the line may be at times, the Rav regarded it as a Rubicon. Unless mandated by the raw halakhic data proper, he was consistently wary of sacrificing formal to teleological considerations. Whether with respect to *bein adam laMakom* or *bein adam la-havero,* he rejected, categorically, inclinations to substitute contextual for normative thinking—unless, again, there was built-in flexibility within the halakhic base. Hence, he enriched our Torah world with a philosophic perception which is both authentic and insightful. The Rav's was an authoritative voice, elucidating the substance of halakha, in all its ramifications, on the one hand, and relating it to general axiological and human concerns, whether personal or collective, on the other. In so doing, he broke fresh ground and put us all very much in his debt.

Sheer novelty or even singularity apart, what, in the Rav's thought and expression, has so powerfully gripped us? In part, of course, the force of his charismatic personality—especially as we have, at times, been alternately overwhelmed and enchanted by it, in the course of mesmerizing *derashot* and stimulating *shiurim*. Ultimately, however, his hold upon us has been far more substantive. W.B. Yeats once commented that a person writes rhetoric about his struggles with others and poetry about his struggles with himself. As an orator, the Rav had no peer in the Torah world. But it is the poet in him which has so touched and enthralled us. He has opened for us new vistas of spiritual experience, vistas within which the drama of human existence, in the form of confrontation with oneself, the cosmos, and, above all, the *Ribbono Shel Olam*—all within the context of halakhic existence in its most rigorous Brisker formulation—is charged with hitherto unperceived force and meaning. It is not as if we had engaged in the quest of *U-Vikkashtem miSham* and had faltered. We had simply never thought in those categories. It is not as if we had felt tremulous anxiety as lonely men and women, but in a minor chord. Mired in the pursuit of mundane daily concerns of faith, most of us had simply never confronted that reality. The Rav did. What we have missed, he experienced—in terms of the dichotomy so cherished by him—at both ends of the scale: *gadlut ha-mohin*, the depth and force of a powerful mind mastering its environment and impacting upon it, and that of *katnut ha-mohin*, the simplicity of the child—not as the epitome of intuited holistic existence idealized by the Romantics, but as the archetype of a helpless humble spirit groping towards his Father and seeking solace in Him and through Him.

Something of that experience he, through various channels, communicated to us; and, in so doing, he has sensitized us to the need for a fuller dimension of our own *avodat Hashem*. Flashes of what he saw and showed both engage and haunt us; chords of what he heard and said resonate in our ears; strains of what he felt palpitate in our hearts. Beyond detail, however, we have been gripped and stirred by *demut diyukno shel rabbeinu*—magisterial but sensitive, winsome and yet, ultimately, inscrutable—and his spiritual odyssey. At home, we have hanging one picture of the Rav with an engaging smile on his face; another of him, bent over pensively, with a somber, almost brooding expression. In looking at the latter, I am frequently reminded of Wordsworth's portrayal of the statue "Of Newton with his prism and silent face, /The marble index of a mind for ever / Voyaging through strange seas of thought, alone." Only not just a mind but a soul, not just thought but experience, and, above all, not marble, but a passionate human spirit.

From the realm of *talmud*, broadly conceived, we move to that of *ma'ase*. Some of the Rav's activity in this sphere might be perceived as *askanut*—quasi-political, in a sense, and yet of genuine spiritual import. Two instances spring to mind immediately. The first is his stand vis-a-vis the Conservative and Reform movements. Hearing some current dilettantes, one might get the impression that the most eloquent and vigorous statement the Rav made with respect to the non-Orthodox was his protracted silence about the Synagogue Council of America. But those who remember the 50's accurately know better. Who issued the radical *pesak* that, if one had to choose between forgoing *tekiat shofar* and hearing it in attendance at a mixed temple, he should opt for the former? Who, in the public mind, gave Orthodoxy intellectual respectability and credibility in its confrontation with other movements? To whom did *me-tukanim she-ba-hem*, right-wing Conservative rabbis seeking to stem the tide of tinkering with halakha—whether with respect to gentile wine or women being called up to the Torah—turn for guidance? Of course, the Rav knew, as we ought to know, that many, rabbis and laymen both, in deviationist movements, are genuine *me-vakshei Hashem*, sincerely seeking the *Ribbono Shel Olam* within the context of *yahadut* as they perceive it; and to these, he accorded both respect and understanding. But, as a custodian of tradition, he was, in thwarting institutionalized revisionism, adamantly unwavering. One can truly apply to him Ramban's encomium, in his letter to the Northern French *rabbanim*, of Rambam: מי הכה הצדוקים אשר היו בגבורים בוסים, מי נתן הביתוסים לשוסים, הלא הרב ז״ל כי ה׳ עמו.[8]

The second instance concerns interfaith, rather than intra-communal, relations, although it, too, had internal ramifications as well. I refer, of course, to the Rav's adamant stand against Jewish-Christian theological dialogue. Concerned, in the wake of Catholic overtures encouraged by the thaw in anti-Semitism mandated by the Second Vatican Council, that the sense of the singularity and uniqueness of *Kenesset Yisrael* might become jaded, both within and without the Jewish world, the Rav fought vigorously against incipient ecumenism. He, and only he, had both the stature and the courage to restrain those who, whether *le-shem Shamayim* or otherwise—the prospect of having one's picture with the Pope appear on the front page of the *New York Times* is no mean temptation—sought the warm embrace of our erstwhile contemners; and the policy he enunciated—assent to dialogue about moral or social issues but rejection of discussions of faith and dogma—has stood the Orthodox community in good stead. In retrospect, some may feel that the Rav's anxiety about missionary impulses and possible mass apostasy was exaggerated. Be that as it may, however, the episode—and it was more than that—boldly manifested the Rav's engagement in communal affairs and the leadership he exercised in that capacity.

Even in the realm of *ma'ase*, however, sociopolitical activity was not the Rav's forte. His primary practical role was realized, rather, through the interface of *talmud* and *ma'ase*—through teaching, which Aquinas aptly defined as the ideal fusion of the active and the contemplative life. This interaction probably lies at the heart of the *Gemara*'s discussion, as understood by Rashi, about the comparative merits of *talmud* and *ma'ase*. Resolving an apparent contradiction about their respective priority, the *Gemara* concludes: לא קשיא הא, למיגמר, הא לאגמורי;. Rashi explains: למיגמר לעצמו, מעשה עדיף, אבל לאגמורי לאחריני עדיף ממעשה.[9] Presumably, the intent is not simply that teaching is more meritorious, qua *talmud*, than *ma'asse*, but rather that, in effect, it incorporates both, in the spirit of *Hazal*'s formulation: תורה ללמדה, זו היא תורה של חסד; שלא ללמדה, זו היא תורה שאינה של חסד.[10]

As regards the Rav, then, his primary practical contribution was as *moreinu ve-rabbeinu*, our master teacher. And this, in two respects. First, of course, in the narrow sense of exposition, explication, and instruction. He often—albeit, at times, with a note of conveniently feigned self-deprecation—described himself as a *melamed*; and that he was, without peer. His capacity for formulating pivotal questions, with an eye to the relation between principle and detail; his sheer pedagogic skill, in stimulating curiosity and insight; above all, his fertile and suggestive solutions—these continually left their imprint upon students, over the span of half a century.

He addressed himself to this task with conscious dedication—dictated, in part, by his professional responsibilities as a *rav ha-ir* or as a *rosh yeshiva*, but driven, far beyond what those duties required, by the impetus of mission, that pervasive sense of *shelihut* of which he often spoke, so fervently and so eloquently. This was, obviously, primarily manifested in the course of regular *shiurim*, whose sheer scope is strikingly impressive; but its also impinged upon his *harbatsat Torah* as a whole. It largely influenced, for instance, the choice of topics for the *Yahrtseit shiurim*—so heavily tilted toward *Orah Hayyim*, and almost wholly devoid of more abstruse areas such as *Kodashim*, which had been his father's forte and, in a sense, his own first love. I vividly recall how one year, several decades back, he began to prepare a *Yahrtseit shiur* to deal with *kinyan hatser*, but then dropped the idea out of concern that the infrastructure might not be sufficiently familiar to many in the audience. In a similar vein, when, in later years, his interest in publication intensified, he was firm in encouraging the assignment of primacy to writings which would serve the general Torah public best, rather than to those which were geared to his indigenous "*lomdische*" constituency.

In the Rav's thought and experience, his role as *moreinu ve-rabbeinu* went in tandem with a second—that of *me-turgeman.* He once remarked to me that, basically, it is the function of *marbitsei Torah,* in each generation, to render its content into the language and categories of their contemporaries; and there is no question but that this facet was an integral component of any self-portrait he limned. That rendering was, of course, interpretation rather than mere translation; and very much in the spirit of the *Gemara* in *Kiddushin*: תניא, ר׳ יהודה אומר, ׳המתרגם פסוק כצורתו, הרי זה בדאי, והמוסיף עליו, הרי זה מחרף ומגדף, אלא מאי תרגום–תרגום דידן.׳[11]

As a halakhic entity, *Targum didan* is related to an area much developed by the Rav, *keriat haTorah.* Explicating a *pasuk* in *Nehemiah,* describing Torah reading upon the return from exile, the *Gemara* explains:

> אמר רב חננאל אמר רב, ״מאי דכתיב, ׳ויקראו בספר תורת האלקים מפורש ושום שכל ויבינו במקרא׳? ׳ויקראו בספר תורת האלקים,׳ זה מקרא, ׳מפורש,׳ זה תרגום, ׳ושום שכל,׳ אלו הפסוקים, ׳ויבינו במקרא,׳ זה פיסוק טעמים, ואמרי לה, אלו המסורות.״[12]

In this connection, the Rav repeatedly developed a distinction between the *keria* of mid-week or *minha* on Shabbat, primarily geared to maintaining continual contact with Torah as a vivifying force, and that of Shabbat morning, intended to provide not only inspiration but instruction and direction. Hence, he contended that *targum* was confined to the latter, as a vehicle for the realization of public *talmud Torah,* for which an intermediary interpreter could be pivotal, in line with the prescription of an oft-quoted *Yerushalmi*:

> כשם שניתנה על ידי סרסור, כך אנו צריכים לנהוג בה על ידי סרסור, עאל רבי יהודא בר פזי ועבדה שאילה, ׳אנכי עמד בין ה׳ וביניכם בעת ההוא להגיד לכם את דבר ה׳.׳[14]

The Rav was central to our weekday and Shabbat *keria* both—as our link to the mesora, infusing us with the substance of Torah, on the one hand, and through creative explication, halakhic and philosophic, relating it to the realities of the modern world, on the other. This dual integrated function of *rav-me-turgeman* is a difficult and delicate enterprise. Interpret too literally, and you run the risk of ossification and obscurantism—*harei ze badai*; range too far afield, and you raise the specter of blasphemous deviation—*harei ze me-haref u-me-gadef.* Only *Targum didan,* traditional creative exposition, in the hands of a thoroughly responsible and richly innovative master, hits the mark. And we are all deeply in the Rav's debt for having embarked on this undertaking.

The Rav's dual role as spiritual mentor was, for him, a source of immense gratification. However, it was also, perhaps inevitably, a cause of considerable frustration. That frustration centered, primarily, on the sense that the full thrust of his total *keria-targum* was often not sufficiently apprehended or appreciated; that, by some, parts of his Torah were indeed being digested and disseminated, but other essential ingredients were being relatively disregarded, if not distorted. In a moment of striking candor, when my colleague, Rav Yehuda Amital, first visited these shores, over twenty years ago, the Rav commented to him: "You know, I have devoted *talmidim*—very devoted *talmidim.* If I were to announce a *shiur* at two o'clock in the morning, they would come *en bloc.* And yet, deep in their hearts, they think I'm an *apikoros.*" The remark was laced with characteristic humor and confined, presumably, to a select group. Nevertheless, it gave vent to a genuine, if painful, sentiment.

The ideological fault aside, however, he often felt—and this, with respect to a far broader group—that even among *talmidim,* some of his primary spiritual concerns were not so much rejected as ignored; indeed, that spirituality itself was being neglected. He was, like Rambam, persistently perturbed by religious vulgarization, practical or conceptual, and by shallow ritualization, of either the "modern" or the "*frum*" strain; and the tension between the subjective and the objective, between action, thought, and experience, was a major lifelong concern. The sense that he was only partially successful in imparting that concern gnawed at him, and impelled efforts to redress the imbalance; but these, too, were only partly successful. After his wife's death in 1967, he initiated intensive *shiurim* for *talmidim* who would come to Brookline to learn during the summer. One day (*ca.* 1969-70), he stunned the group by announcing that, inasmuch as he found them spiritually desiccated, he would now, in addition to the regular *shiurim* on the *massekhet*, learn the *Likutei Torah* of the *Ba'al haTanya* with them; and he started, the following day, with the section on *Ani le-dodi ve-dodi li.* "But," he confided to me subsequently, "it didn't really help."

The most forceful expression of this sentiment is to be found in a brief essay which I regard as the single best introduction to the Rav's thought—all the more so, as it bears the stamp of total genuineness, having been conceived and composed during and shortly after his bout with cancer in the winter of 1959-60. After lamenting that the current Torah world has produced aspiring *talmidei hakhamim* who are intellectually assertive but experientially deficient, he goes on to assign part of the blame to himself:

> Therefore, I hereby announce that I am able to identify one of those responsible for the present situation—and that is I myself. I have not fulfilled my obligation as a *moreh derekh vehora'a* in Israel. I lacked the spiritual energies which a teacher and rabbi needs, or I lacked the necessary will, and did not dedicate everything I had to my goal. While I have succeeded, to a great or small degree, as a teacher and guide in the area of "*gadlut ha-mohin*"—my students have received much Torah from me, and their intellectual stature has been strengthened and increased during the years they have spent around me—I have not seen much success in my efforts in the experiential area. I was not able to live together with them, to cleave to them and to transfer to them from the warmth of my soul. My words, it seems, have not kindled the *shalhevet y-a* in sensitive

> hearts. I have sinned as a *marbits Torah she-ba-lev*, which has been given over in a fashion which has been *me-ma'et ha- Demut* to the point of *katnut ha-mohin*. My error lies with me.[15]

That, too is part of the Rav's legacy. Not just spellbinding *shiurim*, magnificent *derashot*, and electrifying *hiddushim*, but the candid recognition of failure—failure which is transcended by its very acknowledgement. In his own personal vein, so aristocratic and yet so democratic, he has imbued us with a sense of both the frailty of majesty and the majesty of frailty. He has transmitted to us not only *Torat Moshe Avdi*, but the Midrashic image of Moshe Rabbenu constructing and then dismantling the *mishkan* daily during *shivat yemei ha-milu'im*—whose import the Rav interpreted as the fusion of radical, almost Sisyphean frustration with ultimate hope. He has initiated us, far from the admiring crowd, into the anguished quest—unlike Plotinus, he did not necessarily experience it as a flight (as either ascent or escape)—of the alone for the Alone. He has left us not only memories of packed audiences, dazzled by his multifaceted powers, but the riveting sense of the message of the *Mishna*, so humbling and yet so inspiring, מנין שאפילו אחד שיושב ועוסק בתורה, שהקב״ה קובע לו שכר? שנאמר, ״ישב בדד וידום כי נטל עליו.״[17]

The Rav repeatedly referred to this *Mishna* when expatiating upon the experiential character of *talmud Torah*; and the meeting envisioned by it may be regarded as the epitome of the Rav's *talmud* and *ma'ase* both. His quintessential aspiration was the fusion of spirituality and *lomdut*. We, who come after, cannot retrospectively imagine the past half-century without him. Prospectively, as dwarfs on a giant's shoulders, we feel charged to persist, impelled by his spirit, in the implementation of his goals—to learn, to teach, to realize. To the best of our abilities, we are called and we are pledged to continue, in the *bet hamidrash* and in the community, his multi-faceted enterprise—*le-hagdil Torah u-le-ha'adira*.

Notes

1. *Halakhic Man*, p. 23. With respect to the substance of this specific passage, several points may be noted:
   1) The examples subsequently cited all refer to modes of dealing with deviant phenomena, whose failure to materialize, so that the relevant *halakhot* can be applied, is obviously not to be lamented. It does not follow from this, however, that a *talmid hakham* may be equally apathetic about the fate of positive or even ideal elements.
   2) Abstinence from *pesak* out of *yirat hora'a* may not reflect indifference to implementation but, rather, responsible concern about it—and hence, anxiety over possible error.
   3) The statement about the reluctance of *gedolim* to enter the lists of *pesak* probably requires some qualification. It is true of some venues—nineteenth century Lithuania, out of whose tradition the Rav sprang, possibly being a case in point—but, as historical generalization, strikes me as somewhat sweeping.
2. *Ibid*, p. 38.
3. *Ibid*, p. 30.
4. *Ibid*, p. 79.
5. See the account of Reb Haym's method in the Rav's *hesped* of his son, Reb Yitshak Zev, "*Ma Dodekh miDod*," in *Divrei Hagut veHa'arakha* (Jerusalem, 5742), pp. 79-80.
6. How much the formal philosophic discipline—as opposed to general cultural orientation—contributed to the Rav's overall *mahshava* is worthy of study. In *Halakhic Mind*, the impact is of course powerful; but that work, while published only recently, is relatively early (1940's), and the question can be raised with respect to later phases.
7. "The Prelude," III, 61-3.
8. *Kitvei haRamban* (Jerusalem 5746), 1:341.
9. *Baba Kama* 17a; *Rashi, s.v. le-migmar*.
10. *Sukka* 49b.
11. *Kiddushin* 49a.
12. *Nedarim* 37b.
13. See *Shiurim leZekher Abba Mari Z"l* (Jerusalem 5743), 1:100, 5-10.
14. *Yerushalmi, Megilla* 4:1.
15. "*Al Ahavat haTorah uGe'ulat Nefesh haDor*," in *Besod haYahid ve-haYahad*, Jerusalem.
16. See *Rashi, Vayikra* 9:23.
17. *Avot* 3:2.

"For My Grandfather Has Left Me . . . ."

MOSHEH LICHTENSTEIN

HOW CAN A GRANDSON EULOGIZE HIS GRANDFATHER? How dare he assume such a task? Will not fear and awe overtake him? Would it not be preferable to wrap himself in the silence of sorrow and the solace of tears? Can he really hope to accurately portray the departed persona or faithfully describe his personality? The eulogy must be a full and accurate description of the deceased, his personality and acts, the wonderful and unique within him. But the grandson could observe the great creative powers of his beloved grandfather only through the blurry vision of childhood, the veil of youth cast upon his eyes throughout the period of his elder's zenith. Yet, when the grandson matured and ripened, ready to receive his grandfather's bounty, it was too late, for by then the elderly figure had already begun to withdraw, slowly receding from the younger generation. The grandson could see the present, but not the past. Though a glimpse of the towering stature was still discernible, and although retrospection is a form of vision, can it possibly compare to direct contact with the power and intensity of the fully active years?

Rabbi Lichtenstein teaches at Yeshivat Har Etzion in Alon Shvut, Israel.

Furthermore, how can a grandson attempt to eulogize a grandfather who was a supreme master of Torah, a figure who expressed his great personality through force of intellect and breadth of vision as he attempted to penetrate the mysterious and the deep. Who can gather the strength to describe a grandfather who defined the art of eulogy as follows: "It is the duty of the eulogist to present a full, comprehensive description of the greatness of the departed, in reasoned tranquil categories, to stress all the mysterious wonder interwoven in the concrete personal reality. . . . The eulogist is an excellent educator, the agent of the cool quiet intellect, and also an artist representing the irrational, absurd experience. . . . The eulogist explains and interprets, illustrates and creates."[1] Can a grandson rush in, fearless of where he treads, to comply with these rigorous criteria, which have been imposed by his own grandfather, the greatest eulogist of the generation? Even if his inferior intellect supports him in this endeavor, will he be able to control his emotions in the face of his great loss? As soon as he begins to describe his grandfather, powerful feelings will overwhelm him as he remembers their warm and loving relationship and recollects fond memories of the many beautiful hours which they spent together. Moreover, were all these emotions to be controlled, the struggling grandson will, nevertheless, be overcome by a sense of disappointment and guilt for the Torah that he lost and the wisdom which he missed.

However, in spite of all this, how can one not eulogize and lament a grandfather such as the Rav *zt"l*, a genius of halakha and a giant of spirit, a figure belonging to the select group of the Sages of our Tradition (*Hakhmei haMesora*)? Both natural human feeling and the halakhic obligations regarding human dignity (*kevod haberiot*) and the honor of Torah (*kevod haTorah*) require me to set forth upon this endeavor. And though I may be unable to fulfill the task of faithfully portraying his image, the *Mishna* in *Pirkei Avot* has already taught us that a person may not shy away from his charge, even though it is unexpected of him to complete it.

I.

The *Gemara* in *Baba Batra* (59a) relates: "A pipe which drains water to the yard of one's neighbor and the owner of the roof tries to stop it up, the owner of the yard can prevent him. . . . Rav Oshaya said he has the right to prevent him; Rav Hama said he does not have the right to prevent him. They went and asked Rav Bisa, who said he has the right to prevent him. Rami bar Hama said of him, "The threefold cord is not readily broken"—this is Rav Oshaya, the son of Rav Hama, the son of Rav Bisa." The *Tosafot* remark: "There were many such that they and their fathers and their fathers' fathers were outstanding scholars, yet this is not said of them; here, however, all three saw each other."

Thus, it was not merely the fact that three generations of the same family achieved Torah scholarship that so impressed Rami bar Hama, nor was his exclamation due to the uniqueness of this phenomenon. After all, there have been many such families. Rami bar Hama felt that he was witnessing something extraordinary. Rav Oshaya was not merely a member of the group of sages who were fortunate enough to be the sons and grandsons of learned scholars; it was rather that he embodied a special combination that contained the treasures and traditions of former generations. Old and new were integrated within him. His threefold cord wove together his father's Torah learning, fully absorbed and comprehended, with his own great native forces of innovation and creativity. In his youth, he learned Torah with his father and grandfather and debated with them weighty halakhic issues; delving into difficult passages together, he acquired their mode of learning as a lasting possesion. Returning as an adult to these same *sugyot*, he was able to pour new content into them as result of the personal method which he had developed and perfected over the years. The unique strength of the threefold cord is not due to its additional thickness, but to its complexity; each thread adds a new dimension to the cord. Thus, he who builds his personality and learning by combining his native powers and individual approach with those of his fathers can attain a singular level that is not to be found in those who rely solely on their own powers or depend on those of their forebears.

It is the way of the world that a son takes over from his father. One generation passes on the tradition to its successor: "Instead of your ancestors will be your children, you will appoint them princes throughout the land"(Psalms 45:17). A child receives instruction from his father, a student from his teacher. Thus, the torch of traditional learning and scholarship is passed on from generation to generation. The passage in *Isaiah* 59:21, which the *Gemara* in *Baba Metsia* (85a) interprets as referring to Torah, describes and emphasizes this process: "And this shall be My covenant with them, said the Lord. My spirit which is upon you, and the words which I have placed in your mouth, shall not be absent from your mouth, nor from the mouth of your children, nor from the mouth of your children's children—said the Lord—from now throughout all time." No premium can be placed upon the centrality or importance of this transmission, about which God entered into a covenantal relationship with us. Studying with and teaching one's children are the foundation of our tradition, and thus, Torah remains rooted within families. *Tosafot* inform us that there have been many learned families throughout the course of our history. A succession of three generations, a grandfather, father and grandson, all Torah scholars, is an extremely important but not a particularly rare phenomenon and does not justify an exclamation of wonder. Generations may differ or they may resemble one another; what is common to them, though, is that each member is rooted within the Torah world of his time. Whether he applies and continues his learning method as he was trained or develops a different approach, each participant is an additional link in the chain of tradition, a continuation of the previous generation. "Perets begot Hetsron, Hetsron begot Ram, Ram begot Aminadav, Aminadav begot Nahshon, Nahshon begot. . . ." Generations come and go, but tradition remains forever.

Sometimes, though, instead of the usual thread attached to the previous one at its tip—the son taking the place of the father—a unique threefold cord presents itself. A person who carries both his own talents and those of the preceding generations appears. Not only his capacities, but also those of his ancestors are evident in him. Three generations are combined within one individual. The forces of the past and present ferment within him. He succeeeds in breaking the barrier of the present as he weaves together elements of the past's mighty heritage with his own innovations. He does not merely reconstruct the past, nor does he simply cling to his ancestors' Torah. Although every fiber in the layers of his personality is capable of standing on its own, his unique power is created by the integration of all three elements in a single persona. When confronted with a Rav who uses the achievements of the past to create a new method and approach, who is able to draw from the past and impress a new stamp upon it, all shall rejoice and proclaim: "The threefold cord is not readily broken."

Rav Oshaya was such a man. When Rami bar Hama came to the *bet midrash* and found Rav Oshaya ruling—in opposition to his father's opinion—that the owner of the yard has the right to prevent the pipe from being stopped up, he sent for the opinion of Rav Bisa, the grandfather. Rav Bisa determined that the pipe cannot be stopped up unilaterally. This caused Rami bar Hama to wonder: if this is his grandfather's opinion, what is Rav Oshaya adding? Why doesn't he simply cite Rav Bisa's ruling? Does the addition of extra names add any weight to the ruling? He carefully reexamined the issue and understood; Rav Oshaya was not merely repeating his elder's opinion, he was expressing an independent view. A new perspective was being brought to the question. Though his conclusion was identical to his predecessor's, the rationale behind it reflected his own particular approach. Thus, the old and the new were combined to form a new method.

My grandfather, the Rav, was also such a figure. He, too, was an illustrious grandson, an outstanding product of his family's

Brisker school. His mastery of the rigorous analytical method and innovative approach of the "Brisker *derekh*" was complete. A full-fledged member of the inner circle of Reb Chaim's children and grandchildren, he acquired the Brisker way of learning at a very young age. While yet a young boy whose wisdom far exceeded his years, he sent his *hiddushei Torah* to Reb Chaim himself, who proudly exhibited them to others. When he grew older, he engaged in an active correspondence with his uncle Reb Velvel, the Brisker Rav. But the supreme influence upon him in the formative learning years was, of course, the constant, uninterrupted years of study with his father, Reb Moshe Soloveichik, as they sat together day and night, clarifying most of the difficult passages in the Talmud. This marvelous relationship between father and son, linked together in heart and soul, which began in a tiny Byelorussian *shtetl* and remained constant until the day of Reb Moshe's death in New York, created a Torah giant, proficient and creative in the ways of his ancestors.

Though the Rav was born in Lithuania, he died in the United States; though commencing his studies in Chaslavitch, he ended them in Boston. Though clearly a Brisker scion, he was an independent personality who stood by himself, uniquely different from all who preceded him. A threefold cord interweaving the past and the present, the old and the new, Berlin with Brisk, Boston with Volozhin—such a figure was my grandfather, the Rav.

II.

The Rav was a many-faceted individual. A great scholar in many fields, he was a master of halakha and aggada, learning and philosophy, exoteric and esoteric wisdom. However, attempting to delineate his persona and to describe his spiritual world, we must emphasize the world of Torah study and halakha as its prime mover. If there was one feature imprinted upon the depths of his soul, if there was a single primordial experience for the Rav, it was the study of *Torah li-shma*. If I had to describe my grandfather with two words, they would undoubtedly be "Halakhic Man." He regarded himself as a teacher surrounded by students engaging in *Torah li-shma*, a Rav instructing his congregants in the details of halakhic *sugyot* as they all joined together to form the community of tradition. His self-image was neither that of the philosopher, communal leader, or author, even though all these were part of his personality and achievements. Before the holidays he would bless his students that they should be able to experience the *kedushat ha–yom* through the study of its *halakhot*. It was Torah study that supported him during the difficult years in the aftermath of his wife's death, enabling his bleeding soul to find some repose. The enormous energy that he poured into teaching and disseminating Torah protected and preserved him; it may be said of this period that "the Torah of duress is what stood by me." A particularly striking instance of how deeply ingrained Torah was in the Rav's personality is worth relating. In the immediate aftermath of surgery, when medication loosened the grip of his stern, conscious self control and his inner self freely expressed itself, a series of solutions to difficult *Rambams* poured out! The qualities of Halakhic Man, so brilliantly depicted in his great essay, were firmly imprinted upon the depths of his soul.

Let us begin, therefore, with a description of his halakhic enterprise. The rigorous Brisker approach of strict analysis and clarification of concepts, well known throughout the modern Torah world, was masterfully continued and developed by the Rav. All areas of halakha were illuminated by his penetrating analysis. Issue after issue, from the beginning of the *Shas* to its end, were examined, taught, and interpreted.

Actually, he was not alone in this endeavor. Reb Chaim's method, itself a combination of elements long existing in the world of halakha with the vigor and vitality of the new tools of systematic analysis and criticism, was securing for itself the central role in the Lithuanian Torah world. Although surrounded by only a handful of close students throughout most of his teaching career, Reb

Chaim's approach rapidly won over the hearts of the learning public. Despite encountering initial opposition on the part of the senior *rabbanim*, within a generation his method reigned supreme in the Lithuanian yeshivot. All those familiar with the works of the so-called "*Roshei Yeshivas* generation" are well acquainted with the Brisker influence. Thus, the Rav was a partner in an enterprise that many others were also participating in. [Some of the *hiddushei Torah* which he wrote as a youth and declined to publish, as befitting an authentic member of Brisk, were subsequently published by others who had independently arrived at similar conclusions.] Nevertheless, he was superb in this endeavor, producing Torah of the highest quality. An understanding of Reb Chaim's method and its characteristics will enable us to explain and demonstrate the Rav's achievements in this respect.

There are many ways to approach the methodology developed by the Rav's grandfather, Reb Chaim Soloveitchik of Brisk, and it is certainly not our intention here to provide a comprehensive analysis. However, if we limit ourselves to a single point, the core of the method consists in shifting the center of interest from the intent and goal of the halakhic ruling to its actual manifestation in practical terms (*nafka mina*). It is not a hidden rationale or biblical intention (*ta'ama di–kra*) that provides the point of origin for the discussion, but the phenomenon in and of itself. The student places his interest in the fruit of the tree rather than its roots. Thus, unsubstantiated hypotheses relating to hidden matters are eliminated and scholars are prevented from speculating about unverifiable issues which cannot be judged by concrete halakhic phenomena. Torah study is, therefore, placed upon firm ground and criticism established as the cornerstone of the learning activity. Purely speculative hypotheses (*sevarot*) are subordinated, as reasoning is required to account for halakhic manifestations in actual practice. Principles are not accepted unless they grow directly and organically out of the details in the *Gemara* and *Rambam* and are capable of being criticized by them. Disagreement among the *rishonim* must be explained, and if a theoretical distinction is suggested, it must provide a practical manifestation that illustrates the difference. There should be no phenomenon without an explanation and no explanation without a phenomenal expression.

This principle is obviously analogous to the scientific revolution of the early seventeenth century. Here, as there, there is a shift of interest from the "why" to the "what" and "how," from the final cause to the effective cause. In the same manner that the change in scientific outlook led to far reaching achievements, so, too, did the new critical approach of Reb Chaim do so in the sphere of Torah study. The Brisker revolution is the Copernican revolution of the halakhic world.

Part of this process is the increased emphasis placed upon *Rambam* by the followers of Brisk. As long as Torah study focused upon the supposed theoretical reasoning underlying a Talmudic passage, a gap existed between the Talmudic commentators *ad locum* and the *Mishne Torah,* which is essentially a book of applied halakha. Thus, a commentator would ordinarily devote his time and effort to the study of other commentaries dealing with the same text, while a *posek* of practical halakha would deal with the relevant halakhic literature, each remaining within his specific field. [This is obviously a generalization and is not meant to be absolute.] However, as soon as the interpretation of the Talmudic passage itself becomes dependent upon its practical implications, it is imperative to systematically examine the various practical conclusions which may be derived from it. This, of course, is where the *Mishne Torah* enters the picture, for it is the monumental review of the conclusions which have developed out of the Talmudic passages, and, therefore, ideally suited for Reb Chaim's purposes.

To be totally clear and to prevent any misunderstandings, I would like to point out that the emphasis upon the halakhic conclusions of the *sugya* is not meant to arrive at any conclusions regarding practical behavior, but is a purely interpretive enterprise. Therefore, the interest is not neccesarily in the final conclusions, but in the halakhic manifestations throughout all stages of the discussion. The aim of the Brisker approach is the conceptual formulation, not the prescription of behavior, and in this, too, it resembles the scientific attempt to derive abstract laws and concepts from concrete phenomena. However, the abstraction and conceptualization must be sought through the practical manifestations dictated by the Talmudic passage and subject to their criticism. Therefore, the method is equally applicable in all areas of the Talmud—*Kodashim* and *Taharot* as well as *Mo'ed* and *Nashim*. This, according to Reb Chaim's method, is the real meaning of "*le-asukei shemateta a-liba de-hilkheta*": the interpretation of the *sugya* based upon its halakhic implications, regardless of our actual ruling regarding practice.

This approach, which is the foundation of Reb Chaim's method and which gives it its unique quality, also poses a danger. If we focus on the "what" rather than the "why," we have remained faithful to the facts and have been careful not to proceed beyond what is warranted. However, focusing upon the pure structural logic within a *sugya* without examining the plausibility of the conclusions, erecting a halakhic paradigm based upon the concrete details regardless of whether it is reasonable or not, is as serious a defect as pure speculation detached from the details. Both the "speculative fallacy" and the "logical fallacy" must be avoided. The "what" must also withstand the criticism of the "why." Even though two separate alternatives can function as two facets of a halakhic investigation (*hakira*), explaining differences of opinion and enhancing various details, they cannot be accepted if there is no rationale behind them which is reasonable in the context of their topic. The relationship between these two factors must be a mutual one, each engaging and critical of the other element. The point of contact between these two elements is where the problematic aspect of the Brisker approach is exposed. The heavy emphasis placed upon the analytical element may easily undermine the delicate balance between the two factors, since any investigation which postulates two sides to a question and demonstrates their practical implications can be accepted without any further ado.

It is this very point of encounter which enables us, it seems to me, to comprehend the unique quality of the Rav's learning (aside, of course, from his natural intellectual ability). Indeed, many followed Reb Chaim's footsteps and attained important achievements. However, even the most capable of his disciples were not always able to avoid the "logical fallacy." Radical formulations which were logically possible but opposed to any reasonable standard of plain halakhic thinking were adopted on occasion, creating conclusions which were highly implausible, even though valid if judged by *a priori* logic alone. Others, who were not satisfied with merely explaining the phenomena, abandoned Reb Chaim's method altogether and lost the critical anchor of the concrete halakhic expression (*nafka mina*).

The Rav avoided both extremes. Fundamentally faithful to his grandfather's method, his ideas were subjected to the critical control of the actual halakhic case. He was careful not to rashly charge into areas where he could not exercise such control. Nonetheless, he took care to examine the results of his inquiry into the actual halakhic manifestation in the light of simple logic. When one of his students mentioned to him a well known (and seemingly self evident) *hakira* to him, the Rav's response was, "I have no idea what the second option could possibly mean." I vividly remember this tension dramatically expressing itself the first day I was in his *shiur*. We were learning the issues of *gezeila* in the ninth chapter of *Bava Kama* that year. The first *shiur* began with the following statement by the Rav: "There is a well-known inquiry into the nature of the obligation to return stolen property. I don't like it since it is obvious to me that one of the possibilities should be rejected; however, what can I do, it is clear that both sides are represented in a debate between the Ba'al haMa'or and Ramban" [*Sanhedrin* 72a]. Personal logic and common sense must have their say, but if the evidence in the sources indicates otherwise, the evidence must be accepted.

What should be emphasized, morever, is that the Brisker method was not, for the Rav, an acquired technique or a scholarly method which he received from his mentors. His natural thought patterns were forged out of analytic understanding. His initial reading of a *sugya* was an analytic one; intrinsically, he read the passage in such a manner. The prism through which he viewed all issues was an analytic one, exposing the conceptual structure of the text as a matter of course. Thus, his manner of learning was not the application of a technique or the utilization of acquired tools, which may be occasionally employed and occasionally forgotten, accepted at times and neglected at others. His learning was not founded upon sudden flashes of insight or based upon an intuitive reasoning as fleeting as it is sudden. The Rav's Torah was based upon the rock–solid foundation of an internalized systematic thought process, steady and sure, analytic and innovative. Therefore, the Rav's learning did not distinguish between greater or lesser issues, minor or major *sugyot;* whatever he studied was subject to his scholarly critique and intellectual discipline. Brief and minor issues were analyzed in the same manner as weighty, intricate and well-known passages, since the same inner logic applies to them all. Great or small, weighty or trivial, all matters were treated equally.

It is worth noting in this context that the Rav's scholarly net was spread over all areas of Torah learning. I do not mean to claim that he devoted a great amount of time and energy to relatively neglected halakhic sources such as the *Yerushalmi* or the *Sifrei* or that he had a phenomenal memory, but rather that he trained his scholarly eye even upon sources which are not generally considered deserving of halakhic attention. Thus, he gleaned pearl after pearl from the *siddur, kinot* and *piyyutim* and interwove them into his halakhic presentations. My memory still retains, in all its vividness and freshness, the wonderful *shiur* which he gave upon the structure of *tefilat musaf* of the *shalosh regalim,* weaving toether the relevant *sugyot,* passages from the *siddur, keriat haTorah* and *Sefer haMitsvot*. The *Yahrtseit shiur* on the issue of *mehikat haShem* (which was later published in *Shiurim leZekher Abba Mari*) ended with a fundamental distinction (*hiluk*) between two aspects of *yud-he* as a *shem,* which was based, in part, upon a *diyyuk* in *Targum Onkelos*. With his sharp eye, the Rav was able to identify and transform such non-halakhic material, utilizing it for his purposes time after time.

The systematic thought that analytically penetrated everything it took in—great or small, classic or unconventional sources—is what gave the Rav's learning its authority and force. However, a systematic critical ability was not the only quality which characterized his Torah. The Rav was also blessed with an abundance of creative and innovative powers. These burst forth from the depths of his personality, forming a fountain of learning creativity, flowing along the lively new paths of Torah through which their creator channeled them. What he claimed about Halakhic Man—"[he] received the Torah from Sinai not as a simple recipient, but as a creator of worlds"[2]—he was able to achieve in his own person, and what he added there, that "the power of innovation is the basis of tradition," can be seen as an accurate description of his own endeavor, a Torah which is original and innovative, yet deeply rooted in the continuity of tradition.

Thus, the Rav remained firmly rooted in the family tradition of Brisker learning, through his adherence to the mutally controlling relationship between cause and effect, concrete phenomena and analytic conceptualization. The additional quality which he added as a third thread to the existing cord of tradition was an involvement in halakhic areas which unite cause and effect into a single learning unity. The establishment of areas and issues which entwine the two together, in contrast to the usual Brisker opposition between cause and effect, is what characterized his unique contribution. Addressing issues of halakhic import whose primary motive is to be found in the religious experience, he was able to combine his analytic Brisker approach with his philosophical powers, as he interwove the religious rationale with the concrete details to create a unified halakhic entity. The greater the link between halakha and aggada, the more he felt at home in that area. Thus, he laid new foundations in areas such as *berakhot, avelut, keriat haTorah, gerut, tefilla, mo'adim, kiddush ha–hodesh,* and many others. Totally new concepts were created in this manner. This trend can be clearly discerned in some of the opening passages of the book of *hiddushei Torah* which he co-authored with his father, Reb Moshe *zt"l,* while still a youth. This combination would fully blossom later in the *shiurim* which the Rav would deliver on these topics as part of his teaching routine, and attain its most outstanding expression in the *yahrtseit shiurim* which he would deliver in memory of his father. Anyone perusing the two volumes of his book, *Shiurim leZekher Abba Mari,* will clearly see what achievements were realized in these areas and how unique he was in this, both in contrast to his Brisker predecessors and his contemporary colleagues.

Nonetheless, it is important to reiterate that this development did not entail an abandonment of the basic Brisker method, neither in terms of his self image nor in actual substance. Development and innovation are found here, but not a renunciation or disclaim of the fundamental system. This is the secret of the threefold cord.

III.

The Rav's halakhic achievement, his bright white threefold cord, was accompanied by an additional strand of *tekhelet,* the colored thread whose associations remove man from his personal world and garment to contemplate the sea, skies and Heaven, reaching up to the Heavenly throne itself. The personal *tekhelet* which my grandfather affixed to his halakhic *lavan* was a philosophical and experiential acceptance of the natural physical world in which man was placed by God, as well as an involvement with man's complex relationship towards this world as he strives to present himself before his Creator. The majesty and greatness of a dignified human existence accompanied with the proper sense of humility and respect, an ongoing dialogue between man and the Almighty [and between the covenantal community of Israel and its Divine companion], the place of man within a technological society, these and similar dilemmas all appear in his writings. Such were the topics which the Rav dealt with and wrote about, and such were the issues which he experienced in his inner being.

The interweaving of both strands, the blue thread of philosophical enquiry with the white one of Torah scholarship, combined to create a special personality and philosophical approach. Since a eulogy is not the place to deal with the specifics of my grandfather's philosophical outlook, we will confine ourselves here to the essence and aims of his approach. The linchpin of the system is to be found in the synthesis of halakha and philosophy and the Jewish and general worlds which serve both to establish the topics of consideration and as source material for the actual discussions. It is this unique combination which gives the Rav's teachings their vitality and force. The mastery which the Rav achieved in both halakha and Jewish philosophy is itself a notable phenomenon, worthy of mention in an evaluation of his works. Anyone who wants to form a complete impression of the Rav's achievement and versatility must take into account his occupation with such diverse sources as the teachings of Habad (which included *shiurim* which he gave on *Likkutei Torah*) and his epistemological, metaphysical work, *Halakhic Mind.*

However, it must be made clear that it is not the coincidental presence of halakhic and philosophic profundity within a single personality which we are discussing, but rather the fusion of the two into an integrated Torah perspective. Rav Soloveitchik is not a halakhic *gadol*, unaware of the dilemmas of general culture, nor a religously observant philosopher; he is a master of both fields who is able to illuminate both of them with the light of his Torah. An artificial division between the rabbinic and philosophical element within his personality is inconceivable. The two are mutually compatible and complementary. The dilemmas and acts of the God-fearing Jew receive, in the Rav's world, assistance and enhancement from general knowledge, if used with the proper care and attention, while the Torah has within it the capacity to solve questions of pure philosophical interest.

Thus, the Rav portrays Halakhic Man as imposing his Torah upon the natural world which he encounters:

> When halakhic man approaches reality, he comes with his Torah, given to him from Sinai, in hand. He addresses the world by means of fixed statutes and firm principles. An entire corpus of precepts and laws guides him along the path leading to Being.[3]

Halakhic Man addresses not only uniquely Jewish questions or those of interest to a general religious philosophy, but also tackles issues of philosophical import such as epistemology, the status of nature, and other similar topics. All are reviewed and examined, since the answers to these general perplexities can be found in the Torah which God presented to man at Sinai. Not only were righteous laws and religious messages handed down to Israel, but also Divine wisdom which reveals and interprets the world of experience to humankind: ". . . the path leading to Being." The treasury of Torah and mitsvot contains within it remedies for epistemological and ontological problems. The Rav does not merely utilize general wisdom to harness its information for the purposes of Torah, as the medieval Jewish philosophers did; rather, he attempts to fuse the two in a manner that allows each to illuminate the other. Though the rabbis have taught us that wisdom, if not Torah, is to be found amongst the nations, wisdom itself cannot satisfy its own needs without the assistance of the Torah. This very issue was addressed by the Rav at the conclusion of *Halakhic Mind*, where he wrote the following:

> To this end there is only a single source from which a Jewish philosophical *Weltanschauung* could emerge; the objective order—the Halakhah. . . . Problems of freedom, causality, God-Man relationship, creation and nihility would be illuminated by Halakhic principles. A new light could be shed on our apprehension of reality.
>
> Out of the sources of Halakhah, a new world view awaits formulation.[4]

This aspect of the Rav's philosophical enterprise, that which may be called from "Volozhin to Berlin," is a distinctive feature of the Rav's philosophy, not to be found amongst his contemporaries. For though this approach to the relationship between Judaism and general philosophy was also attempted by other Jewish thinkers in the early twentieth century,[5] these figures did not belong to the world of the *bet ha-midrash*, while the Torah scholars, even those who were aware of developments within the general world, did not see the Torah as providing solutions to philosophical problems.

There is, of course, another aspect—the purely religious one. Metaphysical and ontological issues were not the only ones which concerned the Rav. His primary interest was the existential state of the religious individual in the modern world. Actually, his involvement with philosophical concepts was mainly due to their significance for the religious experience. His writings—"Halakhic Man," *"U-Vikkashtem miSham," The Lonely Man of Faith*, and others—are the cry of the believing individual searching for existential meaning as he approaches his Creator in all his loneliness, greatness, pettiness and confusion. These essays reflect and express man's quest for experiental meaning and a living faith within this world, and, unlike *Halakhic Mind*, are not limited to a search for ontological recognition. Thus, the Rav makes the following existential claim in *The Lonely Man of Faith*:

> The trouble with all rational demonstrations of the existence of God, with which the history of philosophy abounds, consists in their being exactly what they were meant to be by those who formulated them: abstract logical demonstrations divorced from the living primal experiences in which these demonstrations are rooted. For instance, the cosmic experience was transformed into a cosmological proof, the ontic experience into an ontological proof, et cetera. . . .
>
> Maimonides' term *le–yda* (*Yesodei haTorah* 1:1) transcends the bounds of the abstract *logos* and passes over into the realm of the boundless intimate and impassioned experience where postulate and deduction, discursive knowledge and intuitive thinking, conception and perception, subject and object, are one. Only in paragraph five [of *Yesodei haTorah* ch. 1], after the aboriginal experience of God had been established by him as a firm reality, does he introduce the Aristotelian cosmological proof of the unmoved mover.[6]

This is the essence of the approach which he advocates to the sensitive individual in his quest for a spiritual dimension within the material world.

In sum, the Rav's philosophy weaves together the approaches of Scientific Man and Religious Man with that of Halakhic Man to provide existential experience and significance to religious life. Halakhic Man, who is also the man of faith, is nourished by the achievements of others in clarifying and elucidating issues of concern to him, while those others are able to receive satisfaction from the halakhic Torah of our sages. To grasp the scope of this phenomenon within the Rav's writings and to appreciate its breadth and depth, one has to go no further than the footnotes which accompany "Halakhic Man." There, summoned by the author, one can meet, side by side, famous *rabbanim* and German professors, Rambam and William James, Minhat Hinukh and I. L. Peretz, along with many other such figures. In the Rav's world, it is possible to use such diverse sources and create a single, coherent, Torah–true whole from them. Lest anyone mislead himself and think that this was an intellectual posture detached from the fiber of his soul, I must emphatically state that this was not so. Many a time did he preach to my brothers and myself, from the depths of a grandfather's loving concern, the importance of acquiring general and scientific knowledge.

Other aspects of the Rav's achievement, such as his use of Kabbala and Habad *Hassidut,* his extraordinary ability to explain such esoteric issues in a plain and lucid manner, his electrifying rhetorical power and masterful *derashot,* all require the space and emotional tranquility which I lack here. Therefore, rather than dwell on these aspects, I will relate to the reader a personal experience which left a lasting impression upon me. The last summer that I had the privilege of learning with my grandfather, we studied Ramban's commentary on *BeMidbar.* It was an awesome experience. Under his steady and sure guidance, we set out to tackle all the issues which Ramban presented to us. Wherever the winding paths of Ramban's multifaceted curiousity took us, there we followed. If it was a halakhic discussion of an issue such as *yayin nesekh* or *tumat met,* we dealt with it. When a purely interpretive or linguistic question came up, there we were, ready to examine it with the proper tools. Whenever Ramban scaled the heights of a philosophical issue, we were able to follow in his footsteps. And when the commentary approached the Torah from the perspective of the *derekh ha–emet* ["the true path," *i.e.,* a Kabbalistic approach], my grandfather explained it clearly and lucidly. Suddenly, Ramban's cryptic hints were transformed into language and concepts accessible to all. I was convinced at the time that Ramban must have known that centuries later there would arise amongst the Torah scholars a man capable of fully appreciating his work, and that to this person, and his peers over the ages, he directed his monumental enterprise. The entire time that we sat learning together, I could not but help feel a silent ongoing dialogue of hidden love between Ramban and the Rav, leaping over the distance of time and place that separated them but by accident. Those who enjoyed the privilege of participating in the *Yarhei Kalla* in the summers or hearing him on many other occasions surely know what I am talking about. All that I can manage to say in conclusion is that my grandfather, the Rav, has left us, and we cannot even study Ramban on our own!

IV.

A transitional figure, the Rav embraced a variety of worlds and periods. Born in a tiny *shtetl* in eastern Europe into a world in which the majority of the Jews were faithful to religious tradition and that had not yet been exposed to the innovations of modern science and technology, he passed through many communities and countries during his lifetime. After spending time in Jewish Warsaw and Vilna as a youth, he lived for a few years in Berlin before settling down, on the other side of the Atlantic, in Boston and New York. Most of his life was spent in places where only a handful of the local Jews remained committed to Torah. The dilemmas and struggles of the believer in the modern world were, as mentioned above, topics which he dealt with in his writings. However, as a source of inspiration and guidance for his contemporaries, the Rav's own person and way of life were no less important than his explicit teachings. A modern man he was, and it was in the modern world that he lived. The Rav led an active life of *Torah li-shma* within the surrounding general world in which he lived, without ensconcing himself or attempting to escape from it into a sheltered environment. He was well acquainted with American society, thoroughly familiar with its language and culture. People confused by the skepticism and relativism of modern philosophy saw him as a figure certain in his faith and convictions even after being exposed to philosophical analysis and scientific theories. For the younger generation, who was so wonderfully attached to him, the Rav was not only a link with a world that had passed, but also a living example and a prototype of vigorously intensive Torah study by a person who related to the world in which they lived. While many other *rabbanim* represented a choice between the world of the past and that of the present, between America and Eastern Europe, the Rav was able to serve as a guide to the path of Torah study integrated into an existence in the present.

Part of this power came from his deep inner conviction on this issue. Thus he thundered forth, in the midst of the years of horror, boldly and confidently:

> I, too, who have just now witnessed the old in all its splendid grandeur, view the new, peeking forth and rising . . . and the spirit shall yet rest upon Israel's community, who rides the firmament and subdues the earth, and it shall be prophetic. Westward, beyond the great ocean, in a new land of freedom and oppurtunity, Israel will be successful, multiplying and rapidly expanding; between tall and mighty walls, in the shadow of skyscraping towers, the laws of personal status will be fervently discussed, as will the halakhot of *kodshim* and *taharot;* there, on the banks of the Hudson, the Torah of Raban Gamliel and his associates will be transmitted. . . .[7]

If all this now seems self–evident in 1995, this is the best testimony to the success of the Rav's enterprise. Fifty years ago, in the America of the forties, matters were not so simple; not even *rabbanim* were sure that Torah could be established in the *"treife medina."*

In the eulogy for his close friend, Rav Chaim Heller, the Rav developed the idea of *"peleitat sofereihem"*—"remnant" scholarly figures, such as Rav Chaim Heller—who live with us in the present but really belong to a past, vanished world. The Rav describes this phenomenon at length and elaborates upon its importance as a vital link in the chain of tradition. His remarks are as fitting for he who said them as for he for whom they were said. However, I must add that the "remnant" scholars and the link they establish with the past are of little help if there are no contemporary scholars to provide elementary leadership and guidance in the present. The past alone is meaningless if it lacks the support and Torah of the present. If the Torah leadership is firmly rooted in the modern milieu and aware of current trends in society and therefore able to penetrate the hearts of the people, then there is beauty and grandeur in the unique link to tradition that the past-oriented souls amongst us are able to provide. Without the Torah scholars of the current generation, the remnants of the previous one are out of touch with their time and place and cannot relate to the concerns of their contemporaries. The basic work is that done by the leadership of the new generation. Though the Rav's personality contained flashes of his past in another world, he essentially belonged to the world within which he lived. His involvement in the American scene was that of a person who felt at home with it. Even the seemingly minor issue of language may serve to illustrate this point. Many outstanding Torah figures who arrived on American shores did not master the language of the country they lived in, thus detracting greatly from their ability to understand and influence the local youth. This, of course, is untrue of the Rav. He spoke and wrote a fluent and articulate English despite having learned the language as a mature adult. When the need arose to teach in English, he made the transition from his mother tongue to an adopted language with ease. This provided him with an opportunity, unavailable to many of his peers, to reach out to a large audience, scholars as well as laymen, Jews as well as non-Jews. Though this is a practical example, the essence of the issue which it represents runs much deeper.

The Rav was a very modest person. His concern for the people and his attachment to them brought him to serve as a shul and school rabbi, a position which he undertook with the fullest spiritual and emotional involvement rather than remaining within the confines of the *bet midrash*. He lived amongst his people and loved them. Anyone who wanted to know the Rav fully had to see him at home, within his community, in Boston. There, he and the members of the community developed a warm relationship of mutual love and care as the *gadol ha–dor* was transformed into the local rabbi, relaxed and at home amongst his *ba'alei batim*.

The Rav's Torah was a *Torat Hesed*. The first steps he undertook in his Boston *rabbanut* were accompanied by a harsh and bitter struggle, involving vicious personal attacks and *malshinut* against him, due to his insistence on improving the work conditions of the abused *shohatim*, mistreated to such a degree that they were compelled to start walking to work late *Shabbat* afternoon.[8] He extended his sympathy and compassion towards both the small and the great, willingly giving of his time to plain people as to famous leaders. If he browbeat his *talmidim*, it was out of the depths of his attachment to Torah and his concern for developing their learning skills and knowledge. Many other examples could easily be added to these to illustrate his modest and unassuming ways, as well as the *hesed* which accompanied his teaching and leadership.

V.

A eulogy, even after twelve months, is meant to describe the figure of the departed and his personality, in order to heighten our awareness of the loss and to enhance our sense of his absence. Neither analysis nor evaluation are the primary aim of the eulogy; its purpose is strengthing the sense of personal involvement and loss for both he who delivers it and for the audience to whom it is addressed. Let me conclude my presentation with a more personal tone. May the reader forgive me if, henceforth, clear reasoning surrenders to a feeling heart.

The intellect has the power to criticize itself. It examines whether love has outdone itself or if claims and issues have been misrepresented. It will do the utmost to remain within the realm of the universal, where all are equal. The public sphere is strictly separated from the private one. One must remain discreet and not display his feelings to the outer world. Not so the heart; its grief bursts forth and pours out. Nothing can stand in its path as it rushes to express its feelings. It recognizes no boundaries and will not rest until it has proclaimed to all its aching sense of loss and grief. It ventures forth into the public square and shouts; it does not restrain itself, though it knows well that there is nothing novel or unique in its loss. A commotion of confused and overwhelming emotion explodes from within the depths of the soul as it struggles with its loss.

Until now, the intellect has expressed itself; now my heart must have its say. Throughout this eulogy I have spoken of "the Rav" and referred to "my grandfather." Neither is how I knew him, though. For me, he was simply "*Zeide*." "The Rav" is certainly a title of honor and respect; "my grandfather" is an appropriate and proper description. Yet, how poor is the emotional attachment of these phrases in contrast to that plain, simple word, "*Zeide*." No title of honor can approach the emotional power of such awesome words as "*Zeide*" or "*Sabba*." I know and respect, value and appreciate the bitter grief displayed by his *talmidim* from the depths of their aching hearts and the sense of loss which pervaded the general public. What can I do, though, if my heart insists on violating propriety and cries out: "I've lost my *Zeide*! Not only a Rav and a great figure, but also my own loving grandfather!" He was with us, and now he is not.

To be sure, I learned with him; I heard his *shiurim* and listened to his Torah. However, we did not only learn together, we lived and experienced together. Not only halakhic discussions, but also the pain and joy which we shared together united us. In his own way, true to his personality traits, he knew how to express the intense love and care of a grandfather to his grandchildren. The opinion of Rashbam (*Baba Batra* 128a) that an ancestor cannot testify against his offspring, no matter how great the generational distance, was one of his favorite quotations. During the Lebanon war, when I was serving in *Tsahal,* he contacted one of the heads of the Israeli goverment, a person who respected Torah and *rabbanim,* and requested that his voice be heard; not as a Rav or communal leader, but as a grandfather. Like Yosef *haTsadik,* he had the privilege of seeing great-grandchildren. When his first great-grandson was born, he added his smiling color photograph to those of his solemn forebears that adorned his study. There, on the walls of the study, the past encountered the present and the former grandson and current sage became the proud grandfather of the future.

The time has come for the grieving grandson to conclude. He began with a description of the great *niftar* as a grandson to his forebears and ended by portraying him as a grandfather to his offspring. Between these two poles of his life, the Rav studied and taught, experienced and led an intense life of Torah and mitsvot. Thousands were his students in halakha, many more in aggada; they heard his teachings and were captivated. More than has been depicted here was found in him. At times he hid himself from us and retired into the innermost recesses of his soul; on other occasions he presented a smiling face to us. The Rav hinted at his secrets but did not reveal them.

The Ark has been seized and removed to the heavens. Our teacher has left us and departed to his place in the world of absolute good. We remain with the blessing of the great light of his Torah which dwells amongst us, continuously burning in our hearts and *batei midrash.* A beacon from the Western Diaspora, it links with those lit by *Hakhmei Yisrael* in previous eras, illuminating our heritage from Sinai throughout time. We shall continue to follow his guiding light, to participate in his Torah and preserve it. We will preserve it by comprehension and enjoyment, development and expansion, debate and argument. His teachings are his memorial. He continues to live among us. We are inspired by he who was with us, we weep bitterly over his loss, and conclude with a prayer that the Torah shall not be absent from his children and his children's children, his *talmidim* and *talmidei talmidim*, now and forever.

Notes

This *hesped* originally appeared in Hebrew in *Alon Shevut-Bogrim*, the alumni journal of Yeshivat Har Etzion, on the occasion of the Rav's first *Yahrtseit*. Though urged by friends to publish an English translation and wanting to do the utmost to honor and respect the memory of my grandfather and *rebbi*, I nevertheless have certain misgivings which I have not been able to completely overcome. First, it would appear from the *Gemara* in *Yevamot* [79a; see also *Ketubot* 103b and *Yore De'a* 394:2] that *hesped* should be performed only within the first twelve months of the *petira*, as the original indeed was. Second, though the formal halakhic problem can be overcome, since it should be understood to refer to an oral *hesped* as part of the process of grief and mourning, the underlying emotional truth that the period of a grieving obsession with the departed—no matter how great or how close—should not exceed twelve months, retains its validity. Thus, my involvement with the English version lacked the sense of immediacy and directness which accompanied the writing of the Hebrew original, which was a cathartic outpouring of a grieving soul struggling to comprehend and express its sense of loss. Despite these misgivings, which I feel a need to share with readers, it was decided to proceed and publish this *hesped* in the hope that it may strike a chord in some hearts and serve as reminder of he who was amongst us and is no longer here.

1. *"Peleitat Sofereihem,"* in *Divrei Hagut veHa'arakha* (Hebrew) (Yerushalayim: *Histadrut Tsionit Olamit*, 1981), p. 139.
2. *Halakhic Man*, tr. by L. Kaplan (Philadelphia: Jewish Publishing Society, 1983), p. 81.
3. *Ibid*, p. 19. The concluding word, *"havaya,"* translated by Kaplan as "existence," has been switched to "Being." This is a key word in the text, as our remarks below indicate, whose significance is in establishing that halakhic man treats Being itself, ontologically as well as experientially, as subject to the halakhic discipline. The same difference of interpretation also dictated changing *"misdakek"* in the second sentence of the quote from "orient" to "address." These changes seem to indicate differing readings of the quoted text which are basic to one of the important aspects of Halakhic Man. The issue certainly deserves attention and requires a more lengthy discussion; this, however, is not the occasion.
4. *Halakhic Mind* (New York: Free Press, 1986), pp. 101-2.

5. See M. Schwartz, *Hagut Yehudit Nokhah haTarbut haKelalit* (Hebrew) (Tel Aviv: Schocken, 1976), pp. 9-11.
6. *The Lonely Man of Faith* (New York: Doubleday, 1992), pp. 51-2.
7. Published in a supplement to the *HaPardes* journal on the occasion of Reb Moshe Soloveichik's third *Yahrtseit* [*i.e., Shevat* 5704 or Jan. 1944]. The title page relates that the published material [a *shiur* and a *derasha*] was originally delivered by the Rav in June 1943. The quoted passage appears on pp. 19-20. The translation is mine.
8. *Cf. Halakhic Man*, p. 95.

A Glimpse of the Rav

MAYER TWERSKY

"Do Not Eulogize Me in Small Cities"

IN 1940, AGUDAT YISRAEL IN AMERICA convened a memorial gathering upon the passing of the universally recognized giant and leader of the generation, Rabbi Chaim Ozer Grodzenski *zt"l*. The Rav *zt"l* was invited to deliver the eulogy. In his introduction, Rabbi Eliezer Silver *zt"l* cited the Talmudic passage[1] which recounts Rabbi Yehuda ha-Nasi's last words to the Sages prior to his passing: "אל תספידוני בעיירות Do not eulogize me in small cities."

The Talmud explains that he instructed them so to uphold the respect and dignity of Torah. Rabbi Silver interpreted Rebbe's instructions homiletically: זייט מיר נישט מספיד ווי א קליינשטייטלדיקע איד. Do not eulogize me in a provincial, small-minded way. Rather eulogize me with breadth and depth, sweep and scope. To ensure just such a moving monumental memorial tribute to Reb Chaim Ozer *zt"l*, concluded Rabbi Silver, we turned to Rav Yosef Dov Soloveitchik to deliver the eulogy.

And so we too, albeit members of an orphaned generation who can not even approach (much less approximate) the grandeur and majesty of the Rav's masterful eulogies, must adhere to Reb-

Rabbi Twersky holds the Merkin chair in Talmud and Jewish Philosophy at the Rabbi Isaac Elchanan Theological Seminary.

be's instructions. Recalling incidents and anecdotes, employing overused and, accordingly, stale superlatives will not suffice. The underlying Torah concepts and magisterial Torah personality must command our attention.

Yet another pitfall must, at all costs, be averted. In our attempt to understand, depict and appreciate a few dimensions of the Rav's multi-dimensional greatness, we dare not lower the Rav *zt"l* to our lowly spiritual station. Our personal religious experience does not provide context or categories for understanding him. Our pedestrian loneliness has nothing in common with his profound spiritual, existential loneliness. Our personal insecurities or ideological inconsistencies must not distract us or cloud our vision of his multi-faceted harmonious genius and greatness. As we soared higher and higher, during the Rav's lifetime, on the wings of his *shiurim* and *derashot* and by force of his majestic Torah personality, so too as he posthumously commands our attention we must be inspired to lofty spiritual Torah heights. Only then can we gain a measure of understanding and appreciation.

"Know whence you came and whither you go"

In undertaking the sacred task of writing about the Rav *zt"l* we assume a dual obligation. First of all, the halakhic imperative of *hakarat hatov* (acknowledging indebtedness and displaying gratitude) embodied in such *mitsvot* as *bikurim*[2] is incumbent upon both individuals and, collectively the nation. Accordingly, our Sages identified and celebrated individuals who made pivotal historic contributions to the preservation and transmission of Torah. "That man will always be remembered favorably, and his name was Yehoshua son of Gamla, because were it not for him Torah would have been forgotten . . . he ordained that teachers of Torah be appointed in every region and city and that students be admitted at age six. . . ."[3] And thus historical consciousness—knowledge of Jewish history and its primary actors (*gedolei Yisrael*, righteous individuals, etc.)—is included in the halakhic mandate of *hakarat hatov.*

The premium which the Torah places on historical knowledge and consciousness notwithstanding, ultimately the Torah's concern is for our present and future. "Know whence you came, and whither you go."[4] The Mishna should be understood as follows: know whence you came, because that knowledge will help you correctly discern wither you go. Historical consciousness provides directives and directions for the future.

In writing about the Rav, we must satisfy both of our obligations. First of all, the Rav's unique and towering historical achievements should be duly noted and rightfully attributed. Above all others, he personified and articulated the belief that Torah can flourish anywhere, even in the "*treife medina*" of the United States. By the sweat of his brow and the force of his magnetic Torah personality and teachings, that belief became a reality. We are all his beneficiaries and disciples, profoundly indebted. Tosafot in *Masekhet Berakhot*[5] explain that all individuals, even those lacking personal contact are considered disciples of the *gadol hador,* presumably due to the formative, repercussive influence he exerts over the entire generation. Thus all of us are the Rav's disciples. His memory deserves to be perpetuated, and we are obligated to eternalize it.

Our primary obligation, however, is to preserve the Rav's teachings as a model and blueprint for eternity so that we and future generations may continue along the Torah path he trailblazed through the murky maze of modernity.

The task of presentation and preservation of the Rav's teachings is not an easy one. The Rav's teachings, as his personality, were profound and precisely nuanced. Consequently, these teachings can only be comprehended, presented and preserved for perpetuity if we study them with spiritual and intellectual largesse, thoroughgoing rigor, total honesty and heightened sensitivity. Sadly, we know empirically that the risks of outright falsification, tendentious interpretation or inadvertent distortion are great. The task looms large. Yet the more difficult the task, the more vital and hallowed it is. May the Almighty help and guide us in this endeavor.

II.

Torah Megila Nitna—Torah Hatuma Nitna

The Talmud[6] records an intriguing dispute. Rabbi Yohanan maintains that "*Torah megila nitna* (Torah was given piecemeal)," i.e., as explained by Rashi, when a section of the Torah was communicated to Moshe he committed it to writing, and at the climax of forty years when all sections of the Torah were completed he connected the parchments with sinews and sewed them together.

Conversely, Rabbi Shimon ben Lakish opines that "*Torah hatuma nitna* (Torah was given as a sealed document)." That is, Torah was not committed to writing at all until the end of the fortieth year when all sections of the Torah had been communicated and those sections which were communicated in the first and second years were arranged orally until he wrote them at the conclusion of the forty years.

Matan Torah, our Sages teach us, is a paradigm for *Talmud Torah.*[7] Accordingly we might paraphrase and say, just as *Torah megila nitna* and *Torah hatuma nitna,* so too for all generations Torah must be studied *qua megila* and *hatuma.* But what approach and methodology are thereby implied?

Torah Megila Nitna

Rabbi Yohanan teaches that Torah was given (that is, committed to writing) piecemeal. Every *parasha* in *Torah she-bikhtav* and topic in *Torah she-ba'al pe* has to be mastered individually. Each has its own unique basic laws, concepts and categories, each has to be mined for its singular subtleties and intricacies. Consequently, one must be totally involved and exclusively immersed in the Torah topic which commands his attention.

"When Rebbe is involved with a particular tractate do not question him about another tractate."[8] The greatness or versatility of our holy master is not being impugned; rather the single-minded intensity of his present pre-occupation is underscored. One's concentration and involvement in any given *sugya* should be so all-encompassing that it precludes any other—even Torah—pre-occupation.

Torah Hatuma Nitna

Yet Rabbi Shimon ben Lakish maintains that the Torah was given as a sealed document, [i.e., written in its entirety at one time]. One cannot fully understand any chapter of Torah or topic of Talmud if it is disjointed from the rest of Torah. In the words of the Tosefta "all of Torah is one subject matter."[9] In a similar vein, the Talmud states that "all of Torah (study) involves drawing comparisons."[10] No *sugya* can be fully illumined in isolation.

"The statutes of God are true, together they are just."[11] When studied comprehensively and viewed collectively, the justice and truth of God's statutes emerge. When grasped as a unified, integrated whole the profundity of Torah shines forth.

Comparisons, applications and extrapolations from the seemingly most remote and unrelated Torah portion or Talmudic passage illuminate the portion or passage presently under study. Moreover, Torah intuition is necessary for detecting latent difficulties, sensing subtleties and unraveling the profound intricacies of any and every *sugya*. This rarefied intuition can only be developed, refined and perfected through mastery of all of Torah.

The great Tosafist, Rabeinu Tam in debating whether the prohibition against performing work on *hol hamo'ed* is biblical or rabbinic, argues "Where do we find a biblical prohibition with so many dispensations?"[12]

This particular proof proffered by Rabeinu Tam does not rely on textual analysis, rather it flows from his Torah intuition. All of Torah must be studied and contemplated in conjunction.

Eilu V'eilu Divrei Elokim hayim[13]

Which opinion do we accept and implement in our methodology of Talmud Torah? Do we follow the microcosmic, particularistic view of R. Yohanan that every Torah topic is conceptually unique? And hence every *sugya* summons us to acclimate to its singular mindset and develop the appropriate cognitive categories? And that our involvement in a particular *sugya* is per force exclusive and exclusionary?

Or do we adhere to the macrocosmic, universalistic view of R. Shimon ben Lakish that Torah is not only spiritually but also intellectually an unified organic whole? And hence the lens through which Torah is viewed must encompass the totality of Torah because otherwise our perception will be skewed?

Eilu v'eilu divrei Elokim hayim. These and these are the words of the living God.

Each constituent chapter of the Torah is unique. This principle of singularity is partially reflected within hermeneutical principles such as "We do not extrapolate from monetary law to ritual law."[14] "Scripture repeated this *halakha* to instruct us that it is an absolute requirement,"[15] a principle which governs the laws of *Kodashim* (sacrificial order) exclusively. Consequently pre-conceived conceptual categories can not be imported and superimposed. Unprompted importation and imposition of universal categories often begets artificially contrived, at times erroneous, conclusions. Rather, singularly appropriate categories of thought must be developed internally within each *sugya.*

And yet the universal perspective is indispensable as well. Not only because, as mentioned earlier, comparisons, applications and extrapolations from the seemingly most remote and unrelated Torah portion or Talmudic passage may, at times, illuminate the portion or passage presently under study. But also because the dialectic of *Talmud Torah* is such that it is precisely the universal focus and orientation which uncover and accentuate the uniqueness of the individual *sugyot.* The process of initially questioning by juxtaposing different (seemingly, differing) *sugyot* and answering by distinguishing between them highlights the distinctiveness of each. The questioning which the macrocosmic perspective affords is not a negative or skeptical act; rather it is part of the creative process. The imperative to question, Rav Chaim of Brisk taught, is contained within the hermeneutical principle that the correct interpretation of two seemingly contradictory verses, cannot be attained until the contradiction is reconciled and resolved by a third verse.[16]

The novelty and significance of the third and synthesizing verse can only be grasped if there is an antecedent awareness of the thesis and antithesis. And this awareness, in turn, ofttimes can result only from creative questioning.

In resolving questions and contradictions from the spectrum of Torah we do not revert to the conceptual status quo prevalent prior to the emergence of the difficulty. Rather, fresh insight has been attained; the depth and distinctiveness of the respective *halakhot,* hitherto undetected, has been discovered and demonstrated.

The Methodology of Rav Chaim of Brisk

And thus it is that these two dimensions, particularistic and universalistic, coalesce within the methodology of Rav Chaim of Brisk. Actually, Rav Chaim did not innovate. He revolutionized *Talmud Torah* by merely reinstating the methodology of the *Rishonim* (medieval exegetes). The Rav *zt"l* vividly described that when he would close his eyes and listen to a passage from the novellae of Ramban he would, in his mind's eye, see Rav Chaim standing before him.

On the one hand, Brisker conceptualization rejects simplistic interpretation, exposes inexact comparisons and penetrates to the conceptual uniqueness of each *halakha* or *sugya,* thus generating the now famous "*tsvei dinim* (two *halakhot*)"; i.e., a conceptually compound *halakha* hitherto oversimplified was resolved into its components or two *halakhot* hitherto problematically juxtaposed were distinguished through conceptual analysis. The particulars of a conceptually compound halakha or the respective uniqueness of two different *halakhot* were established.

Moreover, Brisker methodology deduces and proves the fundamental concepts of each *sugya* internally. The internal logic of the *sugya,* exposed through Brisker conceptual analysis, is always compelling. No strained interpretations or artificially contrived disputes. Rav Chaim rarely adopted the approach of *"leshitato"* to resolve Talmudic difficulties.[17] Every explanation and observation, interpretation and insight is internally compelling. The proofs adduced from the vast Talmudic spectrum not withstanding, Rav Chaim's interpretation is always internally compelling.

And yet, the methodology of Rav Chaim of Brisk cannot exist without integrating the principle of *Torah hatuma nitna.* As mentioned earlier, the questioning which the macrocosmic perspective affords is an indispensable part of the creative process. Initial inexact comparisons invite subsequent exactitude. Phenomenological inconsistency points to conceptual distinctiveness. Macrocosmic questioning is crucial to creative microcosmic understanding because creativity involves dialectic.

But the foregoing discussion of dialectic is entirely inadequate in depicting and delineating the dimension of *Torah hatuma nitna* within the methodology of Rav Chaim of Brisk. After all, dialectic is not the central or distinguishing feature of Rav Chaim's methodology. Most, if not all, schools of Talmudic interpretation employ dialectic, albeit yielding different results. The core and crux of Rav Chaim's methodology of conceptualization is a way of thinking, a keen sixth sense, a pure and pristine Torah intuition born and developed, refined and perfected through assiduous mastery of all of Torah. Rav Chaim keenly sensed the conceptual profundity underlying phenomenological prosaism and the far-reaching implications of seemingly benign *halakhot.* Rav Chaim's Torah intuition discerned subtleties, penetrated beguiling simplicities, and resolved complexities. The conceptual breakthrough was often intuitive; only later was it presented, redacted and formulated analytically. How vivid and poetic is the Rav's portrayal:

> At infrequent intervals the Torah is wed to a person and is united with him. . . . Torah is absorbed in the innermost recesses of his being and merges with him. . . . One who merits this union, has merited an additional soul, the soul of the Torah, whence a spring of blessing issues forth. . . . God grants him not only an analytic soul, but a visionary soul. His *halakhic* and analytic thought is sustained by his pre-cognitive vision, which breaks forth in a torrent, from the depths of his personality which is enveloped in holiness. This *mystical intuition* is the source of his *halakhic* creativity and novellae. The strict and rigorous intellect, author of precise definition and illuminating formulation, thinks only that which the visionary soul provides.[18]

It is crucial to recognize the intuitive and natural character of *hidushei Torah* (Torah novellae). A creative *talmid hakham* from whose lips *hidushei Torah* perpetually issue forth is likened to a *ma-ayan ha-mitgaber,* a self-renewing effervescent spring.[19] This imagery is intended to convey a sense of natural creativity. The Talmud teaches that "Rivers and springs are self-generating."[20] Regardless of how much rain-water is introduced externally, the internal spring waters always preponderate. "He was always as a self-renewing effervescent spring, a source of wisdom and life"—so testified the sons of Rav Chaim of Brisk, writing of their legendary father.[21] The qualities of a *ma-ayan* characterize Rav Chaim and his teachings. A genuine *hidush* (novellum) does not emerge begrudgingly; it can not be forced. A *hidush* flows naturally from within the *sugya,* as waters of a spring. Unprompted, Rav Chaim of Brisk, never routinely subjected *sugyot* to standard analysis. He did not impose preconceived categories (גברא/חפצא, object/subject etc.) and orchestrate *"hakirot"* (investigations) to artificially generate *"hidushim."* Such an approach is antithetical to Rav Chaim's method.

> The halakhic conceptualization of this school of thought must be authentic, original, etc. [The *talmid hakham*] must formulate his novellae in his own terms, and impress upon them the

> signet of his thought. Introducing borrowed logical considerations, employing categories of thought and language coined by other scholars of Israel, adopting prevalent ideas and novellae that every *Yeshiva* student knows, wrapping oneself in a prayer shawl that is not his that he has neither spun nor embroidered, gathering *sevarot* [logical explanations] scattered in the world of Talmudists like fallen leaves on an autumn day in a thick forest without an effort to find a way of independent articulation and sincere personal expression—all these constitute an abomination according to the creative and trusted methodology of Rav Chaim.[22]

Studying an interpretation or novellum of Rav Chaim, one confronts paradox. The Rav *zt"l* poignantly portrayed this paradox.

> "Before the discourses of Rav Chaim, (and his sons) Rav Moshe and Rav Yitshak Ze'ev the students were confounded in the pathways of *halakha,* they were wandering in the forest of creation and did not know where to turn or what to seek. . . . When Rav Chaim and his sons concluded their discourses, the situation had changed entirely. Suddenly a great light shone brilliantly. Confusion disappeared, paths were paved straight, the cycle [of perplexity] was broken. The students felt liberated. Everything was so simple, so lucid, so elementary, to such a degree that they wondered why they had not advanced the same interpretation of the position of Rambam or the words of Tosafot, as did their masters. Why, they would query, did they not grasp the central point. Their teachers had not innovated at all, they merely lifted the veil from the pleasant face of *halakha*. . . ."[23]

Rav Chaim's novellae are awesomely profound, yet apparently self-evident. Previously unknown and unimaginable, retrospectively obvious and virtually explicit. The dialectic nature of his novellae is the trademark of Rav Chaim.

This remarkable dialectic is a natural consequence of Rav Chaim's intuitive and responsive approach. He intuited latent concepts and responded to internal stimuli (points of dispute, difficulty, incongruence, etc.) Consequently, his profound novellae were (retrospectively) self-evident and elementary. As Rav Chaim, blessed with the powers of inspired intuition and brilliant analysis, delved into the *sugya*, conceptual structure and categories emerged internally. Hence, the paradoxical inevitability of previously unfathomed and unimaginable novellae. When one imports and imposes pre-conceived conceptual categories, novellae are (artificially) *generated*. However, when one intuits and internally constructs conceptual categories, novellae are *exposed*. As such, they are simultaneously profound and elementary, previously unimaginable and presently inevitable. And, of course, totally compelling. Novellae, when generated, do not partake of these hallmarks of truth.

In sum, the methodology of Rav Chaim of Brisk can not be captured in stale formulae or static categories of thought. It is a mode of perception and thought, above all a rarified Torah intuition perfected through assiduous mastery of all of Torah. It stems from the dimension of *Torah hatuma nitna*. And yet, paradoxically, it is this Torah intuition which allows us to grasp and appreciate the dimension of *Torah megila nitna*: to expose and exposit the uniqueness of each microcosm within the macrocosm of Torah.

The Spirit of His Grandfather Rests Upon Him

> A large star, brilliant as the sun in its strength, is rising in the skies of the Talmud to illuminate, with the light of the Talmud, the dwellings of the Jewish people. . . . It is (virtually) impossible to exhaust his praise, our teacher and master Rav Yosef Dov haLevi Soloveitchik on whom rests the spirit of his grandfather, the greatest of his age, our master and the master of all Israel, Rav Chaim haLevi Soloveitchik *zt"l*. . . . Like his grandfather, he rules over the waters of the Talmud to their deepest depths, no secret is concealed from him, he raises the hidden and deciphers the concealed and pierces a pathway of light in the most obscure *halakhot*. . . .[24]

Such is the letter the famed Rav of Kovno sent to the United States on occasion of the Rav's emigration. He was not alone in recognizing the Rav as Rav Chaim's undisputed heir. In 1935 when the Rav visited Erets Yisrael, Rav Abraham Isaac Kook *zt"l*, Ashkenazic Chief Rabbi and former student of the famed yeshiva in Volozhin during the era of Rav Chaim, instructed Rav Avraham Shapiro, future Chief Rabbi, to attend every *shiur* the Rav delivered in Erets Yisrael because "hearing Rav Yosef Dov is just like hearing Rav Chaim."[25] Amongst the numerous testimonies which could be collected and cited, perhaps most telling and most authoritative is Rav Moshe Soloveitchick's autobiographical comment: "I wonder if I have merited to serve as a link in the chain of the *hakhmei haMasora*. Then I realize that since I am the bridge which connects my father Rav Chaim and my son Rav Yosef Dov, I too must belong to the *hakhmei haMasora*."[26]

As Rav Chaim's heir, the Rav personified the complementary truths of *Torah megila nitna* and *Torah hatuma nitna*. He too "merit(ed) an additional soul, the soul of the Torah . . . (his) mystical intuition (was) the source of his *halakhic* creativity and novellae."[27] He too was as a *ma-ayan hamitgaber*, a seemingly inexhaustible source of *hidushei Torah*. The Rav was incessantly pre-occupied with divrei Torah, forever immersed in a *sugya*, graphically illustrating the Talmudic description of Rebbe's single-minded involvement. Long after the *shiur* or private learning session had ended, the Rav's concentration remained unbroken. Oblivious to the whirlwind of traffic, he would stop in the middle of crossing the street to share an idea which had just crystallized.[28] He was never complacent, relying on his vast accumulated capital of *hidushei Torah*. He would say, "I do not plagiarize from myself."

A *shiur*, private or public, with the Rav was not merely a learning session but an awesome intellectual-spiritual odyssey. Initially, the *Gemora* appeared to be replete with incongruities, difficulties, and worst of all, random prosaism. Frustrating and unfulfilling. The Rav's remarkable Torah intuition served as a honing device, a form of Talmudic radar. Some questions were critical. Although as yet unanswered, they clearly focused attention on the central issue(s) of the *sugya.* Other questions were peripheral and, at times, dismissed, "This question does not bother me," the Rav would say. The Rav, prompted by internal cues (incongruities, points of dispute, etc.), began to explore and explain, invariably, but not exclusively, with the help of the Rambam. Often he would interject "I heard from [my] father . . ." or "Reb Chaim said . . ." Gradually it became clear that *halakhot* embodied and concretized abstract ideas. Doubts (an איבעיא) in the Gemora were not random or trivial, but conceptually profound and significant. Accordingly, inductive conceptualization provided the key to accurate understanding of difficulties and disputes: conceptualize the *halakha,* revealing its noetic substratum. New perspectives began to emerge, vistas were opened.

At this juncture as well, the Rav discriminated between questions. Some if not successfully answered were potential refutations. Others, though valid, were not threatening. "One does not die from a *kushya,*" the Rav would respond, and the question was deferred. These distinctions were natural byproducts of Rav Chaim's way of thinking, Torah intuition. Unknowingly—the entire process was so natural and compelling—one was transported away from an arid, seemingly bland and random world of facts to a pulsating world of ideas, vivid, fresh and exciting.

Halakhic data and distinctions were no longer perceived as arbitrary and lifeless, but vibrant expressions of profound concepts. Imprecise or superfluous language in reality encapsulated volumes of *hidushim.* Time was suspended, place transcended. The words danced on the page of the *Gemora,* as all present experienced the joy of *divrei Torah,* themselves joyous as when they were given at *Har Sinai.*

Conventionally—in practice, if not in theory—a tripartite division is imposed on Torah. Some areas such as *hilkhot muktseh, seder Taharot* and the like are too technical and abstruse and thus defy profound conceptualization. Others such as *Masekhet Berakhot* and the like are too simple, and thus unsuitable for profound conceptualization. Yet other areas such as sidrei *Nashim* and *Nezikin* present the right mix. In Volozhin and Brisk, no such distinctions were tolerated. Accordingly, the Rav did not specialize. More accurately, all of Torah was his specialty. He did not follow a cycle of *Masekhtot*; he delivered *shiurim* on all *Shisha Sedarim.* And remarkably, *Masekhet Berakhot* was revealed to be as substantive and profound and *Masekhet Keilim* as inviting and enjoyable as *Masekhet Bava Kamma.*

In 1939, in Boston, Mass., the Rav founded and headed one of the first advanced Talmudic institutes [*Kibutz l'Torah*] on American shores, *Heikhal Rabeinu Chayim haLeivi.* (Rav Michel Feinstein *shlita,* future son-in-law of Rav Velvel Soloveitchik *zt"l,* served as his assistant. *Heikhal Rabeinu Chayim haLeivi* was subsequently disbanded when the Rav succeeded his father as *Rosh Yeshiva* of Yeshivat Rabeinu Yitshak Elhanan. Some of its *talmidim* proceeded to form the original nucleus of Beit Medrash Govoha in Lakewood, founded by the legendary Rav Aharon Kotler *zt"l.*) *Masekhet Keilim* was one of the *masechtot* studied. Reminiscing, one disciple commented, "With the Rav, *Masekhet Keilim* was as enjoyable as *Bava Kamma.*"[29]

Just as the Rav's independence and gift of conceptualization yielded brilliant *hidushim* in the theoretical realm of learning, so too in the practical realm of halakhic decisions and hashkafic guidance. He succeeded in integrating within *halakha* phenomena which seemingly lay beyond its pale and thereby defied halakhic categorization. For instance, when asked about the importance of the Yiddish language, the Rav did not spout empty emotionalism or merely wax nostalgic. Instead he invoked the Mishna that teaches *Matsilin tik hasefer im hasefer*—the mantle of the Torah scroll is rescued from fire on Shabbat together with the Torah itself, even if this necessitates overriding certain rabbinic prohibitions against carrying.[30] The Yiddish language, wrote the Rav with characteristic insight and clarity, is comparable to a *tik hasefer.* It is the language in which *gedolei Yisrael* from the Rama to the Gaon of Vilna to Rav Chaim formulated ideas of Torah. Like a physical *tik hasefer,* it deserves to be saved.

The Rav's approach was fresh and original, halakhically conceptualizing a practical issue.

Similarly, the Rav, as only he could, offered an halakhic perspective on the Israeli flag. Though the *halakha* rejects ceremonial symbols and artificially contrived rituals,

> let us not ignore a *halakha* in *Shulhan Arukh* that a Jew killed at the hands of gentiles is buried in his clothing, so that God will see his blood and avenge [it], as is stated [in Scripture], 'though I cleanse, I shall not cleanse their blood.' In other words, the garments of a Jew attain a certain sanctity when they are stained with sacred blood. How much more so that the blue and white flag, which is immersed in the blood of thousands of young Jews who died in the War of Independence in defense of the land and settlement [religious and irreligious, because the enemy, may its name be blotted out, does not distinguish] has a spark of sanctity, stemming from self-sacrifice. We are all obligated to respect the flag and relate to it with proper decorum.[31]

There is yet another dimension to the holistic principle of *Torah hatuma nitna.* A fundamental unity and conceptual interdependence prevail between halakha and *agadah,* the exoteric and esoteric parts of Torah. They operate in consonance. Any authentic *hidush* in *halakha,* explained the Gaon of Vilna, has an esoteric counterpart.[32] Halakhic analysis, employing halakhic methodology and categories, and kabalistic analysis with its indigenous methodology and categories always converge. Our Sages depicted this harmonious relationship between *halakha* and *agadah* by analogizing it to the monistic body—soul relationship.[33]

Moreover, only a broad all-encompassing focus can provide a panoramic view of Torah. Focusing exclusively on either *halakha* or *agadah* offers, at best, an incomplete and impoverished perspective.

Anyone who was privileged to be exposed to the Rav *zt"l* beheld the holistic truth of *Torah hatuma nitna.* As the Rav, in a *shiur, derasha,* or even casual conversation, wove an incomparably, beautifully rich Torah tapestry from strands of Talmud, Rambam, Shulhan Arukh, Medrash, Zohar, Moreh Nevukhim, Likutei Torah, etc., one simply experienced this truth. There was no need for the Rav to advocate or even articulate it. The overwhelming experience of listening to him vividly demonstrated that knowledge of all realms of Torah is a *sine qua non* for revealing and reflecting the true dimensions of its luster and majesty.

III.

Ish ha'eshkolot[34]

A wide range of descriptive epithets should be invoked when speaking of the Rav: Halakhist, Talmudist, philosopher, Kabbalist, orator, humanitarian, etc. Moreover, they should be hyphenated so as not to fragment his persona, and the modifying encomia *par excellence* and *sui generis* added. And yet while this breathtaking characterization rightfully underscores his awesome uniqueness, it is contextually deficient. Because the Rav first and foremost was one of the Sages of the *Masora,* and must be viewed accordingly. Membership in this intergenerational cadre does not, of course, preclude individuality and uniqueness. However, these very traits can only be understood and appreciated in the context of the *Masora.* And thus it is that a properly balanced and nuanced understanding of *Masora* and the role of its sages therein provides an indispensable perspective on the Rav, his most repercussive halakhic decisions and positions.

Masora

The foregoing discussion of *Torah hatuma nitna* has already identified two of the salient characteristics of the *hakhmei haMasora.*

"'You shall teach the words of Torah to your sons'—that you totally and clearly master the entire corpus of Torah."[35] This dictum and lofty goal is fully realized by the *hakhmei haMasora* in every generation. They do not specialize within Torah. They tirelessly toil in all areas of *halakha*, theoretical as well as practical, culminating in mastery of all of Torah.

The *hakhmei haMasora* are distinguished by another unique quality: Torah intuition. Although the Rav underscored Rav Chaim's uniqueness[36] all *hakhmei haMasora* are infused with Torah intuition. Perhaps not equally or uniformly, but they are all guided by a special intuitive sense for the true intent and meaning of the *Masora*.

It is absolutely imperative to recognize this dimension because the Torah intuition of the *hakhmei haMasora* is a central and critical component of the *Masora* itself. Let us focus initially by way of example on the following seminal, repercussive ruling of Hazon Ish, concerning *moridin ve-en ma'alin* (the *halakha* that mandates that certain grievous sinners and infidels are to be thrown into deep pits and left there to their certain fate):

> it would appear that this halakha is only operative when Divine providence is clearly evident as it was when miracles were commonplace and the *Bat Kol* was functional, and the righteous individuals of the generation were under special divine providence discernable to all. In those times heretics perversely provoked themselves to the pursuit of pleasure and anarchy and in those times excising evil people constituted protection of the world because all knew that inciting the people of the generation would bring calamity to the world; it would bring pestilence and war and famine. But now in an era during which God's providence is concealed and the masses are bereft of faith, orchestrating the death of sinners does not repair the breach in the wall of religion, but enlarges it because the masses will view such actions as destructive and violent, God forbid, and since our sole purpose is to be constructive, this *halakha* [of

> *moridin*] is not operative at a time when it does not yield constructive results, and it is incumbent upon us to attract the masses to Torah through love and to position them so that they can experience the radiance of Torah, to the best of our ability.[37]

These words of Hazon Ish are truly remarkable. Not only by dint of substance, but methodology as well. Hazon Ish seemingly did not adduce any textual proofs or invoke earlier authorities. But, in fact, his ruling is supported by the full force of the entire Torah corpus because he was guided by his Torah intuition, formed by a lifetime of devotion to and mastery of that corpus. *Hakhmei haMasora* combine encyclopedic knowledge with intuitive understanding to represent Torah accurately.

The role of Torah intuition is similarly paramount in these famous lines, penned by the legendary Hafets Hayim.

> It would appear that all this [i.e., Talmudic passages prohibiting teaching of Torah to women] was intended for earlier generations when everyone dwelt in the place of their familial ancestral home and ancestral tradition was very powerful amongst all to follow the path of their fathers, as per the scriptural dictum, "ask your father and he shall instruct you;" under such circumstances we could maintain that a woman not study Torah and, for guidance, rely on her righteous parents, but presently, due to our myriad sins, ancestral tradition has become exceptionally weak and it is common that people do not dwell in proximity to the familial home, and especially those women who devote themselves to mastering the vernacular, surely it is a great *mitsva* to teach them *Humash, Nevi'im, u'Ketuvim* and the ethical teachings of our sages such as *Pirkei Avot, Menorat haMaor* and the like so that they will internalize our sacred faith because [if we do not adopt this educational course] they are prone to abandon the path of God and violate all principles of [our] faith.[38]

The phenomenological and methodological resemblance to the passage from Hazon Ish is striking. Again, seemingly no supplementary sources or textual proofs. Torah intuition alone is the lodestar, reflecting the light of all of Torah.

Although countless comparable examples may be adduced to confirm the central role within *Masora* of intuitive interpretation, let us be content with one final illustration. Rav Chaim of Volozhin was asked why he felt it necessary to establish the Volozhiner Yeshiva. What is amiss within the present system whereby youth study in the various local *batei medrash*? Why is it necessary to establish one central Yeshiva? Rav Chaim responded that most Talmudic passages can be comprehended and mastered within the present system. However, some enigmatic statements almost defy understanding. By way of example, he referred to the statement in *Masekhet Pesakhim*: "It is permissable to kill an ignoramus even on Yom ha-Kippurim."[39] Students, explained Rav Chaim, need a central Yeshiva graced by a concentration of *gedolei Yisrael* to comprehend such passages.[40]

There is no dearth of difficult Talmudic passages. Why does this passage from *Masekhet Pesachim* best illustrate the endemic difficulties of Talmud study and the need for mentored guidance? In this instance, textual and conceptual skills alone are clearly inadequate. Above all, an intuitive sense is necessary to detect the authentic meaning of this Rabbinic statement. *Gedolei Yisrael* who will take their place in the chain of *Masora* can only develop if, alongside their formidable textual and conceptual skills and encyclopedic knowledge, they possess a sharply honed Torah intuition. This intuition, in turn, would best be developed through the maximal exposure to *gedolei yisroel* which the yeshiva in Volozhin would afford. Divine providence crowned Rav Chaim of Volozhin's efforts with many points of success. *Inter alia,* it was within his Yeshiva that his illustrious descendent and namesake, Rav Chaim of Brisk, championed his trailblazing intuitive approach.

HaMakh-hish Magedeha

The central role within *Masora* of intuitive interpretation is dramatically underscored by Rambam: "There are three (types of) heretics who deny Torah . . . and also one who denies the interpretation of Torah, i.e. *Torah she-ba'al pe* and who contravenes the transmitters of the oral tradition (*v'hamakh-hish magideha*) . . ."[41]

The Rav underscored Rambam's broad definition of heresy: not only does denial of the *Masora* constitute heresy (*hakofer beTorah she-ba'al pe*), but contradiction of the *hakhmei haMasora* as well (*hamakh-hish magideha*). The reason is evident, the *hakhmei haMasora* do not merely mechanically preserve and transmit. Rather their understanding and interpretation, ofttimes intuitive, form an integral part of the *Masora*. The *hakhmei haMasora* transmit and teach, and their teachings are incorporated into the *Masora*. And thus not only is the *kofer beTorah she-ba'al pe* a heretic but *hamakh-hish magedeha* as well.

This fundamental concept underlies a striking passage in the Talmud.

> Rava taught: initially Torah is referred to as God's possession and ultimately as his own (i.e., the *talmid hakham*'s) as it says "his yearning is for God's Torah, and he meditates day and night over his own Torah."[42]

In what sense does Torah belong to the *talmid hakham*? If, by way of analogy, one masters the discipline of physics, does the subject matter belong to him? Expertise does not grant proprietorship. Clearly *Hazal* are focusing on the interpretive role of the *hakhmei haMasora*. Torah is theirs to authoritatively interpret. Torah is given to their understanding and intuition.

This theme of authoritative, ofttimes intuitive interpretation is also encapsulated in a remarkable passage in the Sifrei. "'You shall not deviate from their ruling either right or left'—even [if they rule that] right is left, and left right."[43]

The penetrating, intuitive interpretation of *hakhmei haMasora* may appear, at first glance, to be counterfactual. *Halakha* teaches that we should precipitate the downfall of certain sinners. Hazon Ish taught that we should embrace them lovingly. The Talmud prohibits men from initiating Torah study for women. Hafets Hayim insisted that such initiatives are vital. Seemingly, these sages ruled that right is left, and left right. Nevertheless, we are obligated to accept their rulings. Perhaps we lack the Torah intuition necessary to recognize the authentic parameters of certain *halakhot,* and correctly implement them. Consequently, we, suffering from nearsightedness, perceive that our sages are confusing right and left. But in reality their far-reaching, intuitive vision has simply exceeded ours, and beheld truths that lie beyond our field of vision.

Sui Generis

The Rav merited a "visionary soul" and "mystical intuition." He was, in our generation, *sui generis* in this respect. He often said that when confronted with an halakhic query he first intuited the correct response, and only subsequently documented it. Here too the testimony of the Rav of Kovno resonates: "the spirit of his grandfather rests upon him."[44]

The Rav's remarkable Torah intuition was coupled with a profound understanding of contemporary man, especially Jewry—its follies and foibles, challenges and crises. And thus he was uniquely positioned to guide Jewry in its confrontation with modernity. His halakhic positions on the seminal, vital issues of his (and our) day reflected his sharply honed Torah intuition, uncompromising devotion to truth, and keen understanding of Jewry in the modern era.

The Burdens of Leadership

Hazal, amplifying the verse "How shall I alone bear your burdens, loads and iniquities,"[45] describe the burdens of leadership very openly and graphically.

> The Jewish people were heretics. [When] Moshe emerged [from his tent] early they said "Why did the son of Amram emerge? Perhaps he does not experience tranquility in his home." [When] Moshe emerged late, they said, "Why did the son of Amram not emerge [on time]? What do you think? He was sitting, plotting and scheming against you!"[46]

The leader assumes responsibility for a burdensome and obstinate people who tendentiously misrepresent his actions and positions. Most ripe for misunderstanding and distortion are the intuitive rulings which appear to confuse right and left. Cries of condemnation are raised and slanderous epithets hurled—'reformist!,' 'modernist!,' etc. Those *hakhmei haMasora* who stand in the vanguard of the fight against assimilation and per necessity speak the language of the alienated and confused masses are most vulnerable. The trouble-filled career of the Malbim, *inter alia,* immediately comes to mind. This spiritual giant who in the eyes of the *Beit haLevi* and Rav Chaim commanded the reverence due to one of the *rishonim* was the object of merciless, vitriolic attack. How bitterly ironic: he devoted his life to combating the pernicious dangers of reform, and himself had to suffer accusations of being a 'reformist.' Sadly, the Malbim was neither the first nor the last amongst *gedolei Yisrael* to suffer such a fate. Such are the burdens of leadership.

The Rav exercised remarkable leadership and also bore with great dignity the burdens and indignities of leadership.

The subtle truth is this: our *Masora* is eternally binding and unchanging. "This Torah shall not be altered, and there will be no other Torah forthcoming from the Creator, may His name be blessed."[47] Regardless of their intensity or velocity, winds of change are powerless against a divine, eternal *Masora.* External change or accommodation is anathema. However, *Masora* does possess an *internal* dynamic. The Torah internally dictates, in some cases, that changing circumstances elicit different directives and responses. The Torah, absolute and unchanging, itself provides individualized guidelines for different epochs. The first Rebbe of Ger, the legendary *Hidushei haRim,* unequivocally formulated this cardinal truth: "In every generation [new] Torah interpretations come to light in accordance with the [people of the] generation and the need to direct them."[48] These interpretations are divined, often times intuitively, by the *hakhmei haMasora.*

IV.

Torat HaRav

Let us, with the benefit of careful retrospective reflection, while rejecting revisionism, study some of the Rav's teachings, especially those which responded to the confrontation of Torah and modernity.

Talmud Torah For Women and the *Mehitsa* Controversy

The Rav advocated teaching *Torah she-Ba'al Pe* to women. He personally taught *Torah she-Ba'al Pe* to his daughters, on his initiative and authority *Gemora* has been taught to girls in Maimonides School,[49] and he delivered a *shiur* inaugurating a Talmud program for women at Stern College. At first glance, the Rav's actions seemingly bespeak a modern instinct and reformist proclivities.

This superficial and simplistic interpretation, however, is clearly belied when we focus on another vital contemporary issue. In the 1950's nascent post-war American orthodoxy stood at a fateful crossroad. Increasingly acceding to societal assimilationist forces, both rabbinic and lay leaders were removing the *mehitsa* from synagogues and abandoning separate seating, in the name of alleged egalitarianism. The sacredness and inviolability of *halakha* were threatened.[50] The Rav responded very forcefully, decrying the Christianization of the synagogue, beautifully articulating the rationale for a *mehitsa,* and absolutely prohibiting entry into such a "modified" synagogue, even if it provided the only opportunity to fulfill the mitsva of *shofar* on *Rosh HaShana*. Here are the Rav's impassioned words as he spoke to that vital issue:

> In particular, I wish to call the attention of the conference to the *mehitsa* problem . . . many of our colleagues choose the *derech ketzarah va'arucha*, the easy way which leads to doom and disaster. I do hereby reiterate the statement I have made on numerous occasions, both in writing and orally, that a synagogue with a mixed seating arrangement forfeits its sanctity and its halakhic status of *mikdash me'at* (sanctuary in miniature), and is unfit for prayer and *avoda she-belev* (the service of the heart). I know beforehand the reaction to my letter on the part of our apostles of religious "modernism" and "utilitarianism." They will certainly say that since a great majority of the recently constructed synagogues have abandoned separated seating, we must not be out of step with the masses. This type of reasoning could well be employed with regard to other religious precepts, such as the observance of the Sabbath, and the dietary laws. However, we must remember that an ethical or halakhic principle decreed by God is not rendered void by the fact that people refuse to abide by it. Its cogency and veracity are perennial and independent of compliance on the part of the multitudes. If the ethical norm, 'Thou shalt not kill,' has not lost its validity during the days of extermination camps and gas chambers, when millions of people were engaged in ruthless murder, but on the contrary, has been impregnated with deeper meaning and significance, then every halakhic maxim assumes greater import in times of widespread disregard and unconcern. The greater the difficulty, the more biting the ridicule and sarcasm, and the more numerous the opponent—then the holier is the principle, and the more sacred is our duty to defend it. In my opinion, the halakhic dictum, *bishe'at gezerat ha-malkhut affilu mitsva kallah kegon le-shinuye 'arketa de-mesana, yehareg ve'al ya'avor* [at a time of religious persecution through governmental decree, even for a minor custom, such as one involving changing a shoelace, let one suffer death sooner than transgress it] requiring of us a

> heroic stand in times of adversity, applies not only to political and religious persecution originated by some pagan ruler, but also to situations in which a small number of God-fearing and Torah-loyal people is confronted with a hostile attitude on the part of the majority dominated by a false philosophy.[51]

The Rav from his earliest youth was trained to be exceptionally sensitive and disciplined in matters of language. An extra word in Rambam's *Mishne Torah* could prompt profound novellae. Rav Chaim rewrote his own *hidushim* a hundred times, every word weighed and measured.[52] The Rav imbibed and lived this hallowed tradition. How striking and revealing then is his language in his devastating critique of religious "modernism" and "utilitarianism." The description of the path of doom and disaster, the analogy to the Nazi abandonment of the precept against murder! The clarion call to martyrdom rather than surrender to a majority dominated by a false philosophy! Let one suffer death sooner than acquiesce to removing the *mehitsa* from a synagogue! In this context, the Rav appears as the ultimate ideologue, author of extreme right-wing rhetoric.

The "third verse" which reconciles the apparent contradiction is this: Truth and men of truth transcend facile classification and defy superficial stereotyping. The Rav was neither left nor right wing, modern nor ultra orthodox. He was a man of Torah, truth. Truth, its underlying unity uncompromised, often undergoes a process of diffraction and manifests itself in a variety of guises. The Rav's position, like those of the Hafets Hayim and other *hakhmei haMasora*, regarding women's education reflected his intuitive understanding of what the *internal* dynamic of *Masora* prescribes for the contemporary predicament.

Pre World War II European Jewry had been in the throes of a religious crisis, a fact omitted in our romanticized histories of the period. The forces of assimilation were very strong, and many succumbed. The crisis was most acute in the area of Torah education for women.[53] Profound corrective educational measures would have been necessary in Europe, the bastion of orthodoxy. *A fortiori* in the United States.

The *halakha* prohibiting Torah study for women is not indiscriminate or all-encompassing. There is complete unanimity that women are obligated to study *halakhot* pertaining to *mitsvot* which are incumbent upon them.[54] Clearly men are allowed to provide instruction in these areas. A father's obligation of *hinukh* relates equally to sons and daughters.[55] The prohibition of teaching *Torah she-Ba'al Pe* to women relates to *optional* study. If ever circumstances dictate that study of *Torah she-Ba'al Pe* is necessary to provide a firm foundation for faith, such study becomes obligatory and obviously lies beyond the pale of any prohibition. Undoubtedly, the Rav's prescription was more far-reaching than that of the Hafets Hayim and others. But the difference in magnitude should not obscure their fundamental agreement: intuitively, it is clear that the guidelines of the Talmud in *Masekhet Sota* were never intended for our epoch. This is not an instance of modernism, but Torah intuition.

Similarly, Torah intuition and reasoning dictated a firm, resolute stand in the *mehitsa* controversy. Firstly the requirement for a *mehitsa* is absolute. Moreover, any *hora'at sha'ah* would be dangerously misguided because succumbing to a religiously and culturally hostile environment, compromising principles and distorting *halakha* can not preserve but only distort Torah. As the Rav underscored, the *mehitsa* issue was representative. If orthodoxy would not remain true to its principles on this issue, no precept would be immune to such religious accomodationism. The Rav keenly perceived and forcefully articulated this truth, and was instrumental in stemming the tide of assimilation and rescuing nascent post-war orthodoxy.

Intra-Faith Co-operation and Interfaith Dialogue

Juxtaposing the Rav's positions on membership in the Synagogue Council, on the one hand, and inter-faith dialogue, on the other, is similarly illumining. For many years the Union of Orthodox Congregations and the Rabbinical Council of America belonged to the Synagogue Council, an umbrella body comprised of orthodox, conservative, and reform organizations. The Rav approved of their ongoing participation. His ruling was not rooted in "tolerance" or "pluralism." Nor did it reflect his alleged modernity.

The Rav's firm stand banning inter-faith dialogue suffices to dispel any such illusions. In the early 1960's in the aftermath of the Vatican's Ecumenical Council, many Jewish groups were eager to engage the Church in dialogue. The Rav adamantly opposed this, eloquently explaining the impossibility of such a venture and subtly exposing the Vatican's invitation as a veiled form of assimilationist entrapment. His counsel was heeded, effectively preempting and eliminating potentially disasterous dialogue between orthodox Jewry and the Church.[56] The following is an excerpt from the Rav's *tour de force*:

> We certainly have not been authorized by our history, sanctified by the martyrdom of millions, to even hint to another faith community that we are mentally ready to revise historical attitudes, to trade favors pertaining to fundamental matters of faith, and to reconcile "some" differences. Such a suggestion would be nothing but a betrayal of our great tradition and heritage and would furthermore, produce no practical benefits. Let us not forget that the community of the many will not be satisfied with half measures and compromises which are only indicative of a feeling of insecurity and inner emptiness.[57]

The Rav's philosophical profundity and prudent eloquence do not obscure the resoluteness of his ban against inter-faith dialogue. It is abundantly clear that the same consideration and rationale presented by the Rav preclude intra-faith dialogue as well. Is bartering fundamentals of faith any less of a sacrilege when dealing with misguided co-religionists?

The Synagogue Council, however, was not a forum for intra-faith dialogues or an instrument for mutual inter-denominational recognition or legitimization. "When representation of Jews and Jewish interest *klapei hutz* (vis a vis the non-Jewish world) is involved, all groups and movements must be united. There can be no divisiveness in this area for any division in the Jewish camp can endanger its entirety. . . . In the crematoria, the ashes of *hassidim* and *anshei ma'ase* (pious Jews) were mixed with the ashes of radicals and freethinkers and we must fight against the enemy who does not recognize the difference between one who worships and one who does not."[58] No relativism or modernism, God forbid, rather pristine Torah intuition.

Some forty years earlier, Rav Chaim Ozer Grodzynski was petitioned to issue an absolute ban on joint communal membership with Reform. The request was occasioned by the publication, a year earlier, of the Reform movement's aggressively heretical manifesto, "Richtlinien." Nevertheless, Rav Chaim Ozer demurred, explaining that there are no absolute halakhic guidelines concerning such membership. Moreover, he personally was unqualified even to express an opinion because only the Sages of the generation who are intimately familiar with prevailing local circumstances can render the appropriate *ad hoc* decision. "Such a doubt . . . cannot be resolved based on Talmudic sources, only on the basis of straight thinking . . ." "complete familiarity and unobscured vision."[59]

The Rav followed this mandate. In his eyes, the actual dangers of disunity and orthodox isolationism in vital Jewish communal interests, the inevitable consequences at that time of boycotting the Synagogue Council, far outweighed the potential dangers of membership possibly misconstrued. The Synagogue Council was charged to act on issues of general concern to the Jewish community, not to recognize or resolve "differences" with non-traditional elements. "A sage is superior to a prophet."[60] Some years later, *inter alia*, the Synagogue Council played a prominent role as Jewish organizations fought successfully to deflect proposed legislation which threatened the permissibility of *shekhita* [ritual slaughtering] in America. As part of that successful effort the Synagogue Council endorsed the Rav as representative of and spokesman for the *entire* Jewish community on an advisory council to the Secretary of Agriculture.[61]

You Shall Occupy the Land and Dwell There

Next let us consider the Rav's affiliation with Mizrachi. The Rav had been an active member of Agudat Yisrael; as late as 1940 he was appointed chairman of its executive committee.[62] Then in 1946, after prolonged, intense introspection the Rav joined Mizrachi, accepting the title of honorary president of World Mizrachi.

In the annals of *gedolei Yisrael* the Rav's support for and embrace of the Mizrachi movement were not trailblazing. Quite the contrary. Such towering, awe-inspiring figures as Rav Meir Simcha haKohen of Dvinsk (the *Ohr Sameah*) and Rav Shlomo haKohen of Vilna (*Binyan Shlomo*), universally recognized *gedolei hador,* wholeheartedly embraced and enthusiastically supported Mizrachi. Nor did they stand alone. Many, many prominent *rabonim,* among them such outstanding figures as Rav Hanokh Henokh Eigus of Vilna (*Marheshet*) and Rav Moshe Shmuel Glazner (*Dor Revi'i*), were avid, public supporters of Mizrachi.[63]

Nevertheless, the Rav's Mizrachi affiliation, by his own account, represented a personal metamorphosis and an apparent break with his family *masora.* "I was not born into a Zionist house. My grandfathers, my paternal home, my teachers and colleagues were remote from the Mizrachi. They also adopted the view of 'what right do you have to meddle in the secrets of divine providence.' My affiliation with Mizrachi came gradually. I had many doubts about the truth of this position."[64]

The Rav's migration to Mizrachi is even more curious in light of his profound reverence for and deep devotion to his personal *masora.* The lens through which the Rav viewed Torah and the world was crafted by his father and grandfather. "My father *zt"l* stood me on my feet, gave me the key to lomdus and *Torah she-Ba'al Pe,* he taught me the method and imparted the approach to understand and analyze, study and teach, . . ."[65] Rav Chaim is "our great master—from [the words of] his mouth we live, and his waters we drink . . ."[66] Once, commenting on the crushing burden of responding to critical queries often involving life and death, the Rav said "I would give my right arm to be able to discuss these questions with my father." Such was the primacy of his personal *masora.* And yet, he seemingly strayed and embraced the Mizrachi movement!

The answer is evident: on some issues, as explained earlier, our *masora* offers individualized directives for different epochs. To mechanically overextend the *masoretic* directive for a bygone era into the new one, ignoring its uniqueness, does not preserve *masora.* To the contrary, it distorts *masora.*

> I feel that divine providence . . . is employing secular Jews as emissaries to enact its plans with regard to the Holy Land. . . . The years of the Nazi holocaust, rise of the state, and the achievements of Mizrachi in Eretz Yisrael, convinced me of the justness of the path of our movement.[67]

Elsewhere, in remarks delivered in 1961, the Rav described even more elaborately the confirmation which historical events provided for his earlier, apparent metamorphosis.

> The first axiomatic truth of our movement is the intuitive conviction that the establishment and thirteen year existence of the State of Israel should be considered a miraculous event of unlimited importance in our recent history. . . . My instinct tells me that just as the sages of the Talmud and Medrash and the medieval sages declared: nature does nothing in vain, in the cosmos everything has a purpose, and the Almighty did not create even the smallest snail in the ocean without a purpose, for nothing; so, I feel, there is nothing in vain in Jewish history,

> and if on the sixth day [of the week], the fifth of Iyar, the Almighty said, 'Let the State of Israel be' his proclamation is not in vain, and his words do not drift aimlessly, God forbid.[68]

The intuitive, *masoretic* impulse which prompted the Rav to join Mizrachi provides perspective on his affiliation. Slogans such as *dat u-medina* distort his support of Mizrachi. Alleging modernism has the same deletorious effect. Mizrachi's efforts to colonize and establish a state in Eretz Yisrael do not compliment Torah; rather they implement Torah. Torah can not be complemented or supplemented because it encompasses all our values. The verse "you shall inherit the land and dwell therein," *inter alia,* is both the imperative and imprimatur for Mizrachi's efforts at colonization and statehood because, as explained by Ramban,[69] *yerusha* implies sovereignty. And, of course, a Jewish state must be worthy of its name not only ethnically, but religiously and spiritually. Hence, Mizrachi's concomitant commitment to establishing a network of Torah schools.

Any lingering doubt regarding the cogency of the halakhic analysis was dispelled by the singularly tragic and ultimately triumphant decade of the 1940's. The malevolent apathy and evil indifference of the "civilized" world to the fate of European Jewry at the hands of the Nazis and their genocidal partners underscored the absolutely vital need for Medinat Yisrael as a haven and refuge for all Jews. Subsequently, the openly miraculous divine intervention which made possible the establishment of the state thereby simultaneously sanctioned it as well.

It should be noted that we have focused exclusively on the Rav's affiliation with and vision for Mizrachi. Although it is impossible in the present context to fully assess whether contemporary religious Zionism is faithful to the Rav's vision, nevertheless we must underscore the following. The Rav's religious Zionism was not infected or even tinged by messianism. (The *mitsva* of *v'yirashtem otah* is operative at all times; the post-holocaust realities necessitating a state are unrelated to messianic considerations or speculation.) His support for Mizrachi and *Medinat Yisrael* was not fueled by messianic activism.

Sadly, the manifold dangers of messianism (as distinct from traditional fervent messianic belief), in all its guises, against which our Sages cautioned us,[70] are painfully evident in contemporary society.

Hokhma Bagoyim Ta'amin[71]

Finally, our attention is drawn to the Rav's attitude towards *hakhma*, secular knowledge. The Rav's emphatically positive attitude earned him a place in a galaxy of *gedolei Yisrael* spanning the generations which, to mention but a few, includes Rav Sa'adyah Gaon, Rabeinu Bachya, Rambam, Rama, Malbim, etc. all of whom pursued, to different degrees and within varying parameters, *hakhma*.

The Rav's pursuit and advocacy of *hakhma* was bi-dimensional—ahistorical and historical. First, the Rav felt that the Torah encourages pursuit of secular wisdom. I recall once questioning whether the time invested in secular studies was worthwhile. The Rav's response was emphatic: *parpara'ot l'hakhma* are valuable.[72] The time he had invested had proved valuable and he encouraged me to do likewise. However, the Rav also stressed the historical component.

> Yosef (whose analogue in this *derasha* is the Mizrachi) of 5662 instinctively felt that the peace and tranquility, quiet and security in which his brothers lived were only illusory. Yosef of 5662 saw in a dream that "behold we are binding bundles," we are integrated into a new economy, the overwhelming majority of Jews will be concentrated in the Western World, where society is founded on science, . . . *all professions require academic education* . . . we must prepare and ready ourselves for these changes.[73]

In truth, the question of secular education in our generation is another act in the drama of the confrontation of Torah and modernity. The Rav's approach was courageous, consistent, and compelling: withdrawal or ghettoization is no solution. Undoubtedly, the dangers inherent in that confrontation are real. However, the consequences of trying to avoid and ignore that confrontation are far more dire. Only a small percentage of *Kelal Yisrael* is cloistered in the *Beit Medrash.* Very few Jews can be contained and saved in a ghetto. (Moreover, is the *Beit Medrash* hermetically sealed against the influx of modernity? Will a ghetto be truly insular? *Inter alia,* the European experience of the nineteenth and twentieth centuries would seem to indicate otherwise.) The Rav firmly believed that we must cultivate a *modus vivendi* for the religious laity who venture into the modern professional world. We must ensure that the pathways to careers in medicine, law, business, computers, etc. do not, God forbid, point away but rather converge with Torah. Otherwise, God forbid, large segments of *Kelal Yisrael* will be lost.

The Rav, in an address to the annual convention of Mizrachi in America that still resonates powerfully, articulated this conviction:

> Those who march under the banner of withdrawal, absolute abstinence, silently concede to the reformers, that in the modern cultural-historical constellation observance of mitzvot and study of Torah are virtually impossible. We reject the policy of abstinence as dangerous for the existence of the (Jewish) nation.

> Under the force of the circumstances which have been created during the past years, when the majority of the Jewish nation was transplanted to the Western World, and has established ties with the general society in linguistic, economic and political matters, the ideology of withdrawal is suicidal. As a consequence of this ideology the danger exists that we would contract and become a small cult, which would not endure. We joyously declare that the principle of the eternity of Torah guarantees us that it is possible to study Torah and observe it, not

> only in the *Beit Medrash* and Ghetto, but in every place in the world, be it a modern house, laboratory, campus, or factory; We do not minimize the difficulties and complicated problems inherent in living a life of sanctity in modern society, rather we believe that "we shall ascend [and conquer it] because we are able."[74]

The Rav delivered this impassioned *derasha* almost thirty four years ago. Surveying the contemporary scene, it is clear that his model and *modus vivendi* have been adopted on a widespread scale. Yeshiva graduates (from a wide array of Yeshivot) have received the necessary academic training and degrees and function productively as doctors, lawyers, businessmen, etc. This quiet revolution is accurately reflected, *inter alia,* in the fact that the question of removing one's head covering at work is increasingly moot. By virtue of their increased numbers and professionalism, *shomrei Torah u-mitsvot* are increasingly accepted as such. In areas with dense Jewish population, the workplace has been sanctified with *minyanim* for *minha* and *shiurim.* The Rav's axiomatic truth and inspired vision have, in large measure because of his influence, became a reality.

V.

Humility

The Torah, in its account of creation and *matan Torah,* teaches us the singular importance of humility. Prior to creating man, God said "let us make man in our image,"[75] employing the plural verb form. Our sages comment that the Almighty did so "to teach proper conduct and the attribute of humility."[76] The lesson of humility was taught and illustrated again when God revealed Himself upon Mount Sinai, the most unimpressive of mountains, and bestowed the Torah. "A person should constantly learn from his

Creator (Rashi's commentary: to love humility)—behold the Holy One blessed be He ignored all mountains and hills, and caused His divine presence to dwell on Mount Sinai."[77] The Torah illustrates the attribute of humility twice, in order to delineate two distinct imperatives. Our obligation to be exceedingly humble is twofold.

First of all, humility forms the core of a religious personality. Its centrality and indispensability, dramatically underscored at the moment of creation, owe to the fact that the Torah conceives of humility not merely as an ethical, but primarily a religious attribute.

Rambam's formulation is striking. "One who is haughty has denied belief in God, as is stated, 'and your heart shall become haughty and you will forget Hashem your God.'"[78] Haughtiness is not merely tantamount to heresy: it *is* heresy.

This remarkable, sobering equation suggests a profound understanding of humility and haughtiness. While humility manifests itself in self-effacing behavior, eschewing honor, and the like, it consists of a firm belief in and acute awareness of absolute dependence upon God. He created and perpetually sustains us, endows us with ability, grants us opportunities for accomplishment, and crowns our efforts with success. How utterly absurd and nonsensical for a totally dependent and vulnerable creature to swell with pride. Pride or haughtiness is only possible if one feels ontologically autonomous and accordingly is self-congratulatory about success. Such a delusional belief forms the substance of haughtiness and is indeed a form of heresy. It is heretical to perceive oneself as ontologically autonomous when in fact God is the sole source of all vitality.[79]

The second imperative for humility is contained within the *mitsvah* of *Talmud Torah.* Our Sages list humility amongst the forty-eight prerequisites for the acquisition of Torah.[80] The omission of other cardinal attributes also mandated by the imperative of *imitatio dei* indicates that, in their listing, our Sages focus exclusively on those attributes which pertain to the process and act of *Talmud Torah*. In this context *anavah* is underscored because *Talmud Torah* requires humility. Accordingly, the Almighty demonstrated once again at *matan Torah* the importance of humility to emphasize its indispensability for *Talmud Torah*.

Moreover, humility is *the* outstanding prerequisite for the acquisition of Torah and defining characteristic of *hakhmei hamasorah*. "Mosheh received Torah from Sinai and transmitted it to Yehoshua, Yehoshua to the elders, the elders to the prophets, and the prophets transmitted it to the men of the Great Assembly."[81] Rav Chaim of Volozhin highlights the correlation between Torah greatness and humility.[82] *Mosheh Rabeinu* was chosen to receive Torah because "the man Mosheh is exceedingly humble, more than any person on earth."[83] Similarly, Yehoshua became *Mosheh Rabeinu*'s foremost disciple and the next link in the chain of *Masorah* because of his outstanding humility, etc.

The reasons for the coupling of humility and Torah greatness are manifold. Let us focus on one of them. The Torah delegates sweeping authority to its sages. As previously explained, Torah is given to their understanding and interpretation. Thus the Talmud tell us of a dispute between the Almighty and the members of the celestial academy which was adjudicated by Raba son of Nachmani, the outstanding Torah sage of his time.[84] On another occasion, rallying behind the cry that "Torah is not in heaven," the Sages upheld the halakhic principle of majority rule and rejected divine intervention.[85] The Almighty Himself, as it were, studies the Torah of his children.[86]

There is, however, one precondition for authoritative rabbinic interpretation. The Torah sage wields authority only if his Torah reasoning and intuition are pure, unsullied and unbiased by the vagaries of an intrusive ego. A haughty person is forever plagued by the influence of his ego which inevitably compromises and contaminates his pursuit of truth. "And you shall not take a bribe, because a bribe will blind the eyes of the wise and distort the words of the righteous."[87] An arrogant person, bribed by his own ego to impress his signet upon truth rather than submit to it, is similarly handicapped. Consequently, Torah can only be acquired by a humble person, and Torah greatness by one who is exceedingly humble.

If anyone in our generation had reason to be proud or touched by arrogance, it was the Rav *zt"l*. His abilities and accomplishments were simply unparalleled. His brilliance was blinding, his mastery of Torah awesome. He was indisputably the greatest *Rosh Yeshiva*, disseminator of Torah, Jewish philosopher and *darshan* of his epoch and yet he was exceedingly humble.

His dress was simple. As his grandfather, Rav Chaim, the Rav did not wear rabbinical garb. He dressed as an ordinary Jew. He did not surround himself with an entourage; he eschewed formality. He would answer the phone himself. He was adamant about helping to clear the Shabbat table upon completion of the *se'udah*. He waited on line in the bakery. He never invoked rabbinical privilege, but was especially careful to accord others proper respect.

Genuine humility manifests itself in profound concern for the unfortunate and the downtrodden. The Rav exemplified this teaching. He was plagued by a chronic bad back, a condition exacerbated by other disabling medical problems in his old age. And yet he was never deterred. A longtime resident of Boston, a *shohet*, was suffering from cancer. The Rav climbed the steps to his second story home to visit him. Another representative anecdote from his later years, when each step could evince pain: he ascended to the third floor to console a mourning family; they were simply speechless at his self-sacrifice. No matter how burdened with myriad responsibilities, somehow he always found time for simple people with prosaic problems—a rift between parents and children, issues of *shalom bayit*, etc.

During the week of mourning, countless individuals came and shared their memories of the Rav. A remarkable, revealing portrait emerged. Although the Rav was universally known and celebrated for his vast Torah erudition and scintillating genius, the members of his community who enjoyed a personal relationship with him—each of whom had his own inspiring story of the Rav's benefactions—viewed him primarily as an emissary of *hesed.*

In this respect as well, the Rav's life mirrored that of Rav Chaim. The Brisker Rav's fame as the Torah genius of his age spread far and wide, but in Brisk he was known simply and lovingly by the diminutive "Reb Chaimke" for his unstinting and unceasing *hesed.*

As befits *hakhmei haMasora,* the Rav's extreme humility was especially pronounced in the context of Talmud Torah. "If you have learned much Torah do not commend yourself because you were created for this purpose."[88] The Rav was never self-congratulatory. He always eschewed praise, and insisted that "whatever Torah I studied is not in my own merit, but rather the merit of my holy forefathers."[89]

Moreover, the Rav's extreme humility allowed for absolute intellectual honesty, which is so crucial for *Talmud Torah.* The Rav often recounted an episode from Rav Chaim's life. A panel of *Gedolei Yisroel* was convened to decide if Rav Chaim would serve, alongside the *Netsiv,* as the second *Rosh Yeshiva* of Volozhin. Rav Chaim, asked to deliver a shiur, did not disappoint. All present were enthralled by his brilliance and originality. Suddenly, in mid-sentence Rav Chaim reminded himself of a passage in the Rambam's *hilkhot melahim*[90] which contradicted his thesis. He abruptly terminated the shiur, retracting all that he had said. The *Gedolei Yisroel* empaneled to recommend a candidate to fill the position of *Rosh Yeshiva* acted swiftly. Their verdict: anyone whose honesty and humility are such that of his own accord he would retract a brilliant shiur thereby seriously jeopardizing his chances for the coveted position is singularly qualified for that post.

Here too the Rav was a most worthy heir of Rav Chaim. He was his own harshest critic—never hesitating to retract a previous statement if he felt he had erred. Once a student interjected a question in the middle of the Rav's *shiur,* eliciting a swift and vigorous response. The Rav unequivocally rejected the student's approach and dismissed the question. After concluding the *shiur,* the Rav sat immersed in thought as the students from the *gemorah shiur* exited, and their counterparts for the ensuing *Yoreh De'ah shiur* entered. Finally the Rav asked for the student who had posed the question. Informed that the latter had gone to eat lunch, the Rav promptly arose and, accompanied by all the students of his *Yoreh De'ah shiur* proceeded to the cafeteria. Spotting the questioner at the far end of the dining hall, the Rav called out loudly, "I was wrong and you were right. Tomorrow we will study the *sugya* according to your approach." With that the Rav turned away, and returned to deliver the next *shiur.*

The Rav could have easily approached or, alternately, beckoned the student to him for a private, quiet discussion. Certainly self-interest dictated such an approach. Instead the Rav conspicuously called out because in the public forum he could most effectively encourage the *talmid,* and demonstrate absolute intellectual honesty.

Beit Hillel's opinions were endorsed by the heavenly bat kol "to teach you that the Holy One blessed be He elevates one who lowers himself."[91] Normative *halakha* flows from the sages who are most distinguished by extreme humility. The famed Rav of Korno reflected this principle when in advance of the Rav's arrival in America, he wrote: "the *halakha* follows his opinion in all areas."[92] This unqualified endorsement testified to the Rav's singular mastery of Torah and to his exceptional humility.

VI.

> Rava taught: When a person is ushered in to his final judgment, he is asked; "Did you conduct your affairs faithfully, designate times for Torah study, engage in procreation, anticipate the final redemption, delve into *hakhma* and induce additional knowledge."[93]

There is, *primo facie*, a glaring omission. Why is there no mention of *hesed*? Rabbi Akiva taught, "'you shall love your neighbor as yourself'—this is a fundamental principle of Torah."[94] Hillel instructed the aspiring proselyte that this verse encapsulates all of Torah; the rest is merely commentary.[95] And yet *hesed* is seemingly neglected in the final judgment.

Let us focus our attention on the question of *"tsipita liyeshua."* What does this *halakhic* imperative entail? The Rambam, in his commentary to the Mishna, enumerating the thirteen principles of faith establishes the belief in *Mashi-ah* (i.e. *tzipiya liyeshua*) as the twelfth. His formulation: "to believe with total conviction that *Mashi-ah* will come . . . and to pray for his coming."[96] Yearning for redemption is not merely a silent state of belief. Our actions must reflect and express our passionate belief and yearning. Ergo the cardinal principle of faith encompasses an obligation to pray for the advent of *Mashi-ah*.

Let there be no misunderstanding. The *halakha* does not look favorably upon messianic speculation or activism which devises and implements messianic strategies to hasten the advent of *Mashi-ah*. Messianic belief should be unwavering and consistent; but the fermentation of that belief is exceedingly dangerous. Messianism is volatile, and the fallout of disappointed messianism is spiritually lethal.[97]

Hafets Hayim also highlighted the need to ensure action consistent with messianic yearning. He invested much energy in a campaign to revive the study of *Seder Kodashim* [the sacrificial order]. He authored three volumes of commentary [*Likutei Halakhot*] and published others towards this end. He founded a special Kollel (institute for advanced study) devoted to the study of *Kodashim*. His rationale: "Do we not wait and yearn at every moment for the coming of *Mashi-ah*—may he come speedily—as we say thrice daily "we hope onto You *Hashem* our God to speedily witness the splendor of your might;" let us listen ourselves to the supplication which we address to *Hashem* our God, because if we truly eagerly anticipate the coming of our *Mashi-ah* certainly everyone would be obligated to arouse himself to prepare his heart to know matters pertaining to the *Beit haMikdash* [Temple] and [its] service . . ."[98]

Rambam stressed the need for prayer, Hafets Hayim for the study of *Kodashim* [i.e., halakhic preparedness]. What other concomitant beliefs or actions are necessary to reflect genuine *tsipiya liyeshua*?

Rambam in *Hilkhot Teshuva* codifies the view of Rabbi Eliezer that "the Jewish people will be redeemed only through repentance."[99] Our belief in *Mashi-ah* is absolute ["I believe with complete faith in the coming of *Mashi-ah* . . ."],[100] and yet his arrival heralding the redemption is contingent upon national penitence. The inescapable, remarkable conclusion is that "our belief in the advent of *Mashi-ah* depends upon our belief in the Jewish people."[101]

Faith in the Jewish people dictates that we must, with empathy and sympathy, embrace all of *Kelal Yisrael.* A secular Jew is one whose precious soul is imprisoned and stifled beneath layers of assimilation. Our sages teach us that even the "sinners of Israel abound with *mitsvot,* as a pomegranate [with seeds]."[102] We must view them accordingly. Not only religious, but secular Jews are worthy of our love. We must practice *hesed* inclusively and bountifully. And, above all, we must disseminate Torah as widely as possible, firm in our belief that Jewish hearts and souls will be captivated by its infinite divine beauty and profundity. A misanthropic or sectarian view which despairs of and abandons large segments of *Kelal Yisrael,* belies authentic *tsipiya liyeshua.*

In man's final judgment *hesed* is not neglected. The question of '*tsipiya liyeshua*' is composite. The heavenly court is, *inter alia,* asking: "did you believe in the basic goodness and resilience of *Kelal Yisrael*? Did you manifest that faith by practicing *hesed* and striving to improve the lot of the Jewish people? And, above all, did you disseminate Torah as widely as possible? Otherwise your professed *tsipiya liyeshua* is flawed and hollow."

The Rav's response to the question *"tsipita liyeshua"* is an emphatic "yes." His concern and commitment encompassed all Jews. One year, on the eve of *Yom haKippurim,* the Rav traveled to the cemetery to visit his wife's grave. He was approached by two non observant Jews. They did not recognize him, but judged him from appearances to be a rabbi. They asked if he would accompany them to their parents' graves and recite a prayer. The Rav obliged. Their brother was also interred in that cemetery, and they asked the Rav if he would accompany them to his grave site as well. Again the Rav graciously complied. Then, declining their repeated offers for remuneration, the Rav wished them well and returned to his waiting car. A cemetery official had witnessed the entire scene. After the Rav's departure, he approached the two beneficiaries and identified the anonymous "rabbi." They were stunned that so great a personage burdened with vast responsibilities diverted time and energy to address the needs of two unknown, non observant Jews. Two weeks later Maimonides School received a cover letter with a thousand dollar contribution enclosed. "Please accept our donation in tribute to Rabbi Soloveitchik. We are the two Jews whom he so graciously and affectionately assisted at the cemetery on the eve of the Day of Atonement." The Rav's *hesed,* an integral part of *tsipiya liyeshua,* was accordingly bountiful and inclusive.

Ten Exiles

As the *Shekhina* prior to the destruction of the *Beit haMikdash,*[103] Torah is also destined to be exiled ten times before the ultimate redemption. The first exile was to *Bavel,* then to North Africa, etc. and the last will be to [North] America. So, according to tradition, Rav Chaim of Volozhin confided in his disciples.[104]

Who is the archetype of *tsipiya liyeshua*? He feels and displays concerns for the physical and spiritual needs of all Jews. He dedicates his life to disseminating Torah throughout the world, but especially in America, the last exile for Torah on its torturous journey to the ultimate redemption. He is confident that Torah can flourish not only in the hallowed *batei-medrash* of Vilna, Volozhin and Brisk, but even in the *"treife medina."* He personifies for twentieth century Jewry the vitality and majesty of Torah. His words of Torah ignite a spark within people, inspiring them to *teshuva*.

"And Yosef Dreamt"

The Rav was the outstanding example of *tsipiya liyeshua* in our age. His confidence in meeting the challenge of fostering Torah growth in America was not nurtured by naivete. No one understood the arrogance and confusion of modern man better than he. No one exposed the spiritual vacuum within contemporary society as eloquently as he. And yet "Yosef dreamt." He beheld a vision for American [and world] Jewry: Torah will be taught and disseminated and its beauty radiated. Jews will be captivated. A devout generation will be raised in America. Not only 'professional' *talmidei hakhamim* (rabbis and educators), but also committed laymen.

The Rav arrived on American shores with this dream. Interestingly, the root ח-ל-ם has two meanings. 1) to dream, as in the verse ויחלם יוסף חלום (and Yosef dreamt)[105] 2) to strengthen, or make whole as in the verse ותחלימני והחייני (strengthen and revive me).[106] The ideal dream is not an idle, but rather a guiding vision. It does not represent a flight from reality, but rather a blueprint for improving it.

As the righteous Yosef of old, the Rav was not an idle dreamer. He combined vision with conviction, prophecy with persistence. Determined to rescue an entire generation, he reached out to all Jews. And many responded.

A young girl from an irreligious home whose hometown had no local Jewish community traveled to a convention of the National Council for Synagogue Youth seeking guidance in living a life of Torah. When questioned about her source of inspiration and conviction, she explained that some time ago her grandfather had given her *Reflections of the Rav* as a birthday present. She read and studied it and resolved to become observant.

On a trip to the Soviet Union in the 1980's, I visited a leading refusenik who headed a major indigenous learning group. The first sight to greet any visitor to his home was a large photograph of the Rav, prominently displayed in the front room. Subsequently another of these remarkable, religious refuseniks explained. "Many of us were inspired to become observant by reading 'The Lonely Man of Faith.' "

Surveying the current religious landscape we remember the dreams that our contemporary *Yosef haTsadik* dreamt for us. Divine providence ordained that the American exile—the last of the ten for Torah—was to endure longer than the span of an individual lifetime. Much work remains to be done. But the seeds of the redemption have been sown and are beginning to flower. The Rav, personifying the majesty of Torah, with his profound *tsipiya liyeshua,* was the Almighty's emissary for the hallowed historical task of planting and nurturing Torah in America.

VII.

Love of God

Rambam in his *Sefer haMitsvot* defines the *mitsva* of loving God. "We are obligated to love Him, i.e. we must contemplate and understand in depth his commandments and actions until we know Him; and in knowing Him experience the greatest pleasure possible; and this is the obligatory love . . ."[107]

Rambam selected his words carefully—"contemplate and understand in depth [נתבונן ונשכיל]." Paying casual attention to and superficial study of Torah do not induce love of God. Our *Talmud Torah* must be probing and scintillating to allow us to achieve that lofty goal.

The Rav exemplified this teaching. His brilliant, effervescent

Talmud Torah was matched by his passionate love of God. His relationship with the Almighty was intensely personal, his experience of God most immediate. The Rav spoke and wrote, often employing anthropomorphic metaphor, of his experience of *kirvat Elokim* (divine closeness). While poring over the *Gemora,* he was not alone. He would feel a hand on his shoulder, encouraging him. In particular, the Rav was sustained by this experience in the dark days and hours of 1967, after his mother, brother and wife all passed away within a three month period.

The Rav's philosophical analysis in his essay *"u-Vikashtem me-Sham"* is also autobiographical.

> Just as awareness of existence in general and personal existence in particular does not involve logical resolutions, rather it comprises the very spiritual essence of man, so too is the experience of God. It is entirely original, the alpha and omega of man's existence. For all eternity it proceeds all logic and deduction, it is the greatest certitude and truth . . .[108]

Inducing Other to Love God

Rambam, quoting again from the *Sifrei,* explains that there is a second component to the mitsva of loving God. "And [our Sages] have already stated that this mitsva also encompasses [an imperative to] seek out and call other people to His service and to believe in Him . . . when you truly love God you will undoubtedly seek out and call heretics and fools to the knowledge of truth which you have acquired."[109]

The two comments of the Sifrei are complimentary and in conjunction define the mitsva of *ahavat Hashem.* We are commanded to love, and induce others to love, *Hashem,* and *Talmud Torah* is the means to both of these ends. If superficial self-study is inadequate for inducing love of God, then surely superficial teaching is equally uninspirational. We are obligated to share scintillating, inspirational Torah with others, thereby infusing them with love of God.

The definition of *mitsvat ahavat Hashem* provides an apt

description of the Rav's career as a *"melamed"* [a teacher, as he always referred to himself]. He did not employ outreach gimmicks or advertising techniques. His formula was simple: teach and study Torah. He did so indefatigably, delivering countless *shiurim* and *derashot*. The Torah he taught was enthralling and invigorating, reflecting its infinite depth and breadth. The Rav rarely traveled outside the Boston—New York corridor. And yet, warmed by his radiant words of Torah and touched by his inspiration, countless Jews from all corners of the earth lovingly embraced the Almighty and His Torah.

VIII.

Conclusion

> To teach you that the demise of the righteous is comparable to the burning of our God's house.[110]

Our sages chose their words with the utmost care. Any equation they formulated is substantive and rigorous, not to be dismissed as merely rhetorical. What underlies the equation between the demise of the righteous and the destruction of the Temple?

The Talmud in *Masekhet Berakhot* teaches that "from the day the *Beit haMikdash* was destroyed, the Holy One blessed be He, in His world, has only the four cubits of *halakha*."[111] The *Beit haMikdash* was an abode for the *Shekhina*. "And they shall construct for me a *mikdash*, and I shall reside amongst them."[112] The temple, as it were, was God's home in this world. The lesson taught by the Talmud is that after the destruction of the *Beit haMikdash*, we can only merit *hashra'at haShekhina* [residence of the divine presence] in the four cubits of *halakha*, i.e., through *Talmud Torah*.

Whenever Torah is studied, the *Shekhina* is present. *Torah megila nitna*—an individual studying but a single section of Torah induces a measure of *hashra'at haShekhina*.[113] But when the Holy One blessed be He graces the world with a righteous person who humbly combines encyclopedic Torah erudition with brilliant creativity and versatility, profundity with piety, knowledge with nobility, and truth with tolerance and tenacity, the *hashra'at haShekhina* intensifies manifold. The *tsadik* who embodies not only *Torah megila nitna,* but *Torah hatuma nitna* as well evokes an *hashra'at haShekhina* comparable to that of the *Beit haMikdash.* Accordingly when that *tsadik* departs this world, his death atones and is comparable to the destruction of the *Beit haMikdash.* In each case, we have been deprived of *hashra'at haShekhina.* Having suffered that calamitous consequence, we are granted atonement.

For close to a century, the Holy One blessed be He graced our world with such a righteous individual, the Rav *zt"l.* And now it is our task to rededicate ourselves to and intensify our efforts on behalf of the Almighty and His Torah. In so doing, perhaps we can be worthy of the Rav's legacy and entice the *Shekhina* to return.

Notes

1. *Ketubot* 103a-b.
2. Deuteronomy 26:1-11.
3. *Bava Batra* 21a.
4. *Avot* 3:1.
5. 31b.
6. *Gittin* 60a. Our analysis of this Talmudic passage follows Rashi's interpretation. Cf., however, Ramban's introduction to his commentary on the Torah for an alternate understanding of this passage.
7. *Vide, inter alia, Berachot* 22a.
8. *Shabbat* 3b.
9. *Sanhedrin* 7:5.
10. *Bava Batra* 130b.
11. Psalms 19:10.
12. *Hagigah* 18a, *Tosafot* sub *'holo.'*
13. *Eruvin* 13b.
14. *Berachot* 19b, as per the view of the Vilna Gaon, cited and interpreted by Rav Herschel Schachter, *shlita, Eretz HaTzvi,* [Yeshiva University Press, 1991], chap. 2. Cf., however, Rashi in *Berachot, ad loc.* sub *'mamona'*
15. E.g., *Zevachim* 7b.
16. Introduction to *Torat Kohanim.*

17. Cf., however, *Hidushei Rabeinu Chaim haLevi al haRambam Hilkhot Shabbat* 10:17 for a notable exception. Nevertheless, even in this instance, the core of Rav Chaim's interpretation is the conceptual distinction between *melekhet mahashevet* and *davar she-eino mitkaven.*
18. מה דודך מדוד, reprinted in בסוד היחיד והיחד, Orot Publications, Jerusalem 1976, p. 218-9.
19. *Avot* 2:8.
20. *Shabbat* 65b.
21. Introduction to *Chidushei Rabeinu Chaim haLevi al haRambam.*
22. מה דודך מדוד, *op. cit.*, p.231-2.
23. *Op. cit.*, p.230-1.
24. The letter is reprinted in *Sefer Zichron HaRav* [published by the Rabbi Isaac Elchanan Theological Seminary, 1994].
25. Rav Menachem Genack, *shlita, Jewish Action,* Summer 5753, Volume 53, no. 9.
26. The comment was recounted to me by Rav Azarya Berzon *shlita* in the name of his father, *zt"l*, who heard it from Rav Moshe Soloveitchik *zt"l*,.
27. *Op. cit.*, n. 18.
28. This example is provided by my brother haRav Moshe Twersky *shlita,* in his eulogy for the Rav. See *Mesorah,* Vol. IX, 1994, p. 36.
29. The comment was related to me by haRav Herschel Schachter *shlita,* to whom it was addressed.
30. *Shabbat* 116b.
31. *Hamesh Derashot* [Jerusalem, 5734] pp. 89-90.
32. Rav B. Landau, *haGaon haHassid me-Vilna* (Hebrew), Jerusalem 5738, p. 135.
33. The analogy is to be found in the *Zohar, Beha'alotkha,* 152a, cited by the Rav in *Ish haHalakha* (op cit.) p. 145, n. 91. Our sages' monistic philosophy is reflected in the dialogue between Rebbe and Antoninus in *Sanhedrin* 91a-b. Monism is an important element within the Rav's expositions of the philosophy of *halakha,* particularly in *Ish haHalakha* and *u-Vikashtem mi-Sham.*
34. *Sota* 47a.
35. *Kidushin* 30a.
36. מה דודך מדוד [*op. cit.*] pp. 212, 218 ff.
37. Hazon Ish, *Yoreh De'ah* ch.2. The position articulated by the Hazon Ish should not be confused with that of Tosafot, Avoda Zara 4b sub *shema mina.* Tosafot state that the *halakha* of *moridin* only applied when the *beit ha-mikdash* was extant. Apparently, Tosafot think that when capital punishment in *beit din* ceased, so too the *halakha* of *moridin* became inoperative. This cessation occurred forty years prior to the destruction of the second *beit ha-mikdash* when the *Sanhedrin* were exiled from their chamber in the *beit ha-mikdash* and the *sine qua non* for capital punishment—

hamakom goreim—was lacking. Thus the *halakha* of *moridin* was only operative in the time of the *beit ha-mikdash.*

At any rate, Hazon Ish does not cite the opinion of Tosafot, a clear indication that it is not relevant to his interpretation.

38. *Likutei Halakhot* Volume II, *Masechet Sotah* p. 21. For further discussion of this passage see my article in *Jewish Action,* Vol. LVII, no. 4.
39. 49b. *Vide Tosafot* sub *ve-yesh* and *Hidushei haRitva ad loc.*
40. The story is retold by my uncle haGaon Rav Ahron Soloveichik, *shlita.* Interestingly, in his epistle Rav Chaim offered other reasons.
41. *Hilkhot Teshuva* 3:8. Vide *Kovets Hidushei Torah,* p. 61 for the Rav's analysis of this passage.
42. *Kidushin* 32b.
43. Deuteronomy 17:11, *Sifrei ad loc.*
44. *Op. Cit.*, n. 24.
45. Deuteronomy 1:12.
46. *Sifrei ad loc.*
47. Traditional, popular summary of Rambam's principles of faith, printed in prayer books after *Tefilat Shaharit.*
48. *Hidushei haRim al haTorah,* Mosad haRim Levine, Jerusalem, 1986, *parashat Hukat.* My father, *shlita,* brought this source to my attention.
49. The *Gemora* curriculum introduced by the Rav focused on *Seder Moed* and *Masekhet Hulin,* i.e. practical *halakha.*
50. See B. Litvin. *The Sanctity of the Synagogue,* 3rd ed. Ktav Publishing House, 1987 pp. xxx-i.
51. *Ibid.* pp. 110-11.
52. See introduction to *Hidushei Rabeinu Chaim haLevi.*
53. My mother תחי' told me that the Rav often shared these memories.
54. *Yoreh De'ah* 246:6.
55. See e.g. *Yoma* 82a.
56. See Louis Bernstein, *Challenge and Mission,* Shengold Publishers, New York, 1982, p. 204.
57. "Confrontation", *Tradition* 1964, Vol. 6, No. 2, p. 25.
58. Quoted in *Challenge and Mission, op. cit.* p. 59.
59. The responsum was printed in *Sefer HaZikaron le-Moreinu . . . Yechiel Ya'akov Weinberg,* Feldheim, Jerusalem, 1969. pp. 1-4.
60. *Bava Batra* 12a.
61. See Bernstein *op. cit.*, pp. 193-202, especially p. 199.
62. *Ha-Pardes,* October 1940, vol. 14, no. 7, p. 28.
63. The history of the Mizrachi movement is detailed by Rav Y.L. Fishman, "The History of the Mizrachi and its Development" (Hebrew) in *Sefer Ha-Mizrachi* (Hebrew), Mosad HaRav Kook, Eretz Yisrael, 1946.
64. *Hamesh Derashot, op. cit.*, p. 24.
65. *Shiurim le-Zecher Abba Mori z"l.*, Vol. 2, Jerusalem, 5745 p. 15.
66. בסוד היחיד והיחד, *op. cit.*, pp. 212-3.

67. *Hamesh Derashot, op. cit.*, p. 25.
68. *Ibid.*, p. 109-10.
69. *Vide* Ramban's list of *mitsvot aseh* omitted by Rambam, *mitsva* 4. The Rav cites and comments on the words of the Ramban in *Hamesh Derashot op. cit.* pp. 88-9.
70. *Sanhedrin* 97b.
71. *Eicha Raba*, Chap. 2.
72. The Rav borrowed the term from *Avot* 3:18.
73. *Hamesh Derashot, op. cit.*, pp. 22-3.
74. *Ibid.*, p. 111-3.
75. Genesis 1:26.
76. *Genesis Raba, ad. loc.*
77. *Sota* 5a.
78. *Hilkhot De'ot* 2:3, based on *Sota* 4b.
79. See Rav Chaim of Volozhin, *Nefesh HaHayim*, Part One, chap. 2.
80. *Avot* 6:5.
81. *Ibid.* 1:1.
82. *Ruah Hayim, ad. loc.*
83. Numbers 12:3. *Vide Sanhedrin* 11a where Hillel the Elder is depicted as being as worthy as *Mosheh Rabeinu* to receive the *Shekhina*. In an apparent *non sequitor*, the Talmud concludes that upon Hillel's death he was eulogized as "O pious one, O humble one, the disciple of Ezra". In fact, however, this postscript provides insight and perspective. Hillel was worthy to receive the *Shekhina* as did *Mosheh Rabeinu* because he too was exceedingly humble.
84. *Bava Metsia* 86a, also cited in the classic introduction to *Ketsot HaHoshen*.
85. *Bava Metsia* 59b.
86. *Gitin* 6b.
87. Deuteronomy 16:19.
88. *Avot* 2:8.
89. Rav Mosheh Tsvi Neri'ah *zt"l*, in his account of the Rav's *shiur* at Yeshivat Mercaz HaRav in 1935, recorded the Rav's demurral.
90. 2:3.
91. *Eruvin* 13b.
92. *op. cit.*, n. 24.
93. *Shabbat* 31a.
94. *Genesis Raba* 24:7.
95. *Shabbat* 31a.
96. *Peirush haMishnayot, Sanhedrin*, introduction to chap. 10.
97. *Vide* n.70 and 78.
98. Introduction to *Likutei Halakhot*.
99. 7:5.

100. *Vide* n.47.
101. על התשובה, World Zionist Organization, Jerusalem, 1974, p.96.
102. *Sanhedrin* 37a.
103. *Rosh HaShana* 31a.
104. Dov Eliach, *Avi ha-Yeshivot* (Hebrew), Jerusalem, 5751, pp. 110-2.
105. Genesis 37:5.
106. Isaiah 38:16. See the Arukh who identifies these two meanings.
107. *Mitzvat Aseh* 3.
108. *HaDarom,* Tishrei 5739, p. 6.
109. *Vide* n. 89.
110. *Rosh HaShana* 18b.
111. 8a.
112. Exodus 25:8.
113. *Berachot* 6a.

On the Halakhic Thought of Rabbi Joseph B. Soloveitchik: The Norms and Nature of Mourning

GERALD BLIDSTEIN

I.

A NOT INSIGNIFICANT BODY OF ANALYSIS, interpretation, and commentary has already been devoted to the writing and thought of Rabbi J. B. Soloveitchik. Attention has been directed to the Rav's homiletic work as well as his topical writings, to be sure; much has been written about the Rav's view of man and of the people Israel. Nor have his discussions of the nature and ends of halakha, his descriptions of the halakhic process and of how one "does" halakha, been ignored either. We now have the beginnings of a serious discussion of the Rav's halakhic ideology, his conception of the relationship of halakhic thought to the world of physical and social phenomena, and of the relationship of halakhic conceptualization to the raw halakhic information available to the thinker.[1] Moreover, it is Rabbi Soloveitchik's description of the halakhic process, his ideology of halakha, if you will, which has stimulated the most trenchant criticism of his work, particularly as regards his denial of the historic character of the halakhic process and his pursuit of analogies drawn from the abstract world of mathemat-

Prof. Blidstein is M. Hubert Professor of Jewish Law at Ben Gurion University of the Negev in Israel.

ics—rather than from the human sciences—to describe the nature and goals of halakha. This, of course, is how it should be, for halakha was at the very center of the Rav's life and work.

Nonetheless, little has been done, I believe, in actual treatment of the Rav's specific halakhic studies. These, ostensibly, ought be the best exemplars of the claims made in more general terms in the programmatic essays, in terms of both content and method. My rather modest intention, then, is to present Rabbi Soloveitchik's thinking on a specific topic, indeed to do not much more than provide a summary of his analysis and conclusions. Naturally, I will also say something about the methodological structure of the enterprise; and I will also try to provide some interpretation of the discussion, to make connections and to render the implicit, explicit. But I will hardly attempt to generalize about the Rav's halakhic method from the case at hand, except insofar as he himself does so. Nor will I attempt to suggest if and how this method departs from—or simply adopts—the method of other halakhists, or to comment on the relationship of the Rav's substantive conclusions with those of others.[2]

The *shiurim* I shall discuss proceed in the traditional mode. The Rav first assembles a list of textual anomalies and contradictions, and then proceeds to solve the series of problems by presenting an overall thesis—analytical, of course, rather than textual or historical—which accounts for the earlier, puzzling phenomena. But if the structure is traditional, the exposition is not: the *shiurim* are expansive, not terse, in the classic style of halakhic writings. Nor is the reader left to form his own judgments; various rhetorical devices are used, points are elaborated, and one senses an attempt to convince. Perhaps the *shiurim* retain some characteristics of oral presentations, though they are also worked literary artifices.

Be this as it may, the literary structure of these essays is traditional. Rabbi Soloveitchik begins with the problematic texts, and then moves to the resolution and synthesis. This strategy indicates, at a most basic level, that the text or behavioral norm is primary—it is the given ground of all theory and discussion. Beginning with the problems is also fair to the listener, who can challenge any solution along the way, or provide his own alternatives: he can be an active partner, not only a passive audience. My presentation of the Rav's work, however, will lean towards the more common style of academic work, as I shall focus quite quickly on the broad theses, though some of the textual material will be provided as well—as proof, if not as matrix. Why? In part, because I wish to make these materials accessible to those unaccustomed to the traditional style. But more broadly, because I wish to present the Rav's halakhic thought as a substantive, coherent statement about significant topics—not merely a series of glittering solutions to possibly disconnected halakhic puzzles. So it is important to note that R. Soloveitchik himself re-works the conclusions of the Talmudic *shiurim* here considered into statements of halakhic phenomenology which are relatively detached from textual issues.[3]

I shall deal with Rabbi Soloveitchik's discussion of mourning. This is a topic to which he returns on a number of occasions, but I shall focus on the two major essays found in *Shiurim leZekher Abba Mari, Z"l.*[4]

II.

The first of our two essays deals with the obligation that priests render themselves impure on the death of any of the seven closest relatives, despite the general ban on priestly impurity. This imperative, R. Soloveitchik argues, is critically different from the apparently similar requirement that both priest and Nazirite—who is also required to avoid impurity—render themselves impure when they encounter an abandoned corpse (*met mitsvah*). This impurity for the *met mitsvah* is functional; that is, it is a function of the obligation to bury this corpse, an act which entails contact and hence impurity. The impurity commanded the priest for his relative, on the other hand, is substantive. In rendering himself impure for his closest relatives, the priest performs an act of ritual mourning. It is not, contrary to what one might assume, a function of the obligation to bury these relatives.[5]

This incisive distinction derives, first, from a close reading of the relevant texts. R. Soloveitchik notes that Maimonides, when describing the impurity commanded the priest/Nazirite for the abandoned corpse, always explicitly mentions its functional quality, saying that the priest/ Nazirite become impure so as to bury the corpse. This proviso is missing in descriptions of priestly impurity for relatives, and the Rav argues that this omission is pointed and deliberate. This distinction also serves to explain a number of halakhic anomalies.

First: one is required to bury even the heretic. But the priestly relative must not incur impurity on his death. All this dovetails with a third halakhic phenomenon, namely, that the death of the heretic does not entail mourning by his relatives. Thus, we see that impurity is a correlate of mourning, not burial. It is substantive rather than functional. My second example is more rewarding. The female priest is not required to render herself impure even though she is required to mourn. This is decidely awkward for the Rav's thesis, as impurity now does not seem to be an aspect of mourning at all. R. Soloveitchik proceeds, however, to utilize just this situation to confirm and indeed deepen his thesis. For Maimonides himself explains that the female priest's exemption from the obligation of impurity is entailed by the fact that she—as distinct from the male priest—is generally not commanded to remain pure. R. Soloveitchik infers from this that impurity is an aspect of mourning only when it violates the priestly status; otherwise, as in the case of the female priest, it is not an act of mourning and is not required. So it is not impurity per se which is desired or which constitutes mourning, but rather the violation of priestly status which impurity accomplishes: this violation is the act of mourning.

Our distinction between the two imperatives of impurity leads to one final, most generative conclusion. R. Soloveitchik claims that since the impurity of the Nazirite is functional and goal-oriented, it is mandated whenever it is necessary for the burial of the abandoned corpse; the Nazirite is expected to incur impurity through contact with sources of impurity other than the corpse itself if these must be moved, say, so as to bury the *met mitsvah.* For the priest, on the other hand, the mandated impurity is not functional at all, but substantive; it is an act of mourning to be performed only in connection with the body of his deceased relative.[6] This conclusion leads to the solution of problems which R. Soloveitchik placed at the very head of his essay, but I shall not pursue this intricate discussion here.

A major substantive implication of the Rav's discussion, one to which he is committed as part of his overall construction of mourning, is that contrary to the usual claim, mourning begins at the moment of death itself, not with the burial. It is only by assuming that mourning begins with death that the Rav can interpret priestly impurity as an aspect of mourning, for it is contracted before burial. Or, put differently: the successful analysis of priestly impurity as an act of mourning demonstrates that mourning begins before burial. Now, we shall return to a fuller discussion of this perspective, but suffice it to say that it promises to illumine, both phenomenologically and psychologically, the normative experience of mourning.

What we have seen up to this point also enables us—indeed, it requires us—to probe the Rav's discussion from a methodological point of view. It should be apparent that the Rav has done more than distinguish between texts or practices only so as to iron out the apparent contradictions and anomalies they present. Rather, he has provided a distinction which attempts something much deeper. In essence, he has posed the question of the basic meaning and purpose of the halakhic norms at issue. The heart of R. Soloveitchik's distinction between the impurity commanded the priest/Nazirite and the priestly relative does not lie in the description of how each behaves but rather in the exploration of why each behaves as he does, or the meaning of this behavior within the normative structure—for it is this meaning which controls and determines the behavior itself, though the details of the how support and express the grand theory of the why. In one case, as we have seen, we are dealing with a functional norm which serves to expedite burial; in the other, we are dealing with a performative aspect of mourning itself.

Now, this normative discourse is also very suggestive as a mode of both structuring and understanding human experience as it confronts death. It might imply, for example, that mourning requires loss of status as well as desanctification. Loss of status, in turn, might express self-abnegation in recognition of human impotence and mortality; desanctification, by preventing the priest's presence in the Temple, might express the mourner's removal from the presence of God, with all that that implies in turn. It should be clear that R. Soloveitchik does not himself make these interpretative suggestions in our essay (though he does elsewhere explore the halakhic aspects of the parallel notions that joy is a correlate of the presence of God just as grief is a correlate of His absence). His explicit topic here is the nature of priestly impurity. This is explored in terms of the halakhic rubric of mourning in a discussion which resolves numerous anomalies, thus transforming them into proofs of the thesis itself.

III.

The essay published in the second volume of *Shiurim leZekher Abba Mari, Z"l,* directly confronts the performative norms of mourning as well as its essential internal correlates and manifestations, and represents the Rav's fullest discussion of *aveilut*. This discussion confronts a number of issues, including the obligation (or ban) of mourning on Sabbath and Festivals; the similarity and dissimilarity of mourning for the dead and the mourning-ritual adopted by the leper; the mourning-ritual of priests; and the differentiation of mourning behavior along its chronological axis. Now, in order to produce a coherent and co-ordinated understanding of these aspects of the mourning-performance, the Rav finds it necessary to present an analysis of mourning itself. Indeed, this very distinction between mourning-behavior and its grounding, and the concomitant demonstration that both behavior and internalization function normatively, would seem to be the matrix from which the rest of the analysis flows. These essays indicate that both performance and internalization are halakhic components of mourning. To be more specific: mourning requires both patterned ritual activity and individualized emotional activity, that is to say: grief. Though one may be expressive of the other, both are equally halakhic. The internalized activity, in other words, is not the "aggadic" correlate of the performed ritual. Rather, ritual and emotion are both normative; indeed, the interplay of the two is a basic given of halakhic discussion and dynamic. This, of course, is a claim which the Rav makes frequently.[6a]

The normative interplay of behavior and internalization, ritual-mourning and grief, is most clearly apparent in the question of mourning ritual on Sabbath and Holidays. The halakhic situation posited here is that mourning is not practiced on Holidays, for the Talmud says, "The communal command to rejoice [or: The command to rejoice communally] overrules the individual's command to mourn [or: the command to mourn as an individual]." Now, mourning and holiday-ritual do not rule each other out as behavioral norms; it is possible to eat the holiday sacrifices while unshod and unshorn. The point, R. Soloveitchik argues, is that both mourning and holiday joy are internalized emotional states before they are performed rituals, and these emotional states are in total conflict. (The proofs for the internalization of holiday joy, a topic of great interest to R. Soloveitchik, will not occupy us here.) For this reason, then, private mourning can be observed on Sabbath, for it internalizes honor and dignity, not joy, and honor and dignity do not conflict emotionally with mourning.[7]

Rabbi Soloveitchik also correlates this discussion with the

fact that a leper observes all the norms derived from the mourning-pattern, even on festivals. (The very imposition upon both the leper and the excommunicate of the norms of mourning offers, of course, an interesting insight into the common qualities of all three situations, and the Rav develops this very point.) Now, this situation is problematic in context, as the festival ought deflect the leper's "mourning" much as it does that of the bereaved. The Rav argues to the contrary that the leper's removal from the community—which the Torah insists upon independent of the rabbinic imposition of mourning-norms—prevents him from entering physically into the festival celebrations and, consequently, from fully participating in the "communal rejoicing" which deflect the "individual's mourning." This is not precisely another example of the interplay of performance and internalization, but it does demonstrate, again, the connection of mourning behavior with broader patterns of action in a context of values.

A further indication of the internalized nature of mourning is the exemption of the high-priest from mourning ritual (an exemption to which only Maimonides does not subscribe). Now, from the fact that he performs the sacrificial Temple ritual even while in the mourning period of *aninut,* the Talmud infers that the high-priest is perennially in the state similar to that of all Jews during festivals. Rabbi Soloveitchik shows that, for Maimonides at least, the high-priest is perennially in the Temple, in some symbolic sense at least (the Rav's demonstration of this point is instructive from a methodological perspective: since Maimonides includes both the ban on all priests to tear their priestly clothes while in the Temple and that on the High Priest to tear his at any time in one and the same negative command, it is argued that they are one and the same ban, and the High Priest is simply considered as always being in the Temple. Maimonidean architectonics participates in the search for the essential.) The festival season and the Temple precincts are correlates, for both locate man in the presence of God, and it is this presence, the Rav claims, which rules out mourning. Indeed, he goes further and asserts (through further analysis of the festival rituals) that existential joy is indeed the response to being in God's presence, while mourning is the experience of His absence. The interplay of normative gesture and normative internalization could not be clearer.

Actually, the claim that grief itself possesses normative status ought come as no surprise. A significant component of the mourning process, after all, is *nihum aveilim* [consoling the bereaved]; indeed, the Talmud measures the bounds of mourning itself by the presence or absence of this phenomenon. *Nihum* presumes, clearly, that grief—to which consolation responds—is normatively present.[8]

If we now turn to the process and structure of the mourning ritual itself as the Rav understands them, we shall see that these dovetail with what we have said up to this point, though R. Soloveitchik does not explicitly draw the connections.

The Rav insists that though most mourning gestures are initiated only after burial, the state of mourning itself commences with the death of the mourned, for Maimonides at least. The major proof for this assertion lies in the fact that Maimonides demonstrates the Biblical status of mourning as a whole from the fact that priests are Biblically banned from participating in Temple worship while in *aninut*, the status of the mourning relative before burial. Now, this inference holds only if Maimonides understands *aninut* to be an aspect of mourning. Yet the period of *aninut* begins with death (as does the command that priests render themselves impure which, we recall, the Rav also takes to be an expression of mourning); and so, the Rav argues, mourning itself begins at the moment of death.

Burial, in this perspective, is merely a functional barrier. The bereaved, simply put, is not expected to engage in all the behavioral gestures of mourning while he is occupied with the task of burial: he is either preoccupied or free of all other positive normative obligations. (The Rav must argue, then, that even the negative gestures—not wearing shoes, for example—are not banned activities, *issurim*, but rather components of the positive structure called mourning.) After burial, however, all the obligations which death itself initiates, become operative. Thus, the Rav notes that these gestures are Torah norms after burial only on the day of death, for it is this latter situation which is generative and crucial. Even the psychological effects of burial as a moment of finality and recognition are not converted into halakhic currency (as they are by others); burial is functional and formal. Death itself contains the fullness of meaning that will be engaged by mourning.

The period from death to burial, then—that period for which the halakha has devised the category, *aninut*—is a situation in which there are no gestures of mourning even though the state of mourning fully exists. In other words, *aninut* renders actual, in "real time," what the Rav describes analytically when he claims that all mourning can be differentiated into performance and grieving internalization. The behavioral aspect cannot exist without an emotional basis (at least insofar as the seven days of mourning are concerned), but internalization is possible without performance—as *aninut* demonstrates. Indeed, the expression "*aninut*" will also be used as a general term to signify the internal aspect of mourning; the *Mishna* rules that the relatives of executed criminals do not perform the rituals of mourning, but they do grieve (*oninin*), for "grief is only of the heart" (*she-ein aninut ela ba-lev*).

It is true, of course, that *aninut* itself has behavioral content: it limits many forms of contact with the Temple and Temple-associated rituals. Indeed, this is the basic content of *aninut*. It seems, however, that the dividing line between Temple-ritual and internalization is thin, or permeable, inasmuch as the Temple concretizes man's standing in the presence of God—a motif which is primarily spiritual. Thus, it is altogether appropriate for the Rav to argue that despite the general assumption that mourning is only a rabbinic norm after the day of death itself, there is in fact a full seven-day Torah-mourning period, which is marked by the ban on mourners' presenting sacrifices to the Temple. This, I believe, is the correlate to *aninut*. What the Rav seems to be saying is that mourning as an internalized activity and norm is, of course, the basis for the behavioral patterns of the post-burial, first day of mourning, but that its independent phenomenological integrity is disclosed in both pre-burial *aninut* and post-burial distancing from the Temple.

The Rav returns to the nature of the *aninut* phase of mourning in a brief discussion of the suspension of normative duties during that period. Here, though, he does not see this suspension simply as a reflex of the task of burial which occupies the mourner; indeed, the radical quality of this situation, in which the mourner is not expected (or allowed) to fulfill any positive norm seems to call for more substantive justification. The Rav suggests that this suspension in fact reflects the existential situation of bereaved man facing death in its most intense and uncompromising brutality, a brutality which threatens to deprive the world of all meaning and, specifically, to dehumanize man himself: ". . . why lay claim to singularity and imago dei ? . . . why be committed, why carry the human-moral load? . . . Our commitment to God is rooted in the awareness of human dignity and sanctity. Once the perplexed, despairing individual begins to question whether or not such distinctiveness . . . exists, the whole commitment expires. Man who has faith in himself . . . was chosen and burdened with obligations and commandments. Despairing, skeptical man was not elected. How can man pray and address himself to God if he doubts his very humanity. . . ?"[9] Halakha, in this case, legitimates man's momentary inability to address God, for it recognizes the coherence of the human reaction to death. One is obliged to say *"barukh dayyan emet"* and bless God at the moment of death, but one is also unable to observe His commands. While this discussion of *aninut* is quite different than the one presented earlier on, both discussions focus on the internalized aspects of the mourning experience. From a more general methodological perspective, this interplay of halakhic norm and religious/existential reality is an excellent exemplar of Rabbi Soloveitchik's claim that halakha is the fundamental authenticator and vehicle of the Jewish world-view.

It should be noted that the Rav's assertion that mourning is both behavioral and internalized does not necessarily reflect a modernizing, Protestantizing bent, which would deny the validity or integrity of behavioral norms unaccompanied by internalization. Thus, despite the modern terminology, the halakhic analysis seems to be autonomous. For one thing, the presence of emotional components in mourning is stressed, as the Rav notes, in certain medieval thinkers—the Tosafists and R. Yehiel of Paris, for example; indeed, this internalization is a consistent motif in the latter's commentary to *Mo'ed Katan.*[10] The Rav also makes it clear that just as there are halakhic topics which fuse the behavioral and the internal—mourning and prayer, for example—so are there topics where this would not be true.[11] Going one step further, he argues that certain components of even the mourning process, such as the thirty-day and year-long mourning periods, lack all internalization. Yet the behavioral-internalized model does seem to have an ideal quality, a halakhic-anthropological richness, for R. Soloveitchik. Indeed, it seems that for the Rav, internalization precedes the halakhic behavior discussed and serves as its basis. He does not describe a situation where behavior is expected to create the appropriate internalization.[12]

Let us conclude our summary at this point. Clearly, there is much that we have not done, both in terms of additional substantive matter and in terms of the analytic treatment involved. Nonetheless and in the light of the limited purpose we set ourselves, I believe we have given a fair summary of the Rav's thought on this topic as well as a fair taste of the method which has produced it.[13]

We have summarized and occasionally interpreted. We have not evaluated or attempted a critique. How, for example, does the Rav read texts? More specifically, how does his "creativity" sit with the textual evidence itself? Moreover, are there different ways of relating to the problems raised? These are not necessarily carping questions; understanding the "roads not taken" contributes constructively in understanding what was done. Nor have we asked whether there are other materials—uncited by the Rav—which support his analysis.

What I think has been made clear, though, is that Rabbi Soloveitchik mounts questions which penetrate to the heart of the topic discussed and molds the myriad particulars of halakhic discussion into a broad, synthetic structure. He deals with detail, of course—no authentic halakhic discussion could ever forego that—but details are not trivia. I recall that the Rav once dismissed a very popular volume of rabbinic studies as "a collection of halakhic eccentricities." The point about the Rav's own work, though, is not merely that he did not produce halakhic eccentricities. It is, rather, that the Rav thought there was no such thing as a halakhic eccentricity, if halakha is properly understood.

IV.

Stepping back a bit from the dialectic swirl, a number of further comments can be made. First, as to the immediate discussion before us, which has frequently focused on the interplay of behavior and internalization. So far as I know, the Rav does not deal at length with the nature of mourning as an emotional, internalized state. In the halakhic writings, it is clear that mourning is opposed to festival joy, that it is a state of deep sorrow. He does not, however, offer a characterization of this sorrow or describe its dynamics. The aggadic writings offer a somewhat richer picture. The Rav describes mourning as the inability ever to communicate with loved ones, the absolute sense of loss. He also discusses the sadness and guilt engendered by the realization that one can never set things right again, that the opportunity to renew a relationship and make it whole is now out of one's grasp forever. This, he writes, is what *Hazal* meant by saying that one mourns one's parents because one has lost the chance to "Honor thy father and thy mother": the Talmudic point is broadly experiential and relational, not narrowly normative. All in all, one does not mourn "the other" who has died; rather, one mourns what has died in oneself.[14]

In the discussion we have studied here, however, grief—the internalization of mourning—is treated as a norm, not as a natural emotion. Just as one is obliged to produce the ritual of mourning behavior, so is one obliged to produce its internalized infrastructure. We seem to be dealing, then, with the interplay of two norms—not with the interplay of norm and human nature. Yet this is undeniably an extreme formulation; it is unrealistic to overlook the basic grounding of mourning emotions in human nature (or the culture we know). Rather, Rabbi Soloveitchik posits the interplay of two norms, one of which is fully a normative construct, the other a norm which bases itself—as do other norms—on the foundation of human nature. (This specific issue leads to certain Maimonidean texts, but that is not our concern here.) The two perspectives on *aninut* given above—as the normative state of non-behavioral mourning and as the normative product of man's instinctive reaction to death—might serve as an analogy.

What, in toto, has the Rav given us here (and I refer to the discussion at hand)? I do not think that terminology like "philosophy of halakha" is very helpful or accurate. In the essays before us, the topic discussed is not "halakha" per se, but rather specific areas of halakhic practice, and it is these areas which are discussed, not the enterprise of halakha in its totality. The term "philosophy" is also not adequate, as it suggests a more systematic and all-embracing presentation than the Rav attempts.

So I think it will be useful to start with the claim that the Rav is presenting an interpretation, in the hermeneutic sense of the term, a sense well described by Charles Taylor: "Interpretation, in the sense relevant to hermeneutics, is an attempt to make clear, to make sense of, an object of study. This object must . . . be a text or a text-analogue [I shall later revert to the question of whether the Rav, in the essays before us, discusses texts or text-analogues], which in some way is confused, incomplete, cloudy, seemingly contradictory—in some way or other, unclear. The interpretation aims to bring to light *an underlying coherence or sense* [italics GJB]. . . . What are the criteria of judgment in a hermeneutic science? . . . It makes sense of the original text: what is strange, mystifying, puzzling, contradictory is no longer so, is accounted for."[15] Naturally, as Taylor continues, such success presumes some commonly-held view as to what "coherence" and "sense" are, some common "language" spoken by participants in the enterprise. This stipulation, Taylor remarks, is but another way of noting the familar problem of the "hermeneutic circle." I think we can agree that the adjectives assembled by Taylor do, in any case, describe the goals of Rabbi Soloveitchik as he approaches halakhic materials; they certainly describe the state of mind created in his listeners.

Now, what is it that the Rav is making "coherent"? The immediate answer would apparently be: "his texts," which are rescued from their inner contradictions. The "objects of study" are the Talmudic text and the Maimonidean materials. In the process, these texts are not merely freed of their contradictions, but are shown to possess an inner conceptual structure, meaning, and depth. In one sense, this is patently the case: the materials discussed are all quotations from these and other textual sources. Yet I would argue that at least in the essays we have discussed, this answer is not sufficient, that more is at stake. Let us recall that halakhic texts are not philosophical disquisitions, but rather, discussions of normative patterns, that is to say, patterns of behavior. Indeed, they attempt, in large part, to structure behavior. We ought, then, to reformulate our earlier description of what the Rav is attempting. He is not only providing a coherent "text"; rather, he is attempting to "interpret" halakhic ritual behavior, to render this "text-analogue" coherent and meaningful. And so the Rav's discussion moves within the framework of a language which is "common" to both himself and his listeners in two senses. It is, of course, the common "language" of halakhic intellectual discourse within a given analytic conceptual millieu. But it is also the "language" of behavioral coherence within a given normative pattern. The Rav is engaged, in a sense, in the hermeneutic of halakhic behavior—a hermeneutic which draws upon halakhic concepts, values, and, in our case, psychological and emotional facts.

For an example, let us return to our earlier synopsis of the Rav's discussion of impurity: the priest's impurity for his relatives and the impurity of the priest/Nazirite for the abandoned corpse (*met mitsvah*). We recall that the Rav distinguished between the two, arguing that the former was a substantive act of mourning while the latter was instrumental to the responsibility for burial. We also pointed out that especially as regards the priest's impurity, the Rav was not only concerned with how the priest behaved but with why he behaved in that way, that is to say, with the meaning of his behavior: it was an act of mourning. We realize immediately, now, that the Rav's discussion was not only about texts, but about ritualized experience, the ritualized experience of mourning. The "language" of mourning, then, found new and richer expression through the Rav's hermeneutic of impurity than it had earlier possessed. And, having subsequently explored the Rav's argument for the internalized infrastructure of behavioral mourning, we would now assume that impurity—which implies a violation of sanctity and not merely a levitical state—was also related to that infrastructure, giving us further access to both the behavioral pattern and its internalized base. The claim that Rabbi Soloveitchik provides a hermeneutic of halakhic behavior is even more patent as regards his discussion of the interplay of mourning behavior and the emotions of mourning.

In the studies we have considered, then, the Rav is interested in texts which translate into experience. Perhaps the success of these studies lies in the dual coherence which is achieved. There is, first, the immanent normative coherence: rules and the supporting discussion are integrated with other rules; consistency is achieved; broad over-arching patterns of meaning emerge; straggling trees are shaped into a clearly discernible forest, and phenomena become a cosmos. Each individual detail gains depth, coherence, and conviction; each is rooted in a significant generalization. Second, there is the matter of experiential coherence, for behavior itself is interpreted. The behavior with which these studies deal may be purely ritualistic, constituted as it were by normative rules (as is the case with impurity). Or it may be behavior which, while governed by norms, is expressive at a more universal human level (as is the case with various normative gestures of mourning expressive of grief). In either case, one rises from a reading of these studies with the feeling that the Rav has made halakhic experience more humanly coherent; indeed, that human experience is deepened as it is shaped and molded by the normative performance.

If halakhic concepts and norms do shape and inform the gestures of mourning, if the interpreter of these gestures can successfully turn to this realm of meaning so as to understand the basis of halakhic behavior, it may be useful to descibe Rabbi Soloveitchik's efforts in terms similar to those in which Clifford Geertz describes what he calls "interpretive explanation": "Interpretive explanation . . . trains its attention on what institutions, actions, images, utterances, events, customs, . . . mean to those whose institutions, actions, customs, . . . they are. As a result it issues . . . in constructions like Burkhardt's, Weber's, or Freud's: systematic unpackings of the conceptual world in which condottiere, Calvinists, or paranoids live."[16] The key terms and assumptions sound familiar. One deals with meaning as it is intrinsic to those whose culture is being interpreted. One looks for the "systematic unpacking of the conceptual world" which the participants of the given culture live in their behavior.

Having wandered this far into hermeneutic territory, it is difficult not to push on a bit further, though my comments will be introductory and even telegraphic. Here I will not restrict myself to the specific topic of mourning but will address the broader claims made in *Halakhic Man*. There, as is well known, R. Soloveitchik develops the idea that the halakhic personality perceives reality through the lenses of halakhic categories; the story of Reb Moshe's vision of sunset on *Yom Kippur* (. . . "This sunset differs from ordinary sunsets, for with it, forgiveness is bestowed upon us for our sins") is the famous instantiation of that assertion.[17] It is frequently said that R. Soloveitchik owes this understanding of halakha as an epistemological tool which enables man to approach and indeed grasp reality, to his Kantian training. Now, this may be true on a biographical level, given the fact that *Ish haHalakha* was published in 1944, and that *Halakhic Mind,* written about the same time, applies similar philosophical concepts to the physical world.

Yet it is difficult, speaking in the 1990's, not to be struck by the congruence of the perspective provided by *Halakhic Man* with other facets of the work of people like Berger, Geertz, Taylor, Walzer, and others. We may safely disregard the relativistic position of the proponents of "local knowledge" or "communitarianism," which is not relevant to the point I wish to make; indeed, it can even be claimed that their materials and analysis need not necessarily lead to this relativistic position.[18] What we ought pay attention to, I think, is the way norms are taken, in the body of this work, as tools for world-building and world-perceiving. Cultures and peoples, in this view, do not merely regulate their behavior, their interaction with an existing world, through normative patterns. In some sense, rather, reality itself is perceived and structured by the normative pattern; or to quote Geertz again, "They do not just regulate behavior, they construe it."[19] Though this may sound too extreme for Rabbi Soloveitchik's understanding of halakha, it does capture something of what is going on in *Halakhic Man.*

Notes

This paper was originally presented at the Third Summer School for Jewish Studies, Institute for Advanced Study, Hebrew University, Jerusalem, and its oral quality has been retained in part. All citations are to the work of Rabbi Joseph B. Soloveitchik, unless otherwise indicated.

1. L. Kaplan, "Rabbi Joseph B. Soloveitchik's Philosophy of Halakha," *Jewish Law Annual* 7 (1988), pp. 139-198.
2. Though see at nn. 5, 6, 8, 10, for comment on some details within the overall treatment.
3. Thus, compare the problem-oriented discussion in section 3, *infra*, with the synthetic discussion in *U-Vikkashtem miSham* (Jerusalem, 1979), pp. 209-212, n. 19.
4. *Shiurim leZekher Abba Mari, Z"l*, I (Jerusalem, 1983), pp. 40-49; II, (Jerusalem, 1985), pp. 182-196. A. Rosenack's interesting discussion of *aveilut* in the work of the Rav came to my attention after this essay had been prepared; see his *Hashpa'ot shel Modellim Filosofiyyim al haHashiva haTalmudit shel haRav . . . Soloveitchik* (Hebrew U., M. A. Thesis, 1994), pp. 104-116.
5. See R. Meir Simha of Dvinsk, *Or Same'ah* to *H. Avel* 3, 8. This understanding of mandated priestly impurity is extremely explicit in *Sefer ha-Mitsvot, Ase* 37 (which, surprisingly, the Rav does not cite), where such impurity is simply identified with the imperative of mourning and serves as its Scriptural base. In *H. Avel*, on the other hand, this nexus is somewhat weakened: the Scriptural status of the imperative of mourning is demonstrated through *Leviticus* 10:20 (see on), while priestly impurity serves more as argumentation (*H. Avel* 2, 6); this impurity, moreover, serves to underscore the importance that one "occupy oneself with (*she-yitasek*), and mourn for" the deceased, seemingly blurring the clear distinction between responsibility for burial and mourning. This blurring is even more accentuated in *H. Avel* 2, 7, where mandated impurity for a wife follows seamlessly after the impurity for other relatives, though she is explicitly described as *met mitsvah*—which implies that the impurity is functional, as we have seen—and the identical *la* (see n. 6) is used for her case as for the latter.
6. I have not found an explicit Talmudic or Maimonidean statement to the effect that the impurity of the priest for his relative must be occasioned through contact with the body of the deceased relative itself (and given Rabbi Soloveitchik's understanding of the meaning of this commanded impurity, the point could be moot), but the Talmudic anecdotes on this topic all concern impurity generated in that way. Apparently the terms *lo* and *la* in the second chapter of *H. Avel* are to be taken as signifiying "through him (or her)," not "for him (or her)." The discussion in *Sema-*

khot 3, 7, ed. Higger, p. 118 (codified in *H. Avel* 2, 8), as to whether this impurity must be contracted before burial or even afterwards (a most interesting debate in its own terms) must then be understood as implying the option that the burial-cavern would be re-opened so as to allow the priest to be contaminated, much as in the explicit anecdote following, where it is opened so that he may look at the deceased.

6a. See, *e.g.*, *Al haTeshuva* (Jerusalem, 1965), pp. 40-45, and elsewhere. Y. Gottlieb's useful paper, *"Al Gishato haHilkhatit shel haRav Y. D. Soloveitchik," Shana beShana* 5754, pp. 186-197, came to my attention after this paper was prepared.

7. The Rav apparently alternated between the idea that *kavod* (honor) and *oneg* (delight) of Sabbath possessed internalized correlates and the position that they were purely behavioral: see, as well, *U-Vikkashtem miSham,* n. 19 on p. 211; *Shiurim* I, pp. 63ff.

8. See, *e.g.*, *Moed Katan* 22a; note as well S. Dickman, ed., R. Menahem Me'iri, *Bet haBehira* to *Berakhot,* 2nd ed. (Jerusalem 1965), p. 56, top (to *Berakhot* 16b). There are many other topics in classical halakha which involve the interplay of behavior and internalization, and yet others where this interplay is moot.

9. "The Halakhah of the First Day," J. Riemer, ed., *Jewish Reflections on Death and Dying* (New York, 1974), pp. 76-78. (It is not easy to find a Talmudic-rabbinic source for this explanation of our norm, though it may be possible: see *Tosafot Berakhot* 17b, *s.v. patur,* which applies, however, only to *keriat shema* and *tefillin.*) In essence, this is a psychologized variation of the argument already offered in *Halakhic Man,* trans. L. Kaplan (Philadelphia, 1983; first published in Hebrew in 1944), p. 31: "Authentic Judaism . . . sees in death a terrifying contradiction to the whole of religious life. . . . 'One whose dead [relative] lies before him is exempt . . . from all the precepts . . . in the Torah.'"

10. Among *ahronim,* see R. Isser Zalman Meltzer, *Even haAzel* to *H. Avel* 1,1-2.

11. See *Al haTeshuva,* p. 40, and n. 7 above.

12. See B. Anderson, *A Time to Mourn* (Penn State U. Press, 1991), pp. 1-18. The issue goes much deeper than the specific question of mourning-ritual, of course.

13. See n. 2 above.

14. See, *e.g.*, *Al haTeshuva,* pp. 178-181.

15. C. Taylor, *Philosophy and the Human Sciences* (Cambridge U. Press, 1985), pp. 15-17. There is much sense, to be sure, in Hillary Putnam's objection: "I do not know just what 'coherence' is nor do I know where the criteria of 'coherence' are supposed to come from—do they too only have to 'cohere'? If so anyone can reasonably believe anything, provided he has just the right notion of 'coherence'" (*Realism With a Human Face*

[Harvard U. Press, 1990] p. 157). But let us recall that the Rav is not concerned with convincing us of the reasonableness of halakha, but simply with interpreting it.

16. C. Geertz, *Local Knowledge* (New York, 1983), p. 22.
17. *Halakhic Man*, p. 38; see also pp. 20-24 for other instances. Clearly, though, the halakhic norm is not the exclusive mode by which reality is perceived, as the incident concerning R. Hayyim (p. 36) indicates.
18. See, for example, the comments of H. Nussbaum, "Non-Relative Virtue: An Aristotelian Approach," in H. Nussbaum, ed., *The Quality of Life* (Oxford U. Press, 1993), 260ff.
19. *Op. cit.*, p. 215. Note also Geertz' comment about the "imaginative, . . . constructive, . . . interpretive power . . . of culture." (Perhaps Cassirer is a kind of bridge between this hermeneutic school and Kant; the role of Cassirer has been discussed at length by Rosenak, I now note.) The analogy I am suggesting here has already been noted by Kaplan, *op. cit.*, p. 162.

Learning with the Rav: Learning from the Rav

STANLEY BOYLAN

MORE THAN A YEAR AFTER HIS PASSING, the articles concerning the legacy (or more properly legacies) of Rabbi Joseph B. Soloveitchik continue to multiply. While most, if not all, have tended to emphasize the impact of the personality of the Rav, or the richness and originality of his thought, few have dealt with the unique features of the Rav's approach to the study and teaching of Talmud. Despite the undisputed influence of the Rav as a philosophical thinker and outstanding leader in the renascence of American Orthodox Jewry, the Rav's ultimate authority stemmed from his Talmudic mastery and halakhic authority. My intent here is to focus on the Rav as "*rebbi*" in the classical sense, as Talmudic expositor par excellence, master of "*lomdus,*" dedicated advocate of the *Brisker derekh* and creator of countless "*hiddushei Torah.*" Because there is already a new generation "who did not know of Joseph," who were never exposed firsthand to the Rav's brilliance and *gadlut*, such an account is all the more necessary.

In attempting to address the unique facets in the Rav's approach to *lomdus*, I base my comments largely on personal experiences during the sixties, when I had the privilege of studying with the Rav at Yeshiva. Recognizing the great gap in *lomdus* between

Rabbi Boylan is Dean of Faculties at Touro College.

ourselves and the Rav, we in the *shiur* could not help but be somewhat amazed at his presence among us and the dedication he demonstrated in traveling from Boston to New York on a weekly basis. In a very real sense, the transmittal of Torah—the *mesora*—was the Rav's defining purpose in life and it was through the *shiur* that this purpose was realized. The Rav's search for *"amita shel Torah"*—for a deep and profound understanding of the *Torah she-Be'al Pe,* and the transmission of this Torah—was of the intensity of an issue of life and death.[1] The excitement of discovery, the search for the truth at its profoundest level, and the encounter with an intellect both open to *hiddush* yet rooted in *mesora,* gave the *shiur* an urgency and intensity unparalleled as a Torah learning experience, for which I will always be grateful.

The *Lamdan* and The *Melamed*

As is well known, the Rav liked to call himself a *"melamed,"* a teacher, which, he pointed out, is an appellation by which the Almighty Himself is known: *"HaMelamed Torah le-amo Yisrael."* The Rav's genius as a *melamed,* as expositor and mentor, in some ways rivalled his genius for interpretation and innovation. Because so much of what we, the *talmidim* of the Rav, know of the Rav's teaching and Torah, derives from the Rav's public and regular *shiurim,* (as opposed to his writings, which have had less exposure), it is impossible to totally separate the two great capacities of the Rav—*lamdan* and the *melamed.*

The Rav's *shiur* was an unforgettable intellectual and spiritual experience. It was, first of all, a *shiur* in every sense of the word, not a college class or professorial lecture. The Rav's fire was the fire of Sinai; no *esh zara,* no alien flames, burned upon his altar of Torah. The Rav's one concession to the changing American scene was a willingness to change the language of instruction from Yiddish to English,[2] because some *talmidim* knew little Yiddish. In all other respects, the *shiurim,* which could easily run from five to six hours daily, three days a week, were modeled after those offered in all *yeshivot*, but were offered with the Rav's unique dynamism, clarity and special pedagogical approach.

As in many other matters, the Rav seemed to base his unique approach to the teaching of Torah on principles of Rambam.[3] Firstly, Rambam (in *Hilkhot Talmud Torah,* Chapter I) incorporates within a single commandment the obligation to teach Torah (*le-lamed*) and the obligation to learn Torah (*li-lmod*). Indeed, the *primary* obligation according to Rambam is that of teaching Torah—"*Ve-limadtem otam et beneikhem.*" The obligation of learning Torah is posited by Rambam as a self-instructional experience: "For, just as one is commanded to teach his son, so one is commanded to teach himself" (*Hilkhot Talmud Torah* I, 4).

Cognizant of this linkage, the Rav organized his *shiur* as an exercise wherein we, the *talmidim*, were invited to share in the Rav's experience of "teaching himself," as it were, the *sugya* or halakhic text to be mastered, with the learning and teaching experience merging as one. Thus, the Rav would force himself to approach a *sugya* as if for the first time,[4] developing with us the various opinions, problems and possibilities embedded in the text, compelling us to confront with him the difficulties of various approaches, sharing with him in the resolution of these problems.

In the fourth chapter of *Hilkhot Talmud Torah,* Rambam further spells out another principle of the *rebbi-talmid* relationship. Maimonides places upon the *rebbi* not only the responsibility of transmitting Torah knowledge, but also of assuring the seriousness and diligence of the *talmid* in mastering the details of the *shiur*: "Therefore, the *rav*, the master, is never to behave frivolously before the *talmidim*, not to eat and drink before them, so that they should remain in awe of him, so they may learn from him quickly." Indeed, the master is enjoined not only to separate himself, but also to publicly admonish *talmidim* who do not devote themselves to Torah with sufficient seriousness.

The Rav took these strictures of Rambam seriously in the demands he made on his *talmidim* and in his personal awareness of the responsibilities placed upon him as an ultimate source of halakhic authority for so many of his contemporaries. The great esteem, awe, and simple fear which the *talmidim* felt in the presence of the Rav reflected the demands which the Rav himself made on us and mostly on himself. "The Lonely Man of Faith," a title the Rav chose for his marvelous essay concerning the problems of modernity, was mistakenly taken by many of us to describe the Rav himself. He was indeed not truly lonely, but singular and awesome.

Maimonides (*Hilkhot Talmud Torah*, IV,6), based on several examples in the Talmud, allows the master to purposely mislead his students by questions or actions in order to sharpen their sensitivity and thinking. On at least one occasion, the Rav candidly admitted to the *shiur* that he had indeed followed this dictum of Rambam in purposely presenting an inapt halakhic comparison. He then used the occasion as a springboard for deeper investigation of the issues involved.

In reality, this principle of Rambam is also essential in defining the *rebbi-talmid* relationship, for it illustrates that the *rebbi* must develop the skills of *talmidim* and not content himself with merely broadening their knowledge base. Indeed, the Rav's objective of developing his students' talmudic skills was always pre-eminent in his *shiurim*. The Rav's particular didactic methodology, starting from the beginning of a *sugya* and working it through as if from scratch, was at once dedicated to "*amita shel Torah*"—and yet somewhat deceptive. The Rav was, of course, always highly prepared for his seemingly initial examination of the *sugya*. His "*hasmada*" and "*ameilus baTorah*" were legendary; his *bekiut* was amazing. That the Rav could approach a *sugya* from a fresh vantage point was an enormous act of will.

The contribution to the skills of each *talmid* from this seeming deception was immense. Yet in truth, there was no deception; the process we observed and participated in was an authentic learning experience for both the *talmidim* and the Rav himself. As Rambam notes at the end of the fifth chapter of *Hilkhot Talmud Torah,* students serve as kindling to set ablaze the imagination and inspiration of the master, drawing forth from the *rav "hokhma mefoara,"* splendid wisdom. So, too, the Rav's interaction with the *talmidim* allowed him and required him to define and refine the concepts which would illuminate the text at hand.

To some extent, if the Rav sought to teach us by teaching himself, he himself became a member of the *shiur* and he was at once his own most brilliant student and merciless critic. After presenting a masterful analysis in which he seemed to have resolved all the problems he had raised, the Rav himself would often raise serious objections which had been overlooked by all those present. He valued *"amita shel Torah"* above all else and subjected his own Torah to this standard at all times. Where others might have been quite satisfied with an elegant resolution of a problematic *shita* or halakhic opinion, the Rav would return to the problem at a later date, bringing new ideas to bear, questioning, contesting, refuting, disputing and reformulating a previous day's *shiur.* The desire for *"amita shel Torah"* which the Rav inspired in his shiur was so intense that those rare occasions when he would pronounce a *hiddush "amita shel Torah"* were marked with profound satisfaction.

Towards the end of the *shiur,* the Rav, the consummate pedagogue, would often summarize succinctly the day's discussions: "What did we learn today?" In other *shiurim,* such a question might be a signal to begin to put away one's books for another day. The Rav saw the need to summarize one's conclusions as another challenge. The Rav's review sometimes took on a life of its own, changing or recasting the *shiur* once again, clarifying issues which might have been left ambiguous or unclear. After the *shiur* was completed, the Rav would, of course, remain for further questions and discussions.

In retrospect, it is clear that the very dynamism of the Rav's thinking can pose special problems. Those seeking to understand the Rav's Torah on a particular *sugya* and those seeking to reconstruct the Rav's teachings from notes taken by dedicated *talmidim* are confronted by the nature of the Rav's didactic approach, his willingness to explore new approaches, his readiness to refine and redefine. The Rav's public lectures, where he more often seemed to provide conclusions, had their own educational objectives (see below), and may not necessarily represent his definitive view on a particular matter. As a consequence, establishing what the Rav actually maintained on a particular *sugya* is often a difficult task.

The Rav often repeated a family maxim which reflected his attitude toward publishing Torah. According to this dictum, "Not everything that one thinks, should one say; not everything that one says, should one write, and not everything that one writes," the Rav would add with a smile, "should one publish." In this, as in other matters, the Rav followed the tradition of Rav Chaim, *zt"l*, whose *hiddushim* were published posthumously. The Rav was very reluctant to publish his *hiddushei Torah*, and much of what appears in print in his name are distillations of *shiurim* reconstructed from notes. The nature of note-taking, even if done well, however, tends to reduce a *shiur* to its bare bones—*heftsa, gavra, ma'ase, halot*, etc., leaving out the flesh and blood. The effort to convey the Rav's teachings is an intellectual and spiritual undertaking of the highest order. The task itself is a daunting one, which runs the danger of reducing the Rav to the dimensions of the *talmid*. Let the reader of works ascribed to the Rav recognize, in the words of the *kohen gadol* on *Yom haKippurim*, that *"Yoter mi-ma she-karanu ketuvim kan"*—"More than we have read is written here."[5] The Rav's Torah, in its splendid variety and multi-dimensionality, remains largely, as he wished, a *Torah she-Be'al Pe*, rather than a *Torah she-bi-Khtav*.

Despite all the above, it would nevertheless be wrong to assert that the Rav's Torah has not been properly transmitted or conveyed merely because the Rav's conclusions in a particular *sugya* are ambiguous. The Rav taught that *hatan Bereishit* was greater than *hatan Torah*,[6] and that the purpose of a *siyyum* was to mark one's ability to start anew with greater wisdom. The Rav's approach to opening up a *sugya*, explaining a *Rambam*, defining a *mahloket*, may be ultimately more important than the particular fashion in which he resolved individual problems in a definitive manner. Like Rashi (as quoted by Rashbam at the beginning of *VaYeshev*), the Rav viewed Torah as an unending process. To understand the Rav, therefore, we must understand his unique approach to learning, rather than merely reflecting on his conclusions; his "*hava amina*" is crucial even when we may never be sure of his "*maskana*."

Hiddush and *Mesora*

Two underlying and seemingly contradictory impulses are apparent in the Rav's approach to learning (and indeed in his very persona): on one hand, a search for *hiddush*, and on the other, a scrupulous devotion to *mesora*, to that which has been imparted. The Rav's individual Torah legacy, derived largely from his sainted father and grandfather, Rav Moshe and Rav Chaim Soloveitchik, *zikhronam li-vrakha*, followed a *derekh* which at the time of its initial adoption revolutionized Torah learning. The Rav viewed himself as a link in this chain of *mesora* and adopted the "*Brisker derekh*" in his general approach to *lomdus*.

Before Rav Chaim, the Rav often commented, *lomdus* was seen as an attempt to reconcile contradictions between differing texts, to resolve apparent discrepancies between opinions. The *Brisker derekh* redirected the focus of attention from these apparent contradictions in texts, to the *a priori* questions of structure and relationship which provide the conceptual underpinnings of a *sugya* or text. In this methodology, a *mahloket* is analyzed in terms of fundamental conceptual differences rather than the particular application at hand. Given a proper orientation regarding the abstract or conceptual basis of an opinion or position cited in a text, apparent contradictions may indeed be resolved, but the ultimate end is the insight gained into a proper conceptual formulation.

With its emphasis on abstract reasoning, the *Brisker derekh* places major emphasis on proper definition, structure and relationships, and the application of universal principles (such as *da'at, kavana, li-shma,* and *ba'alut*) to particular situations. The role of the *lamdan* is to organize and understand the *sugya* as it relates to the general concepts, and to explore both the particular situation and the application of universal principles to the *sugya* being studied.

Under this definition of *lomdus,* the goal of the *lamdan* is not so much to resolve *setirot,* contradictions, but rather to pose *hakirot,* potential conceptual models with which to better understand and define the *halakha* or *sugya* in question. The *setira* is thus transformed into a tool whereby the *hakira* may be resolved. Whereas classical *lomdus* before Rav Chaim concentrated on the *setira* and sought to resolve the *setira* in a variety of fashions, the *Brisker derekh* is dedicated to the *hakira,* the investigation of potential conceptual models.

The Rav was, of course, the master of the *hakira,* with an amazing ability to delineate a wide variety of conceptual possibilities. Equally, however, he maintained that the true *lamdan* must be scrupulously careful concerning the proper understanding of text and almost pedantic in pursuing the consistency or contradiction of opinions as a tool to clarify and classify *shitot.* In the Rav's methodology, the skills of classical *lomdus* were an intrinsic component of the true *lamdan*'s capabilities.

The *Brisker derekh,* in essence, seeks to analyze particular halakhic or textual problems in a conceptual framework. The framework itself is the given, its definitions, axioms and internal relationships largely developed by Rav Chaim and elaborated upon by Rav Moshe Soloveitchik, *zt"l,* Rav Velvel Soloveitchik, *zt"l,* and others. In formulating the *Brisker derekh,* Rav Chaim created, in the Rav's description in *Ish haHalakha,* the framework in which the world of talmudic thought can be analyzed and categorized, and in which the universe itself is to be perceived.

The Rav's personal *mesora,* his legacy of Torah from his distinguished forebears, played an essential role in his approach to any given talmudic or halakhic problem. This *mesora* sometimes expressed itself explicitly in terms of the Rav's direct exposition of an analysis which he had received from his father or grandfather. This analysis then served as the starting point of the Rav's own analysis, bringing proofs to the *Brisker* position, raising problems involved and suggesting possible alternative resolutions.

In some *shiurim,* the Rav would turn to the classical *Brisker* canon (of which he was a master) for a paradigm to use to resolve a problem which had not been directly addressed by Rav Chaim or his father, *zt"l.* In these instances, the *talmidim* would be exposed to a classic *Brisker hakira* in one *sugya,* and the Rav would then apply the *hakira* to the material at hand. In this way, the Rav combined his vast creative talent with the power of his *mesora.*

In all *shiurim,* the structural framework of analysis remained as formulated by Rav Chaim, *zt"l.* The Rav's commitment was to extend this analysis to areas and problems not previously addressed and to explore alternative definitions and categorizations within the overall *Brisker* framework.

The Rav took great pride in the *mesora* he received from his father and grandfather. A maxim which he utilized on a number of occasions, "In order to be a *gadol,* you have to grow up among *gedolim,*" reflected more than family pride. The Rav's aspirations in Torah, his commitment to *"amita shel Torah,"* and the unrelenting demands for excellence and intellectual honesty which he maintained for himself and others had been inculcated in him from his childhood on.[7] On an intellectual level, the Rav had an innate sense concerning the internal logic of halakha against which he measured potential approaches, rejecting some as absurd and pursuing others as potentially rewarding. This intuition, as well as an ability to discover interesting problems within the seemingly routine, were also part of his special heritage. Even his commitment to *hiddush* can be traced to his personal *mesora,* which was a *derekh* which revolutionized Torah learning throughout the world.

While we were in the *shiur,* rumor had it that the Rav had inherited from his father Rav Chaim's notes and *hiddushim* on many *masekhtot*. Indeed, on one occasion, the Rav brought to the *shiur* a copy of Rav Chaim's *hiddushim* on the *sugya* being learned. The Rav would also quote personal family anecdotes, which illustrated the *hashkafa* of *gedolei Yisrael* on particular issues. Rav Chaim, according to the Rav, was a "*mahmir* on *pikuah nefesh*," scrupulously careful regarding any threat to human life, and consequently was more lenient when human life might be at risk. On the other hand, with regard to the permissibility of risking one's own life to save another, the Rav reported how Rav Chaim directed family members to minister to the severely ill during a diphtheria epidemic, although doing so involved risk of contracting the disease. Based on his reading of *Rambam*,[8] Rav Chaim felt that halakha placed a special responsibility for *pikuah nefesh* on *gedolei Yisrael*.

The Rav also highly esteemed the role of *mesora* in halakhic decision-making, *pesak halakha*. In the midst of a *shiur* in *Nidda*, the Rav once reported to us a *kabbala* which Rav Chaim had received in the name of the Gaon of Vilna regarding the proper *shiur* (measurement) of a *gris*, the minimum measure for *tumat ketamim* (menstrual stains). This *gris* was the size of a specific Polish coin, which was between the size of a nickel and a quarter. On another occasion, the Rav addressed the question of the *tekhelet* which had been introduced in the last century by the Radziner Rebbe. The Bet haLevi had rejected the *tekhelet* because it lacked a *mesora* of halakhic practice to verify it, and no other halakhic evidence could substitute for this *mesora*.[9]

In matters of halakha, the Rav was guided not only by a technical mastery of the various *shitot* regarding a particular issue, but also by an intuitive sense of *pesak*, which motivated him in organizing the various *shitot* of *poskim*. With regard to *minhagim*, his special family inheritance often determined his personal practice. (This would not always determine his *pesak* for others, however, which would weigh other *shitot* and common practice.)

The Rav's desire to apply the *Brisker derekh* to areas which had not been previously addressed extended also to *minhagei Yisrael* as described by *poskim*. Just as the Vilna Gaon sought talmudic and midrashic sources for the *minhagim* cited by *Shulhan Arukh*, the Rav would analyze *minhagim* along the lines of the *Brisker derekh*. The Rav was particularly interested in *minhagei tefilla* and the various *nusha'ot* of *tefilla*, examining the differences between their halakhic and theological implications.

One of the unique aspects of the Rav's Torah was its dedication to the unity of Torah, in his attempt to apply a uniform methodology to *kol haTorah kula*. His view of Torah was not fragmented but unified, drawing a principle of *lomdus* from one area to illuminate another. Instead of restricting his attention to the standard canon of *Nashim* and *Nezikin*, the Rav would undertake *masekhtot* far outside the usual range of "*yeshivishe masekhtot*." Thus, the Rav said *shiur* in the Yeshiva on *Eruvin, Succa* (from the beginning), *Sanhedrin, Nidda, Hilkhot Nidda, Halla*, on *Minhat Hinukh* (*e.g. Hilkhot Mila, Tefillin, Tsitsit*), *Masekhet Shabbat* (including the latter *perakim* involving *muktze*). During the summers, the Rav would hold *shiurim* for a *kollel* in Boston, during which he would learn yet other *masekhtot*, including *kodashim*.

Of course, the Rav also said *shiur* on such standard "*yeshivishe masekhtot*" as *Baba Kama, Baba Metsia, Baba Batra, Gittin, Kiddushin, Yevamot, Hullin* and *Yore De'a*. During *Elul*, his *shiurim* might focus on *sugyot* from *Rosh haShana* and *Yoma* (particularly focusing on *Avodat Yom haKippurim*). One *Elul* in Boston, the Rav even said *shiurim* on *Likutei Torah* of the *Ba'al haTanya*.

I have heard from Rav Ahron Soloveichik that Rav Chaim, *zt"l*, did not believe in a hard-and-fast separation between halakha and aggada. Certainly, the Rav well understood the unity of halakha and aggada in Jewish thought, and his approach to *derush* played heavily on their interrelationship. The Rav felt that aggada too needed the strong intellectual underpinning which could be provided only by a halakhic emphasis utilizing *Brisker* methodology.

The Rav's *Yahrtseit shiurim* were generally constructed upon a number of halakhic problems, which the Rav would attempt to resolve using a particular principle. After the resolution of the halakhic issues, the Rav would explore a topic in *aggadta* which was generally related to the halakhic discussion.

A similar pattern might apply at the Rav's *teshuva derasha*, which the Rav gave publicly during the *asseret yemei teshuva*. The text to be examined would usually be a passage from *Rambam Hilkhot Teshuva*. In this *derasha*, which was an extremely moving experience for all participants, the unity of halakha and aggada was even more pronounced.

These public *shiurim* were masterpieces of structure, with all of the disparate problems and discussions coming together in an integrated whole. In most years, the topics dealt with relatively popular or accessible areas such as *tefilla, keriat haTorah* or *mo'ed*. On some occasions, the Rav's *Yahrtseit shiur* might address issues he had addressed in his weekly *shiur*. The *Yahrtseit shiur* was more focused and organized, but by its very nature could not explore all the possibilities the Rav had raised in the weekly *shiur*.

As is obvious from the tremendous breadth displayed in *shiur*, which literally touched upon "*gants Shas*," the Rav had a remarkable *bekiut*, encyclopedic knowledge, which was dwarfed only by his *harifut*, his analytical acuity. The Rav's *bekiut* was in some sense all the more remarkable because of the somewhat circumscribed focus of his primary attention. The Rav once told us that Rav Chaim's definition of a *lamdan* was "one who knows *peshat* in every *Rashi, Tosefot, Rambam* and *Ra'avad* in *Shas*," listing these *rishonim* because they are the ones who themselves wrote on *gants Shas*. With some hesitation, the Rav then added *Ramban* and *Rashba* to the list. With some additions (*Ba'al haMa'or, Maggid Mishne, Minkhat Hinukh*, and *Rebbi Akiva Eiger*), these constituted the main focus of the Rav's attention during *shiur*. The Rav told us that Rav Chaim's personal set of *sefarim* was quite limited, consisting of a *Shas*, a *Tur-Shulkhan Arukh*, and an extremely limited set of *aharonim*. In *Bi'ur haGra* on *Shulkhan Arukh*, the Vilna Gaon had refocused *pesak halakha* on *mekorot halakha*—on *Shas Bavli, Yerushalmi*, and *rishonim*, and on careful readings of text. The *Brisker derekh* incorporated a similar attention to *mekorot* in its reformulation of *lomdus*, to allow for a fresh examination of basic texts without preconceived notions.

With a sensitivity to the nuances inherent in the words of the *rishonim*, the Rav taught us to carefully analyze the various commentaries with regard to the conceptual differences between them. Although the Rav (and the *Brisker derekh* generally) was focused on his own redefined area of study, his *bekiut* reached out to classic halakhic problems and sources illustrative of a particularly *hakira* or supportive of a particular formulation. Whenever relevant, the Rav might well introduce an interpretation of the *Ketsot haHoshen* or *Netivot* on a certain issue. The Rav was more reluctant, however, to add newly discovered *rishonim* (such as *Meiri*) to the recognized canon, except when the *rishon* himself had been cited previously in sources such as *Shita Mekubbetset*.[10] This reluctance sometimes proved a validation of the Rav's *derekh*, when positions only hinted at in *Rashi, Tosefot* or *Rambam* were explicitly taken by *rishonim* which the Rav had never studied. Using his remarkable intuition, the Rav could discern the possible approaches of *rishonim* even when he had never studied them.

After a hiatus of a number of years away from the *shiur*, I returned briefly to once again sit in on the Rav. At that time, I recall being struck by the Rav's demands for absolute precision of definition (which I could not possibly duplicate on my own) and his insistence on interpreting *rishonim* literally, even when common sense dictated that they could not possibly have meant what they seemed to be saying. In "*milhamta shel Torah*," there are times when prudent retreat (or even surrender) seems our only recourse. But the Rav could take difficult *shitot*, and by refusing to retreat or surrender, he would eventually triumph, with electrifying results.

The Rav's greatest strength was in the area of *hiddush*, in proposing new insights and approaches to a *sugya*. One of the outstanding *talmidei hakhamim* at Yeshiva, Rav Nisson Alpert, would often discuss the Rav's *hiddushei Torah* with *talmidim* in the Rav's *shiur*. He would sometimes point out that others before the Rav might have offered similar *svarot* or *peshatim*. Even in these instances, however, the Rav's approach was generally more comprehensive and insightful. It was indeed indisputable that if one searched thoroughly in *aharonim*, one might at times find approaches similar to that of the Rav. (Rav Hershel Schachter's invaluable notes of the Rav's *shiurim* sometimes refer to such sources. Of course, the Rav would not himself have utilized these sources in developing his *shiur* or arriving at his conclusion.

The Rav once related to us an anecdote concerning his grandfather's reaction when he was told a *"shtikel Torah"* by other *talmidei hakhamim*. If he disagreed with the *peshat*, rather than enter into long discussions, Rav Chaim would politely say, *"Ikh hob okhet azoy gezogt, a bissele andersh"* ("I also said similarly, a bit differently."). Of course, the *"bissele andersh"* of *Brisker* Torah can make all the difference in the world. Working within a highly structured discipline of strictly defined concepts, *Brisker* Torah, if it is to excel, depends on finely nuanced arguments and well-articulated distinctions. More importantly, *Brisker* Torah seeks to analyze the particular in terms of universally applicable principles. The Rav's *hiddushim* flowed naturally from this integrated view of Torah and were not designed to address merely the problem at hand. In this way, the Rav's *hiddushim*, even when they seemed similar to those of other *aharonim*, remained *"a bissele andersh."*

Two anecdotes related to us by the Rav exemplify distinctions between himself and even other *Brisker lamdanim*. In trying to differentiate the *mesora* of the Brisker Rav from that of some other disciples of Rav Chaim, *zt"l*, the Rav quoted a family witticism, that if Rav Chaim had made the obscure statement, "A table is like a cow," the Brisker Rav would have explained that the table is like a cow in that both have four legs. On the other hand, another disciple might very well have milked the table!

The Rav, of course, never "milked the table." He highly esteemed the Brisker tradition, but recognized the need to properly interpret this tradition in the manner in which Rav Chaim, *zt"l*, intended. The Rav contributed through his great powers of *hasbara*—of exposition and explanation—to the preservation and explication of this tradition.

It was the Rav's practice to actively solicit possible solutions from the *shiur*, and on a number of occasions, the *talmidim* were successful in providing the *Brisker* formulation which he sought. On one occasion, perhaps to prevent hubris on our part, he turned to the *shiur* with the familiar metaphor of the monkeys in the British Museum, who, given enough time, would eventually type out the works of Shakespeare. "Yes," the Rav said, "if you throw around enough of the familiar terms—*heftsa, gavra* . . . you might very well occasionally come up with the proper formulation. The difference is that I understand it!"

The Rav wished to warn us of the potential to reduce Torah (and even *Brisker* Torah) to manipulation of words or phrases in a mechanical fashion, independent of a higher intelligence to harmonize the particular within the universal. The reduction of each case to individual *halakhot* carries with it the risk of an atomization of Torah to an incomprehensible collection of special situations. The Rav's special gift was creating *"lomdisher" hakirot* which not only were useful in resolving textual problems, but more importantly, were of *a priori* interest, independent of any given text, and in formulating solutions with an intuitive sensitivity regarding *kol haTorah kula*.

The Legend and The Legacy

The *Mishna* in *Sota* (Chapter 9, *Mishna* 15) relates, "When Rabbi Meir died, the era of *moshelei meshalot* (creators of parables) ended." This seemingly trivial eulogy is a strange way to describe the greatness of Rabbi Meir, who was the primary, if anonymous, formulator of the *Mishna* itself (*"Stam Mishna Rabbi Meir"*). I would suggest that the *Mishna* relates not only to Rabbi Meir's practice of combining within his well-attended public *shiurim* halakha, *aggadita* and *meshallim* (parables), but also to Rabbi Meir himself, who through his greatness transformed himself into a mythic figure, into Rabbi Meir Ba'al haNes. In Rabbi Meir's relationship with *Aher,* in his survival in the *mayyim she-ein lahem sof,* in his wanderings to escape the Roman authorities, and of course in his heroic efforts to preserve *Torah she-Ba'al Pe,* Rabbi Meir captured the imagination of the Jewish people of his generation and all generations. In all of the retrospectives concerning the Rav, it is obvious that he too has been a metaphor for the *talmid chacham* par excellence struggling with the modern age and triumphing. In examining the legend and legacy of the Rav, I believe, we can gain insight, therefore, from a further comparison with incidents in the life of Rabbi Meir.

Rabbi Meir possessed a remarkable talent as a scribe and was able to write *sifrei kodesh* with great clarity and precision (sometimes even without a source text). To prevent inadvertent changes to the text, Rabbi Meir was in the habit of adding calcanthum (vitriol) to the ink to assure the impression would be indelible. Rabbi Yishmael, Rabbi Meir's rebbi tells him, "My son, be exceedingly careful in your labors, for your work is the work of heaven, lest you subtract or add a single letter, thereby destroying the entire world." Having set such a high standard, Rabbi Yishmael then adds that one cannot *possibly* add calcanthum to the ink of the Torah, for the potential for erasure and correction is an intrinsic requirement of writing a *sefer-Torah.*

While directed towards the specific requirements of the writing of *Torah-she-bichtav,* Rabbi Yishmael's injunction to Rabbi Meir has equal relevance to his historic role in the preservation of *Torah she-Be'al Pe.* Having lived through the martyrdom of his father-in-law, Rabbi Chaninah ben Tradyon, and his rebbi, Rabbi Akiva, Rabbi Meir took upon himself the mission of the preservation of the *Torah she-Be'al Pe* itself. With his remarkable memory for detail and holistic view of Torah encompassing *kol haTorah kulo,* Rabbi Meir became the formulator and ultimate source of rabbinic authority expressed in the "Stam Mishneh" preserving the *Torah she-Be'al Pe* for eternity.

The second part of Rabbi Yishmael's injunction, on the need to incorporate the possibility for change and amendment in inscribing the Torah was also adopted by Rabbi Meir in his approach to the oral law. So great was Rabbi Meir's talent for explicating variant possibilities within the halakha, that the gemara in *Eruvin* 13b posits this as the ultimate reason why he could not be designated as the supreme halachic decisor, *"shelo yochlu haverov la'amod al sof da'ato"*, because his colleagues could not discern his final conclusions.

Like Rabbi Meir, the Rav and his contemporaries also confronted an historical challenge to the continuity of the *Torah she-Be'al Pe*, after the wholesale slaughter of countless Torah scholars, the extirpation of European Yeshivos and the culture which sustained them and the martyrdom of much of the rabbinic leadership. It called upon them to struggle to preserve the continuity of Torah in an alien environment, calling for an intellectual commitment to the truth of the mesorah together with an openness to innovation and change in presenting this mesorah to an alienated modernity.

Rabbi Meir's most controversial decision entailed maintaining his relationship with Elisha ben Avuya, after his transformation to Aher, the apostate. While ultimately vindicated by the Talmud (*Chagiga* 15b), Rabbi Meir was an object of scorn and mockery for learning from such as *Aher*. Later, in times of other difficulties, Rabbi Meir's relationship with *Aher* would continue to haunt him, as his opinions were designated anonymously as *"aherim"*.

Rabbi Meir himself was likely motivated by two overriding considerations, each reflecting a different aspect of Rabbi Meir's relationship with *Aher*. *Aher* was first of all Rabbi Meir's *rebbi*, a source of *Torah she-Be'al Pe* particularly as transmitted by Rabbi Akiva, which might have been otherwise lost from the mesorah if not captured from *Aher*. Secondly, *Aher* was seen by Rabbi Meir as a *talmid*, who could yet be taught by him the path to *Teshuva*.

The Talmud relates how Rabbi Meir was presenting a *shiur* in the Beth Medrash in Tiberias one Shabbat, when he was told that his *"rebbi" Aher* was outside, riding on a horse. Rabbi Meir follows *Aher* on the horse, discussing Torah with him, until *Aher* tells Rabbi Meir to return because they had reached the *Techum Shabbat* (the boundary of the Sabbath), which *Aher* had measured by the paces of his steed. Rabbi Meir pleads with *Aher* himself to return to the Torah, but *Aher*'s attempt at Teshuva is frustrated when the children of the Beth Medrash reject him.

Both Rabbi Meir and *Aher* are aware of the boundaries and limits in this interchange. Rabbi Meir leaves the confines of the Beth Medrash, to the mocking of his colleagues, to draw *Aher* back. *Aher* seeks to ride away beyond the boundary of Shabbat, leaving Rabbi Meir behind. Refusing to recognize the limits set by *Aher,* by the children of the Beth Medrash and by life itself, Rabbi Meir pursues *Aher* until his return, and according to the medrashim, even beyond the grave into the world-to-come.

In seeking to preserve his own particular *mesora,* his special Torah legacy, the Rav too saw the need for an emphasis on Teshuvah. He addressed not one *Aher,* but all the *"aherim"* of the contemporary world. It was his view that, Torah could transcend the boundaries erected by society and that modern man could indeed be brought to Torah. To this struggle, the Rav dedicated his formidable intellectual skills, his intense religious charisma and abiding belief that "sof Yisroel la'asot Teshuva".[11]

In his efforts, the Rav became larger-than-life, a truly legendary figure. Many of those who have written about the Rav have written of the legend but not the man himself. There are, of course, variants or distortions of the legend devised by many who did not know the Rav, never had the privilege of learning from him or his Torah, or those who sought to use the Rav to justify positions which he himself never espoused—*talmidim,* perhaps, *"shelo amdu al sof da'ato,"*. who never fully comprehended his total world view.

Those who learned from the Rav, those who came to love and venerate him, inevitably made him part of their lives and their souls. We must all be careful, however, not to recreate the Rav in our own image. The Rav was a *rosh yeshiva,* not merely a professor of Jewish Philosophy. He taught *Talmud Bavli* and *Shulkhan Arukh,* not some branch of Hebraic Literature; the Rav knew *gants Shas,* not Chekhov and Pushkin. The Rav sought not to embrace modernity, but rather to transcend it. The Rav fought valiantly against the secularization of Yeshiva. Let us fight just as valiantly against the secularization of the Rav himself.

Of course, part of the legend was the Rav's genius both in Torah and secular studies.[12] Certainly, the Rav was as rich and complex an individual as any *sugya* which he taught us. But the core of the Rav's existence remained his dedication to *limud Torah* and *yirat shamayim.* The ultimate lesson we must learn from the Rav is that this great genius devoted his outstanding intellectual energies so that Torah might be learned and preserved among us. The burden of his legacy to those who knew him best, those who learned his Torah, is to see to it that this Torah is preserved and learned by future generations and that we remain true to that which the Rav taught us throughout his life and through his life. Then we will have shared with others the privilege and glory of learning with the Rav.

Notes

1. See the comments of Rambam, *Hilkhot Rotseah uShemirat haNefesh,* (VIII,1) in explaining the obligation of the master in following his *talmidim* into exile: *"ve-hayyei ba'alei hakhma u-me-vaksheha be-lo talmud kemita hashuvin"*—"For the lives of the masters of wisdom and those who search after it are considered like death, without study."
2. I am told that the Rav's change of language came at the request of Rabbi Daniel Greer, who was a student at the time. Frankly, some of the students were under the impression that the language of instruction had been changed to Latin.
3. An emphasis on the analysis of *Rambam* in order to ascertain Rambam's understanding of the *sugya* being studied was a constant of the *shiur.*

Based on *Rambam, Sefer haMitsvot, Mitsvat Asei* 5, the Rav saw *talmud Torah* and *tefilla* on a continuum of *avoda she-ba-lev*. Toward this end, the *lomdus* of *talmud Torah* (and *tefilla*) was especially significant for the Rav.

4. On one occasion, the *shiur* studied the *sugya* of *migu*, and the Rav grappled for a *hakira* with which to analyze the *shitot* of *Tosafot*. I tentatively offered the Rav the well-worn *yeshivishe hakira* as to whether *migu* was a "*birur*" or "*ne'emanut*." The Rav reacted as if he had never heard of such a *hakira*! I was not able to explicate it to his satisfaction, and the *shiur* moved on.
5. *Mishna Yoma* (7:1).
6. See the *peshat* cited in the Rav's name at the conclusion of "*Reshimot Shiurim she-Ne'emru al yedei Maran haGaon Rabbeinu haRav Yosef Dov haLevi Soloveitchik Shelita al Masekhet Succa*," HaRav Tsvi Yosef Reichman (New York, 1989).
7. The Rav related to us during the *shiurim* on *Yevamot* a story about Rav Chaim in which Rav Chaim was being evaluated as a potential *maggid shiur* at the beginning of his teaching career in Volozhin. Rav Chaim had been saying *shiur* on his *peshat* in *Rambam* concerning "*kol ha-ola le-yibbum ola la-halitsa*." Suddenly, Rav Chaim remembered the *Rambam* in *Hilkhot Melakhim* concerning the *sugya*, which contradicted what he had said. Rav Chaim then closed his *gemara*, explained he had been in error, and dismissed the class. "Needless to say," the Rav added, "Rav Chaim kept his position."
8. See *Rambam, Hilkhot Shabbat*, (Chapter II, 3).
9. This aspect of *mesora* is discussed by the Rav in "*Shiurim leZekher Aba Mari, Z"l*," vol. I. (Jerusalem, 1983), pp. 220-238.
10. See "The Role of Manuscripts in Halakhic Decision Making: Hazon Ish, His Precursors and Contemporaries," Moshe Bleich, *Tradition* 27:2 (1993), for a review of the position of *gedolim* with respect to newly discovered manuscripts.
11. See Rambam, *Hilkhot Teshuva*, 7:5.
12. The Rav was, of course, aware of his reputation for genius and made fun of it. Once, the Rav told us, he received a call from a desperate *ba'al habayit* with a puzzling problem. Could the Rav help him find *Masekhet Makkot* within the *Shas* which was in his bookcase? He had already searched at the end of *Shavuot*, where it is often found, and had similarly eliminated inclusion within the volume of *Avoda Zara*. Reaching back to a *Shas* he had once seen years earlier, the Rav suggested he look after *Baba Batra*. The grateful *ba'al ha-bayit* checked and came back to the Rav with the familiar refrain, "Rabbi Soloveitchik, you really are a genius!"

The Halakhic Rebbe

EMANUEL FELDMAN

IT IS A SCENE NOT LIKELY TO BE REPEATED for a long time to come: a large assembly hall with several thousand people in attendance—young and old, men and women, learned rabbis and scholars, members of the academic community, Orthodox and non-Orthodox Jews. They listen intently. Tape recorders whir, pencils take rapid notes.

On the podium is a tall, lean, gray-bearded figure delivering a *shiur*/lecture on the fine points of *halakha* and Jewish thought. His subject is complex and subtle, but he will hold his diverse audience in thrall for two to three hours.

The speaker is Rav Joseph B. Soloveitchik, a *rosh yeshiva* enigmatic yet open, charismatic yet unaffected, distant yet accessible. Born in Poland in 1903, scion of several generations of world-famous Talmudic luminaries, Rav Soloveitchik was one of the preeminent and most intriguing Torah personalities of the twentieth century, a *mitnaged*'s *mitnaged* with a taste for *hasidut*, an analytic philosopher with a gift for the poetic.

Emanuel Feldman, editor of Tradition, *is Rabbi Emeritus of Congregation Beth Jacob in Atlanta, Georgia. He presently resides in Jerusalem.*

When the mysterious resurrection of American Orthodoxy in the twentieth century is recorded by historians, they will give due recognition to the various great *roshei yeshiva* and hasidic *rebbeim* who, together, with the newly arrived immigrant survivors of World War II, brought with them the stubbornness and the vision which were the catalysts for the renewal of Torah in America. The schools they founded, the *yeshivot* they nurtured, the attitude of self-confidence and pride which they created, the personal examples that they set—all gave birth to the committed corps of Jews who are the vanguard of today's renewed Orthodox Judaism.

At the same time, the historians will have to note a more subtle truth: that it was the unique approach and background of a *rosh yeshiva* like Rav Soloveitchik that provided the intellectual framework that was uniquely suited to present classical Judaism to twentieth century men and women. More than any other religious leader, he was able to demonstrate to a wide audience the intellectual rigor and discipline of halakha as well as the profound world-view inherent in the minutiae of the daily halakhic regimen—a world-view which addresses itself not only to the mind but also to the troubled heart and soul of the lonely modern man.

This demonstration of the universality of Torah, presented with such clarity and passion, also contributed immeasurably to the morale of an Orthodox community which, in mid-century, was being buffeted on all sides and was beset with self-doubt and dispiriting retreats on many fronts.

In particular did he have a major impact on the American-trained Orthodox rabbinate. Not all of them studied under him at *Yeshivat Rabbeinu Yitzhak Elhanan*/Yeshiva University, but they all benefited directly from the spiritual support and inspiration which his teaching provided at a critical juncture in American Jewish history. The undersigned, not a student at Yeshiva University, can directly attest to this. Not only did Rav Soloveitchik help keep at bay those debilitating forces of modernity that threatened to overwhelm and drown the fledgling Orthodox; he was also a major architect of the bridge upon which many marginal Jews were able to return to the tradition.

• • •

That he was able to touch the contemporary soul was in great measure due to his recurring themes. The motif of alienation is sounded regularly in his work. We hear of "the dark night of the soul"; the meaning of death and mourning in human life; loneliness (prayer as a dialogue between the lonely Jew and the lonely God); defeat, despair, retreat and anguish; the absurdity of existence without God: the entire lexicon of contemporary existential thought. Whether it be in the moving eulogy for the Talner Rebbetzin or a theoretical excursus into the realm of spiritual authority, the listener is caught up short by the recognition of his own inchoate vexations and anxieties. The message is clear: it is only the saving quality of Torah and halakha which makes it possible for dust-and-ashes man, whose life without God is inherently tragic and whose physical end is in the grave, to reach out confidently to the King of Kings.

Rav Soloveitchik's ability to strike responsive chords within his listeners was in great measure due to his unique gift for language. Whether he spoke in his native Yiddish or in his adopted English, his use of words was at once precise and poetic. His great intellect was expressed in a corresponding gift of articulation and communication. This fusion of rigorous thought and lyrical language is at the heart of Rav Soloveitchik's power, and made him a teacher par excellence, both on the public platform and in the confines of a classroom. In fact, he often described himself not as a philosopher or professor, but as a *rebbe* and a teacher.

In the era of the seven-word-sound-bite-and-on-to-the-next-commercial, the very idea of an audience sitting entranced for several hours at an arcane lecture is astounding. On the lecture platform, he was a study in the use of voice, gesture, inflection, pathos, humor—all done without artifice and guile. Although he crafted his lectures meticulously, rewriting and editing mercilessly, his talks were marked by a deep passion, by a spontaneous, incisive wit, by questions to the audience—particularly an audience of rabbis—which were not simply rhetorical, but to which he expected answers from his listeners; by an affect and emotion which did not hesitate to bare his personal life and upbringing. He was a consummate platform teacher.

Perhaps most striking about Rav Soloveitchik was his independent and innovative persona. He once wrote that he had

> a liking for pioneers, for experimenters, for people who do not follow the crowd. I have always admired the first ones, the beginners, the originators. Even in my *derashot* I prefer to speak about those who defied public opinion, disregarded mockery and ridicule, and blazed new trails leading men to God.*

He was a traditional *rosh yeshiva* with a doctorate in philosophy from the University of Berlin; a brilliant Talmudic authority who was *au courant* with contemporary thought; a preeminent authority on Maimonides who also was familiar with Kant and with Kierkegaard. Deeply religious, he was the classic *rebbe*, giving regular *shiurim* in Talmud and relentlessly teaching his students the underlying logical core of halakhic discourse. But, perhaps symbolic of the maverick within him, he eschewed the traditional garb of the *rosh yeshiva*: the *kapote* and the black hat or Homburg. While constantly upholding the supremacy of Torah learning in all its manifestations, and while emphasizing the strict, disciplined, and uncompromising allegiance to the totality of halakhic living, he did not hesitate to call upon the resources of secular thought whenever they could undergird or clarify his message.

**Rabbi Joseph H. Lookstein Memorial Volume*, ed. Leo Landman (N.Y., 1980) p. 338.

It was because of this attempt to create a symbiosis between the classic world of Torah and the world of contemporary thought that he was occasionally viewed askance by the mainstream world of *yeshivot.* They recognized his formidable genius and scholarship—one great *rosh yeshiva* once told this writer that those who carped at him "do not come close to him in learning and do not understand him at all"—but they were skeptical about his attempts to apotheosize the secular into the sacred.

His life was precisely the epitome of the religious pioneers he so admired. Shunning publicity, unconcerned with what others might think of him, authentically humble before God and man, he blazed new trails in the understanding of every aspect of Torah and in the application of that understanding to the modern world.

Rav Soloveitchik was many things: a *rosh yeshiva,* a *rebbe,* a halakhic decisor, a *ba'al mahshava,* a philosopher, an orator. In each of these he was extraordinary. But over and above all else, he was a genuinely religious personality. For him, Torah and halakha were not abstractions nor platforms for exciting intellectual gymnastics. They were not philosophy or mathematics or physics, all of which he was fond of citing, but all of which were for him merely subjects for study. Torah and halakha were not intellectual subjects, but life itself, the voice through which the soul of Israel speaks, and the prism through which the God of Israel is apprehended.

The Rav as Maspid

MARVIN FOX

AMONG THE VARIETY OF FORMS WHICH RAV SOLOVEITCHIK *ZT"L* chose for his writings, one of the most striking and instructive is the *hesped,* a eulogy given in memory of a recently departed figure of outstanding stature in the world of Jewish life, learning, or leadership. The corpus of his published works includes six such eulogistic essays, each one a carefully crafted study which is a source of illumination and instruction.[1] I shall try to show that an analysis of these eulogies opens up dimensions of the Rav's thought and method which have not been sufficiently noted in the literature about his work. Each of them is of intrinsic interest and importance, making them eminently worthy of careful study. These *hespedim* should not be confused with the annual *yahrtseit shiurim* which the Rav gave in memory of his father, or with lectures that he gave on similar memorial occasions. The eulogies which we shall study are of a quite different genre. In this essay we can do no more than make a first attempt to open up this fascinating area of Rav Soloveitchik's thought.

Although each of the six eulogies has its own distinctive character, there are certain common qualities which they share. First, they are all informed by the Rav's understanding of what the halakha defines as the nature and function of every true *hesped*. As he puts it, a *hesped* must fulfill two separate but related functions. It

The late Dr. Fox was a founding member of Tradition's *editorial board.*

must cause us to feel deep sorrow over the loss we have sustained, and it must make us aware intellectually of the depth and significance of that loss. A *hesped* "seeks, first of all, to make people weep. . . The Halakhah did not like to see the dead interred in silent indifference. It wanted to hear the shriek of despair. . . ." But in its other dimension, "the *hesped* turns into *kilus*, eulogy, informative and instructional. Instead of addressing ourselves to the heart . . . we try now to contact the mind. We no longer try to arouse emotions. We seek to stimulate thoughts by telling a story . . . the life-story of the deceased."[2] The Rav introduces this same distinction in the opening of his eulogy for R. Hayyim Heller. The *maspid* must cause the sounds of agony to be heard and tears to flow as he makes his audience aware of their loss. At the same time, he must serve as a pedagogue, using calm reason to teach the people the full significance of the personality whom he eulogizes.[3]

Yet, there is a nearly insoluble problem, which is the second feature held in common by all these eulogies. Rarely do we manage during the lifetime of a person to come to know him or her thoroughly and deeply. Even when we are in frequent contact with an individual, we tend to have only a superficial sense of the complex and subtle elements which constitute a human personality. This is true of our efforts to understand ordinary individuals; how much more so of the attempt to grasp the inner reality of great figures, scholars, teachers, moral guides and leaders. Only when they have left us do we begin to realize how little we really knew them. How then can we eulogize them? As a paradigm of this dilemma the Rav cites a talmudic episode in which the disciples of a great sage discovered, to their distress, how little of his teaching they had mastered. Returning from his funeral, they sat down to eat and could not resolve a seemingly simple problem about the laws of grace after meals. With all they had learned from their teacher, they were now aware that they had barely scratched the surface of his vast scholarship. Usually, it is only after we sustain the loss of a loved one or a great teacher that we become painfully aware that there is so much we now want to know that we failed to learn. During life we maintain a distance even from those to whom we are closest, which leaves us, after their death, ignorant of what they knew and of what constituted their true inner being.

This imposes on the *maspid* a very heavy burden, for he must uncover the secret recesses of the inner life of his subject, and he must do so with full responsibility for the accuracy and the perceptiveness of the picture which he paints. The Rav cites an extended talmudic passage concerning the last rites for Rav Huna (*Moed Katan* 25a), from which he draws the sharp conclusion that we may eulogize only if we are able to depict the deceased accurately and perceptively in his full reality. Under no circumstance should we eulogize if we diminish in any way the stature and personality of the deceased. We must not reduce great men to fit into our limited conceptions and understanding. We must rather elevate ourselves and the audience to the point where we are capable of some sound understanding of the nature of the departed.[4] With characteristic modesty, the Rav repeatedly expresses his sense of his own inadequacy to create a full and accurate picture of his subject. Yet, he is so aware of the failures of others that he is driven to try. One thing is certain. In his depictions of his subjects he avoids the trite language, the cliche-laden rhetoric, which he finds so offensive in ordinary eulogies. In an expression of frustration with the limits of all language, Nietzsche somewhere observes that "The word dilutes and blunts; the word depersonalizes; the word makes the uncommon common." Struggling against this problem, the Rav understands that he must use language to overcome language, that as a *maspid* he must be not only a rational teacher, but a creative artist. With rare skill, his artistry makes itself manifest in each of his *hespedim* as he penetrates, intellectually and emotionally, into the depths of the individual personalities. His rational discourse transcends itself to become poetry, poetry which teaches us by stimulating the imagination while arousing the intellect. If it is possible to use language effectively to portray a human personality in its hidden inner reality, then the Rav has achieved rare success in his efforts.

A third feature common to these eulogies is the Rav's familiar practice of dealing with a problem by formulating archetypes which provide the architectural framework within which he then carries on his eulogistic work. It is well known that such typology is a central feature of much of the Rav's teaching. We see it in these eulogies in its full flowering. Let us consider some examples. He illuminates the personality of R. Yitshak Zev, his uncle, through the distinction between the *Rosh haShana* and *Yom Kippur* personality types. *Rosh haShana* is associated with public divine revelation, while *Yom Kippur* is characterized by private divine revelation. The *Rosh haShana* prototype is Aaron, while the *Yom Kippur* prototype is Moses. The Brisker Rav is then described as a Moses type, and it is from this perspective that we are helped to understand him.

Similarly, the account of R. Zev Gold is located within the distinction between the *kedusha,* the holiness, of the Sabbath and Festivals, and the *kedusha* of *Rosh-Hodesh.* The former is public and the latter is hidden and private. Rabbi Gold is then described as a *Rosh-Hodesh* type. The personality and the leadership of R. Hayyim Ozer is exemplified by the distinction between two of the vestments of the high priest, the *tsits* and the *hoshen.* The former was worn on the front of the elaborate headdress of the high priest, while the latter was worn as a breastplate. The *tsits* is located on the forehead of the *kohen gadol,* a location which associates it with the center of intelligence and knowledge. The *hoshen* is worn over the heart, the center of love and devotion to the people of Israel whose tribal names are engraved upon it.[5] The role of R. Hayyim Ozer as Jewish leader is then explicated through these archetypes. Unlike conventional leaders, he represents a unique combination of head and heart, of learning and love of Israel. This combination determines his decision-making process so as to assure that it flows from the teachings of the Torah and is simultaneously determined by an overflowing love of the Jewish people.

As we noted, the method of understanding various phenomena through the delineation of archetypes is a central feature of the Rav's work. It is present not only in his eulogies, but also in his philosophical- theological essays, and, with certain variations, also in his purely halakhic discourses. If we reflect on the way in which this method is used in the *hespedim,* we can gain insight into its meaning and purpose in the other genres of the Rav's writings.

There are two features of the Rav's thought which come into play at this point. As is well known, the Rav consistently insisted that the halakha is the only source of authentic Jewish ideas. Thus, we must always seek the halakhic foundations of any doctrine which he sets forth. Furthermore, central to all of his methodology in the analysis and exposition of Jewish texts is conceptual formulation and clarification. These features are immediately recognizable by anyone who ever attended a *shiur* which he gave, no matter what the subject or what texts were being studied. We must ask ourselves what is the relationship of articulating typological distinctions to the process of formulating and clarifying basic concepts. My contention is that we can come to an understanding of this method and its significance if we pay close attention to what the Rav did in his *hespedim.*

We begin from a premise that I believe is basic to the Rav's thinking, although it has not been widely noted in the literature. Early in 1959, Dr. Hillel Seidman published a very important and rich account of a discourse which the Rav had recently given. His text was based on his careful notes of the Rav's presentation, and he assures his readers that the final text was "reviewed and authorized by the Rav."[6] In this discourse the Rav argued that to achieve a proper halakhic understanding of the question, "What is a Jew," we must focus on the fact that in the halakha, the individual Jew is regularly treated on the model of a *Sefer Torah.* A few examples will make the point clear. The rule is that when one is present at the time of the death of a fellow Jew, he is required to rend his garments. The *Gemara* explains that this is comparable to being present when a *Sefer Torah* is destroyed by fire.[7] A second example: a *Sefer Torah* which disintegrates from age or use is to be buried next to a *talmid hakham*.[8] The two are perceived as sharing certain common qualities. We rise in respect for a *Sefer Torah* as we do for the scholars who devote themselves to the study of Torah.[9] The point of these halakhic examples is to establish that in halakhic-conceptual terms, a Jew is to be understood as analogous to a *Sefer Torah.* It then follows that the concept, "Jew," receives its clarification and formulation from the concept, "*Sefer Torah.*" The Rav further supports this contention by citing aggadic passages in which the same analogy is drawn. When R. Eliezer's pupils visited their teacher during his illness, R. Akiba found them crying bitterly. When he asked why they were crying, they answered that if one sees a *Sefer Torah* suffering, it is impossible not to cry.[10] Finally, the Rav sets forth a whole series of the halakhic manifestations of this analogy. From the *halakhot* of preparing the parchment, writing a *Sefer Torah,* and giving it the sanctity which it requires, the Rav teaches us a series of *halakhot* that pertain to the life of the Jew as if he were himself a *Sefer Torah.* This is not the place to elaborate further on this essay, but we should stress that it is eminently worthy of careful study.

We can now begin to understand the significance of the Rav's stress on the law of *hesped* which requires the *maspid* to give a full account of the personality of the deceased. If a Jew is a *Sefer Torah,* then to know an individual Jew requires the same kind of intellectual effort, the same kind of conceptual formulation and elucidation as does every other topic in the study of Torah. The more eminent the person, the greater and deeper his learning, the more exemplary his virtue, the more creative and sound his leadership, the more sensitive his piety, the greater the intellectual challenge in understanding the departed personality. To give an accurate and adequate account of that person, the *maspid* must employ the same processes of analysis and exposition that he uses in explicating any passage in the halakha. Moreover, understanding the person is a step toward the knowledge of God. Every man is created in the image of God, but that divine image is present in a unique way in the personalities of *gedolei Yisrael.* "The attributes of the Holy One, blessed be He, descend to the lower realm and are concretized in *gedolei Yisrael,* the Sages of the sacred tradition. . . They serve as a dwelling-place for the *Shekhina*. . . A great man becomes the instrument through which one of the divine attributes is actualized [here on earth]."[11] Thus, the study and exposition of the essence of a particular human personality constitutes a major step in the study of Torah, which is, in turn, a necessary condition for the knowledge of God. The acquisition of that knowledge is the first positive commandment in Maimonides' listing of the *mitsvot*. Study of the Rav's method in formulating a *hesped* provides us with a model for understanding his method in straightforward halakhic analysis.

A striking example of this method is found in his characterization of the mode of Torah knowledge of R. Yitshak Zev, the Brisker Rav, and of his father, the Rav's grandfather, the incomparable R. Hayyim Brisker. I have discussed this in more extended form elsewhere,[12] and shall simply summarize briefly here. The Rav begins from the halakhic distinction between *erusin*, betrothal, and *nissu'in*, marriage. In the former state, the couple constitute two separate entities, closely related, with intimate knowledge of each other, but still separate. In the latter state, all the barriers have been broken. In a true halakhic marriage, the couple are as one. They share a common essence; their hearts beat with a common rhythm; their knowledge of each other is not simply discursive, but immediate, intuitive, and deeply perceptive. Providing us with prooftexts from the classical sources, the Rav analogizes the relationship of a *talmid hakham* to Torah to the relationships of *erusin* and *nissu'in*. The former represents a great achievement, but is still purely discursive. It relies on all the tools of the highly developed intellect to grasp and give structure to each topic in Torah learning. A few rare individuals may be said to be married to the Torah, not just betrothed. Blessed with the highest qualities of intellectual depth and acuity, they transcend the limits of intellect to understand Torah by way of direct intimacy. Their knowledge is intuitive. Their intuitive formulations will subsequently be verified by discursive analysis, but they could never be achieved by such analysis alone. If we perceive R. Yitshak Zev as married to the Torah, then we have the indispensable key not only to his way of Torah learning, but to his entire personality.

There is in these eulogies a dialectical movement back and forth between pure halakhic categories and the elucidation of the individual personality that has been taken from us by death. The distinction between *Rosh haShana* as public revelation and *Yom Kippur* as private revelation provides the general halakhic-conceptual framework. This in turn generates a way of understanding Moses and Aaron. The Priest is the open man of the people, and the Prophet is the withdrawn figure, his face covered by a veil that hides his shining brilliance. The priest is mourned by all the people, while the prophet only by the limited number who have some sense of who he truly was.[13] R. Yitshak Zev is now characterized as a Moses/*Yom Kippur* figure, and the Rav sees more than symbolic significance in the fact that he died on *Yom Kippur.* He was a hidden personality, living, like Moses, behind a cloud that kept him from being accessible to the general public. The people "sensed intuitively that this was a holy man who walked among them, however, only a very small number of select individuals knew and understood him."[14]

Having placed his uncle appropriately in the typological framework, the Rav now confronts the question of what this characterization teaches us about R. Yitshak Zev as student and teacher of Torah. This is the essential question, since it was Torah learning which was the chief defining force of his life. Here the Rav introduces us to a second typology which we have already discussed, namely, the distinction between being betrothed to the Torah and married to the Torah. Having set out the halakhic grounds and implications of this distinction, he turns first to his grandfather, who presents us with the ideal model of one who is married to the Torah, and then helps us to see how this characterization helps us to gain insight into the personality of R. Yitshak Zev. In the course of this extended presentation, there are a number of intricate and technical discussions of complex halakhic topics. This is not the place to expound on these discussions, but it must be said that any reader who is at home in the literature of halakha will have no difficulty in seeing how all of these discussions connect to the central theme of the *hesped*. In turn, these discussions illuminate for us the connection between forming basic concepts in halakha and forming conceptual structures for understanding a great Jewish personality.

In the *hesped* for R. Hayyim Heller we find a similar methodology. I shall mention only one common characteristic, the description of R. Hayyim's way in Torah learning. Here we are introduced to the familiar halakhic categories of long and short forms of benedictions, *berakha aruka* and *berakha ketsara*. These categories are then applied to other areas of halakhic practice, in particular to the procedures of the priests in the Temple service. There is a setting in which the ritual involves an extended procedure, and another in which the procedure is short and direct. This is then applied to styles of learning, and finally to the method of R. Hayyim, which was direct, concise, compressed, immediate and intuitive. Although this may sound very much like the *erusin/nissu'in* distinction that was used to illuminate R. Yitshak Zev, it is not fully identical. While the Rav had unlimited admiration for both of these great luminaries, he saw that each had his own defining characterisitics. It would be presumptuous to try to spell out the full and exact nature of their differences and how these are implicit in the different typologies, since the Rav did not choose to do so himself.

There are, however, three striking differences that come to the fore as we study these eulogies. One is that R. Hayyim Heller, unlike most classical *talmidei hakhamim*, was a great and creative master of the Bible as well as rabbinic literature. Second, he was unique among such figures in his knowledge of semitic and classical languages and in his application of this knowledge to a defense of the integrity of the *Tanakh*. Third, the Rav stresses the special importance of R. Hayyim Heller as a last living link between the earlier generations of Torah learning and the generations that followed him. In this discussion, the Rav introduces historical concerns into the mix of halakhic typology with which he illuminates the personality of R. Heller. He does so by giving us other examples from Jewish history of figures, such as Serah bat Asher and Ahiya haShiloni, who were indispensable links between earlier and later generations.

Even this historical perspective emerges from a quasi-halakhic description of R. Hayyim Heller by Dr. Samuel Belkin. Using the language of the liturgy, Dr. Belkin speaks of R. Heller as belonging to a special group known as "*peleitat sofereihem,*" the remnants of the Scribes of Jewish antiquity. The Rav gives a historical account of the meaning of the term "remnant." No matter how many great Torah scholars adorn any given generation, they cannot be truly connected to the great chain of tradition unless there is among them at least one figure who is a remnant of the past, who alone is able to bridge the abyss which separates the later generations from the earlier. In this sense, we have in R. Hayyim Heller the necessary connecting link which authenticates and authorizes the present generation of scholars by joining them with their past. R. Heller, by the Rav's reckoning, had intimate connections with three generations of the greatest Torah scholars that preceded him, and he transmitted not only their formal teaching, but their inner reality, to the generations which followed him.

The *hesped* for the Talner Rebbe reveals essentially the same characteristic methodology as well as a certain commonality of themes with those that we have already discussed. Yet, what should occupy the attention of the careful reader is what is distinctive in each case. We saw how, despite similarities, R. Hayyim Heller is carefully delineated in ways which distinguish him from

R. Yitzshak Zev, so that he emerges as the unique Torah personality that he was. Both are differentiated from R. Hayyim Ozer, who shares their learning but also assumes a role of public leadership which was alien to the others.

In his learning, in his piety, and in his love of Israel, the Talner Rebbe is similar to the other great figures whom the Rav eulogized. The most obvious distinction is that while the others represent the great tradition of *mitnagdim*, the Talner Rebbe was the scion of one of the great hasidic dynasties. Superficially, it would seem that the Rav does little more than follow a by-now familiar pattern in his *hesped*, but closer reading shows us that this is not a sound conclusion. There is the usual expression of regret over the failure to know the person in sufficient depth during his lifetime, and the gnawing, agonizing questions, "Who was he? Whom did we lose?" This is preceded by an extended halakhic discourse in which two types of mourning are carefully defined and distinguished. The first stage is *aninut*, which is the initial "spontaneous human reaction to death. It is an outcry, a shout, or a howl of grisly horror and disgust. Man responds to his defeat at the hands of death with total resignation . . . Beaten by the fiend . . . man begins to question his own human singular reality. . . He starts downgrading himself. He dehumanizes himself. He arrives at the conclusion that man is not human, that he is just a living creature like the beast of the field."[15] In this state, the halakha frees man of all *mitsvot*. The reason, as the Rav explains, is that "our commitment to God is rooted in the awareness of human dignity and sanctity." When a despairing individual questions all that makes us distinctively human, there is no longer any ground of human dignity and no foundation on which to view man as uniquely bound by God's commandments.[16] If we are merely animals, then we have no more obligation, no more divinely imposed duty, than do animals. Following the burial, the stage of *avelut* begins. Here the halakha requires man to overcome his self-rejection, to reaffirm his own humanity and to grieve without allowing his distinctive humanity to disintegrate. Thus, we begin with an illuminating halakhic typology from which we learn much about the formal laws of mourning but even more about the conceptual world, the world of religious ideas, which underlies these *halakhot*.

There is here another motivation which is more explicit than in some of the other eulogies. The Rav had already eulogized the Talner Rebbe at his funeral. There he raised the question, "Who was he?" but failed, in his own judgment, to answer it properly. "Of course, due to the fact that I was in a state of total confusion and despair, I could not pursue the analysis in an orderly manner."[17] In other words, in the condition of *aninut* it was not possible to supply the mode of discourse which could answer the question adequately. Now that *aninut* has yielded to *avelut*, it is not only emotionally and intellectually possible, but obligatory, to answer the unanswered question through a proper *hesped*. Here the halakhic analysis serves as a direct mandate for practical fulfillment of an obligation.

At this point, the Rav is able to turn to an account of the qualities which made up the personality of the Talner Rebbe. "All our great leaders, both hasidic and mitnagdic, were preoccupied with and committed to one task—teaching. The teacher, the rebbe, has been throughout the generations the central figure within the covenantal community. The teacher towered above any other figure—king, warlord, or high priest."[18] In this respect the Talner Rebbe was similar to the other great Jewish leaders whom the Rav has eulogized. The task of the *maspid*, however, is to help us understand what is distinctive about his subject, what constituted the essential nature and contribution of the person whose death we are mourning.

To achieve this end, the Rav introduces us to a new typology, the distinction between the "king-teacher" and the "priest-teacher" or "saint-teacher." The king-teacher "addresses himself to the mind. He teaches both pure halakha and applied halakha. He teaches disciples how to conceptualize, how to classify, how to reconcile texts and opinions, how to systematize, to infer, and to analyze." This king-teacher is concerned, above all, with the use of the tools of the intellect and with forming the capacity of his students to use their own intellectual powers creatively to understand and systematize every topic in the study of Torah. He is concerned with what the *Zohar* describes as the outer garments of the Torah. This study is of vital importance for the religious life of the Jews. It is indispensable, not only as a *sine qua non* for the fulfillment of our obligation of *limud haTorah,* but also as a central element in Jewish spiritual life. The great models of this king-teacher type are Rambam, the Gaon of Vilna, and the Rav's own ancestors.[19]

The saint-teacher, in contrast, "focuses his attention upon the invisible, intangible letters, the soul of the Torah. . . the saint-teacher speaks to the heart, communes with the heart and tells the heart how to attune its own excited accelerated beat to that of the Torah. The saint-teacher teaches man the art of catharsis, how to cleanse and purge the heart of vulgarity and inhumanity, of unworthy sentiments, uncouth emotions and selfish desires. How can a man merge his soul with the soul of the Torah if his inner life is unclean?"[20]

In making this typological distinction, the Rav has succeeded in teaching us who the Talner Rebbe really was. In fact, he teaches us what constitutes the nature of the life and service of the true hasidic rebbe, in contrast to that of the classical mitnagdic *talmid hakham.* His learning may be no less than that of his king-teacher colleagues, but there is an added dimension which defines him as saint-teacher. He is concerned with transmitting intellectual understanding of the Torah to his disciples, but even more with forming their characters. He guides them so that they hear not only the words of the Torah, not only the intense rational discourse of Talmud study, but shows them how to penetrate to the non-verbal, perhaps super-verbal, soul of the Torah. He creates not just great Talmudic virtuosos, but virtuosos of the spirit, who are so fully purified, so refined in character, so delicate in sensitivity, that the soul of the Torah expresses itself through them and in them. To achieve this end he directs himself, not only to a highly select intellectual elite, but to every Jew, however humble. "Hence, the teaching of the saint-teacher is exoteric, democratic, understandable and accessible both to the simpleton and to the philosopher." While other hasidic dynasties came to so intellectualize their teaching that they lost their democratic touch, the Talner Rebbe and the Tchernobil dynasty of which he was such a glorious representative remained faithful to the original charge of teaching every Jew and uncovering the spiritual capabilities of even the most ordinary disciple.[21] The *maspid* places his subject into the general framework of understanding which is part of the apparatus for knowing the essential reality of any great Jewish leader. He then brings to our attention those special characteristics which define the uniqueness of the particular person whom he is eulogizing. In this process, he never abandons that part of the art of *hesped* which requires him to serve as the poet who arouses our deep sense of loss, even while he is serving as the rational teacher who illuminates for us in intellectual categories the nature of the person whom we have lost.

In the eulogy for R. Zev Gold we find the stress on another distinctive characteristic. The opening moves seem to be one more variation on the themes to which we have already been introduced. A distinction is drawn between the *kedusha* of two types of holy days, *Shabbat* and *Yom Tov,* on the one hand, and *Rosh-Hodesh,* on the other. The former is holiness which is open, public, evident to everybody, while the latter is holiness which is hidden, not immediately apparent. This general description is based on halakhic sources which are rigorously examined and carefully illuminated. Following his principle, which we discussed earlier, that the Jewish personality is to be understood on the halakhic and theological model of the essence of a *Sefer Torah,* the Rav uses the typology of the holy days, which he has set forth, as a paradigm for a typology of human holiness. "In the holiness of man there are also two types: publicly revealed holiness and hidden holiness.

. . Both of them flow from the deepest recesses of the human soul and from the spiritual dimension of the personality."[22]

Those great figures who embody the Sabbath/Festival type of holiness are fortunate in being immediately recognized and revered. Their holiness is evident in their life-style, in every aspect and dimension of their being. As a result, they need not struggle for public regard, since they have an immediate and indelible effect on every person with whom they come into contact. All grasp their special distinction and deal with them in humble submission. *"Ashrei ha-adam she-kedushato me-shava'at mitokho u-mezaza'at et ha-zulat."* Even the coarsest and the least learned are profoundly affected by the holy light which shines forth from them.[23]

The *Rosh-Hodesh* types, those whose *kedusha* is hidden, are far less fortunate when it comes to public recognition and reverence. Like *Rosh-Hodesh,* they give little direct evidence of the holiness which permeates every fiber of their being and which makes them persons of unique spiritual worth and importance. Their outer garb is so ordinary that it hides from public view the luminous inner reality of their sanctity. R. Zev Gold is represented by the Rav as such a personality type, whose holiness was generally hidden from public view. The Rav confesses that these *Rosh-Hodesh* types have a special attraction for him. He grew up among such types in his own family, particularly his father, the sainted Rabbi Moshe. It is hard to imagine a higher tribute from the Rav than to identify Rabbi Gold as belonging, in this respect, in the category of his own immediate forebears.

A *hesped* for a great Jew whose holiness was hidden and not widely noted presents a special challenge. The *maspid* must open up that which was suppressed. He must bring to the consciousness of his audience the holy reality of the deceased person, a reality of which they had almost no awareness during his lifetime. "My task is to dig up the coffin of R. Gold, who was buried in such unseemly haste, to open it up and to examine carefully the image of the person hidden there. . . to penetrate to the interior of his hidden holiness, and to find, beyond the external cloud of obscure darkness, the *Rosh-Hodesh* man."[24] The description which follows is based on a three-fold distinction. R. Gold is described as a man of three great loves, one in whom there burned with high intensity three flaming fires: the fire of his love for Abraham, the fire of his love for *Erets Yisrael,* and the fire of his love for the people of Israel.

There is no need to set forth here the details of this description. They are readily available to any reader of the text. We shall concentrate on the exposition of one of these three loves, because it is here that we see what the Rav understood to be the distinctiveness of R. Gold. The love of Abraham implies a thorough knowledge of the tradition which derives from Abraham and forms the spiritual reality of the Jewish people, for without knowledge, love is empty and meaningless. This brings the Rav to raise a startling question: was Rabbi Gold a genuine master of Torah learning, that is, was he truly a master of the classical sources? It is inconceivable that he should have raised such a question about any of the other figures whom we have discussed. Each was a great *talmid hakham,* known and acknowledged as such in all circles. Why then raise such an unseemly question about R. Gold? And why find it necessary to answer it publicly and positively? The reason is easy to come by. R. Gold was quite different from the other *gedolim* whom the Rav eulogized. He was a world leader of Religious Zionism, a fact which was in itself enough to cast suspicion on him in certain religious circles. He was a superb orator whose appearances drew large and enthusiastic crowds of fascinated listeners. He was an incomparable master of the interpretation and exegesis of midrash and aggada. In all these regards, he was different from the types of great Jewish figures to whom the Rav was usually drawn. In his *hesped* he both explicates for us who this unusual figure really was and explains his personal admiration and affection for him.

After assuring us that R. Gold had deep mastery of classical talmudic learning, the Rav draws our attention to the full significance of his area of special achievement, the mastery of midrash and aggada. Anyone who ever learned in a typical yeshiva is aware that mastery of the aggadic portions of the Talmud was not required. In fact, excessive preoccupation with this material served to call into question one's intellectual seriousness. It is, then, not surprising that Rabbi Gold was not recognized as a member in good standing of the elite fraternity of great and creative Torah scholars. The Rav sees it as his task to teach us how mistaken this attitude is.

He makes the point by telling us that as a youngster he once heard an address by R. Gold and was overwhelmed by the experience, not simply by the powerful oratory, but by the intellectual force of the presentation. "On that night this American rabbi opened up for me the gates of the hidden inner meaning of the aggada. Suddenly I understood that "*drush*" is not only a matter of "*maggidut*," of preaching. . . that we must present the words of the Sages in accordance with their exact structure; that we must stress the central motif in their text and explicate their words just as we explicate a verse in the written Torah. Proper stress on a single word can shed new light on the entire pericope."[25]

If we are to take the Rav at his word, and there is every reason why we should, this experience of hearing R. Gold interpret a rabbinic aggada was a transforming moment in his own life. To appreciate the full significance of this moment, we must remember that the youngster who was so affected that night by his newly won insight into aggada emerged in later life as one of the greatest masters of the exposition of midrashic and aggadic texts. Who better than the Rav could, on mature reflection, appreciate the significance of R. Gold as a *ba'al aggada*? Who better than he could appreciate the extent to which this aspect of R. Gold's life accounted for at least part of the hidden *kedusha* of this paradigmatic *Rosh-Hodesh* man?

There is an important lesson to be learned from this discussion. In the *hespedim* which we have been studying, as in very much of his own public teaching, the Rav gave a prominent place to reflection on midrashic and aggadic texts. This great master of halakha was an equally great master of aggada. In general, when he dealt with a topic, he joined halakhic and aggadic analysis together in a kind of inseparable unity. This is true of the *hespedim* that are before us, but it is no less true of almost all his published work. It was certainly the case in most of his public discourses, with the possible exception of his regular Talmud *shiurim*. My contention is that he wanted to teach us that proper understanding of aggadic materials requires the same kind of intense intellectual effort that is required by halakhic materials. When he learned in his youth from Rabbi Gold that expounding a *midrash* is not just a matter of "*maggidut*," he became aware of the seriousness of aggada as a branch of the Torah. I believe that he assigned to aggada a place of critical significance in the whole body of Torah literature. This by itself may be a conventional enough attitude. What is distinctive is that, as I understand him, the Rav wanted us to learn that we need to bring to the exposition of aggada the same intellectual tools that are required in the study of halakha. Conceptual formulation and analysis, systematic structuring, proper classification, exact understanding of language and terminology are demanded by the study of aggada as they are by the study of halakha. These must be informed by a feeling for the poetic, by literary imagination, by artistic sensitivity. They do not, however, take the place of the intellectual/analytic tools which are so characteristic of the Rav's treatment of a talmudic *sugya*.

Basically, I am arguing that in the *hespedim*, but not only there, the Rav has taught us one more aspect of the meaning of his well-known affirmation that the halakha is the only authentic source of Jewish ideas and doctrines. This is not a rejection of aggada, nor is it a denial of its importance in the formulation of Jewish doctrine. On the contrary, his own practice provides the strongest evidence of the high value that the Rav assigned to aggada. What he tried to teach us is how to treat aggada with the same intellectual seriousness as halakha, a methodology which transforms discussions of aggada from pretentious sermonics to intensely serious explorations of fundamental Jewish doctrines and values. We might say that in this way the aggada is absorbed into the world of halakha, that the boundaries which separate them are diminished, if not eliminated. In eulogizing R. Gold, the Rav made it clear that, in his view, there cannot be a responsible expounder of aggada who is not, at the same time, a master of halakha. Midrash and aggada are inseparable parts of Torah, not separate realms of Torah discourse. In these eulogies, as in much of his other work, the Rav showed us how to integrate aggada into halakha, how to give to aggada the rigorous structure which entitles it to be treated with the highest seriousness as a source of Jewish self-understanding.

Finally, we must take note of the Rav's *hesped* for the Talner Rebbitzen. Here we seem to have a very different model before us. The deceased was not a world-class rabbinic scholar or Jewish leader, although she was certainly a woman of great piety and unusual learning. Because of his family relationship to her and because for many years he saw her almost every day, the Rav had a special understanding of the character of this remarkable woman. As we might expect, he approaches the task of eulogizing her with the same tools and the same sense of great responsibility that he does in all the other cases. He sets forth a halakhic account of the obligation of *hesped*, followed by the familiar question, "Who was this woman?" As the Rav says, "We were always under the impression that we knew her well. Apparently, this assumption on our part was just an illusion, a mirage. . . the woman we met and greeted every morning—'*Gut morgen, rebbitzen*'—was a cryptic figure, kind of a mystery. . . Now we ask ourselves, who was the woman who never omitted *tefilla be-tsibbur* [participation in communal worship], who never could catch up with the congregation, and who continued to recite her prayers long after the worshippers had left the synagogue?"[26] We see that the same problem which we face in knowing *gedolei Torah* of the first rank confronts us when we reflect on the personality of a woman of no such public standing and recognition, but of no less piety and perhaps of no less intellectual attainment. One suspects that the Rav would face this problem with any person. Rarely can we be confident that we truly know any individual, even one with whom we have been in close contact. The problem is intensified when the individual is a person of rare stature, of great depth, of profound spirituality, and of serious learning, such as the Talner Rebbitzen.

To meet the double obligation of causing us to sorrow over our loss and to teach us to understand whom we have lost, the Rav uses here the same devices that we saw in the other eulogies. He establishes formal classifications into which he then fits the Talner Rebbitzen. He makes an important distinction between the Torah we learn from our fathers and that which we learn from our mothers. He calls upon his own experience to clarify that distinction, and then calls upon his personal knowledge of his subject to show us how effectively she lived her life as a transmitter of the tradition, and specifically of *torat imekha,* that which can be taught with unique understanding and effectiveness only by mothers.

The final step is to set forth a threefold account of the character and essential nature of the Talner Rebbitzen. She was a wise woman, a great woman, a dignified woman. The first two characterizations are based on biblical verses, and the third on a talmudic expression. Each is expounded with examples and anecdotes from her life. Through them the Rav paints a striking portrait of the Talner Rebbitzen, and in the process gives us a careful exposition of the meaning of the three traits which he ascribes to her. The same deep learning, the same penetrating insight, the same sense of loss which moved the Rav in his *hespedim* for the great figures whom he eulogized earlier, are fully present in this eulogy for the Talner Rebbitzen.

There is also an even more intimate dimension than in the other eulogies. In his admiration for her, the Rav saw in the Talner Rebbitzen more than just the rare individual that she was. He saw her also, as we might expect, as an archetype of the essential Jewish woman, the true Jewish mother. "Quite often when I extended '*gut*

Shabbos' greetings to her, I used to think of the great women through the ages who represented with wisdom, greatness, and dignity the *torat imekha*. Consciously or unconsciously, I greeted not only her, but her mother and her mother's mother, the entire community of mothers who kept our tradition alive. I felt as if all of them had been assembled in the dining room of the Rebbitzen, as if *Shabbat haMalka* herself had been present there. The room looked the way I imagined Sarah's tent must have looked. It was enveloped in a cloud, and there was a burning candle; there was the *Shekhinah*." Thus, he perceived the Talner Rebbitzen simultaneously as an individual whom he knew well and whom he saw daily, and as an embodiment of the archetype of the ideal Jewish woman/mother first embodied in the matriarch Sarah.

Our preliminary examination of the Rav's printed *hespedim* should serve to make us aware that a rich body of material awaits further serious study. These eulogies are wonderful personal tributes. They are at the same time treasure houses of Jewish learning, of methodological sophistication, of poetic creativity, and of human sensitivity. In the hands of this incomparable master of halakha and aggada, these eulogies are important creative treatises of Jewish learning and models of how to approach the understanding and evaluation of a human personality. Reasoned analysis and poetic portrayal are held in tight balance. A tearful sense of loss is fully integrated into brilliant halakhic exposition. The intersection between halakha and aggada is established, explored and exploited for the purposes of the eulogy. Even though the subjects were almost all people whom the Rav knew well and for whom he felt deep attachment, there is never a moment of false or excessive sentimentality. With this body of material, the Rav put us further into his debt, leaving us an added legacy of precious texts to study and models to imitate.

Notes

1. The six eulogies to which reference will be made in the course of this essay are as follows: *"Ma Dodekh miDod,"* contained in Pinchas H. Peli, ed., *BeSod haYahid ve-haYahad* (Jerusalem, 1976), pp. 189-254; this is a eulogy for the Rav's uncle, R. Yitshak Zev Soloveitchik, the Brisker Rav; *"Peleitat Sofereihem," ibid.*, pp. 255-294; this is a eulogy for R. Hayyim Heller; *"BaSeter u-vaGalui," ibid.*, pp. 295-330; this is a eulogy for R. Zev Gold; *"Nose'ei haTsits ve-haHoshen,"* contained in essays of the Rav under the title, *Divrei Hagut veHa'arakha,* (Jerusalem, 1981), pp. 187-194; this is all that was published of an apparently longer eulogy for R. Hayyim Ozer Grodzenski; "A Eulogy for the Talner Rebbe," in Joseph Epstein, ed., *Shiurei haRav,* (New York, 1994, reprinted from edition of 1974), pp. 66-81; "A Tribute to the Rebbitzen of Talne," *Tradition*, 17(2), Spring 1978, pp. 73-83. Most of these eulogies have been reprinted in other collections of the Rav's writings. A bibliography containing many of these references may be found in Zanvel E. Klein, *"Benei Yosef Dovrim*: Rabbi Joseph B. Soloveitchik, zzl: A Bibliography," *The Torah U-Madda Journal*, Vol. 4, 1993, pp. 84-133. All references in this essay are to the editions listed above.
2. "A Tribute to the Rebbitzen of Talne," pp. 73-74.
3. *"Peleitat Sofereihem,"* pp. 259-260.
4. *"Nose'ei haTsits vehaHoshen,"* pp. 188-190.
5. *Ibid.*, pp. 191-192.
6. *"Yiddishe Ferzenlikhkeit iz Geglikhen tsu a Seifer Torah," Die Yiddishe Vokh,* Jan. 30, 1959-March 20, 1959, seven installments.
7. *B. Shabbat*, 105b.
8. *B. Megilla*, 26b.
9. *B. Kiddushin*, 33b.
10. *B. Sanhedrin*, 101a.
11. *"Ma Dodekh miDod,"* pp. 199-200.
12. M. Fox, "The Unity and Structure of Rabbi Joseph B. Soloveitchik's Thought," *Tradition*, 24(2), Winter 1989, pp. 56-58.
13. In a brilliant insight, the Rav calls attention to the difference of one word between *Num.* 20:29 and *Deut.* 34:8. The former reports that *all* the people mourned the death of Aaron, while the latter reports only that the people mourned the death of Moses. Aaron is the revealed personality, known and mourned by the entire nation. Moses is the hidden personality, known and mourned by the small elite that was capable of gaining some understanding of his essence and his greatness.
14. *"Ma Dodekh miDod,"* pp. 209-210.
15. "A Eulogy for theTalner Rebbe," p.66.
16. *Ibid.*, p. 68.
17. *Ibid.*, p. 74.

18. *Ibid.*
19. *Ibid.*, pp. 75-76.
20. *Ibid.*, p. 76.
21. *Ibid.*, pp. 77-78.
22. *"BaSeter u-vaGalui,"* p. 305; for the previous discussion, see *ibid.*, pp. 297-304.
23. *Ibid.*, p. 306.
24. *Ibid.*, p. 317.
25. *Ibid.*, p. 320.

Walking with Ramban

MENACHEM GENACK

MOST PEOPLE TEND TO IDENTIFY THE RAV, Rabbi Joseph B. Soloveitchik, *z.t.l.*, with Rambam (Maimonides). After all, as part of *Bet haRav*, the Rav thrived on Rambam's works and made them an integral part of his Talmudic analysis. Moreover, like Rambam, the Rav was an intellectual giant who was at home in the worlds of Torah, science, philosophy, and communal leadership. Rambam was not only a teacher, model, and inspiration for the Rav; he was also the Rav's comrade and friend. Rambam's concise but lyrical language not only captivated and intrigued the Rav's intellect, but was a song that touched his soul.

Yet, I always identified my Rebbe with Ramban (Nahmanides). Indeed, the Rav said that we could find the genesis of the Brisker *derekh*, his grandfather's rigorous analytical methodology for interpreting halakha, in both Ramban and Ravad.

Ramban was an incredible genius. He wrote *Milhamot Hashem*, one of the most profound works in the halakhic writings of the *rishonim*, when he was only sixteen.[1] His approach was both analytical and abstract, and his "school" (Rashba, Ran, Ritva and Ra'a, among others) represents a significant core of the *rishonim*. The Rav would take special satisfaction after he had mastered a complex *Milhamot*. He would marvel at how Ramban could marshal

Rabbi Genack is editor of this volume.

his proofs from all over the Talmud, but would become so terse when he came to the critical breakthrough.

Ramban's laconic phrasing and economy of language reflected his laser-like, insightful mind. He resolved perplexing questions and seeming contradictions by analyzing the inherent logic of the halakha. Yet, though he was a revolutionary with a creative, analytical approach and a wide depth and breadth of knowledge, the remarkable fact is that everything Ramban wrote was to defend the old tradition.[2] He authored *Milhamot* to defend Rav Alfasi against the attacks of Ba'al haMa'or. He wrote his comments on *Sefer haMitsvot* to defend Bahag's enumeration of the *mitsvot* against that of Rambam (although on most issues, he is more in line with the principles of Rambam). He wrote *Sefer haZekhut* to defend Rav Alfasi against Ravad. His brilliant commentary on the Torah follows closely the tradition of *Hazal* and he is, therefore, most critical of Ibn Ezra, who veers away from interpretations of *Hazal* in the search for *peshat*.

In all of this, the Rav is modeled after Ramban. Though the Rav appeared to be a revolutionary, he too was profoundly conservative. His purpose was to defend the ancient, hallowed tradition of Torah and allow it to survive and ultimately to prosper in a new and in many ways inhospitable environment.

The Rav believed that keeping Jews loyal to Torah required relating to them in the current scientific and cultural milieu. In the 1920's, many people became cynical about religion in general and Judaism in particular. They considered it a meaningless anachronism in the context of the modern, technologically advanced culture. The fact that the greatest halakhist of the time had mastered contemporary philosophy and was able to speak in the current scientific idiom was for many the ultimate affirmation that neither faith and reason nor ritual and modernity were mutually exclusive. Some view the Rav's doctoral studies in mathematics and philosophy at the University of Berlin as revolutionary and a clear break from family tradition. In fact they were, in a broader sense, conservative, contributing mightily to preserving a generation in their commitment to Torah.

The Rav would often speak of the Biblical Joseph.[3] He was drawn to him because his life was in many ways modeled after his ancient namesake. Like Yosef *ha-tsadik,* he was misunderstood by his brethren, who did not understand their gifted, indeed prophetic brother, who saved the emerging nation of Israel from starvation.

Speaking to a Mizrahi convention, the Rav explained the brothers' antagonism to Yosef's dreams. They were shepherds, but Joseph spoke of sheaves of wheat and celestial bodies—a new economic and social order. The brothers were loyal to their traditions, but Yosef saw that they would soon be in Egypt and faced with a new environment. "We can render Abraham's heritage triumphant in alien surroundings, too," Yosef told his brothers. "Abraham's Torah is very powerful, but only when we are prepared for the conflict and know exactly what to do in the new environment" (Five Lectures, p. 28).

> The Biblical Joseph was not persuaded that "and Jacob dwelt in the land of his father's wanderings" (Gen. 37:1) would endure for long. The words "for your seed shall be a stranger in an alien land" (Gen. 15:13) kept tolling in his ears. He saw himself and his brothers in an alien environment, far from the land of Canaan, in new circumstances and under new conditions of life.. Basically he dreamt of a new framework within which the unity of the family could be preserved, even in the far places where the Creator of the universe would scatter them. His constant preoccupation was the continuation of Abraham's tradition amidst a new economic structure and civilization.
>
> The brothers did not understand him, for they looked upon the future as a continuation of the present. They perceived all problems from within the framework of their life in Canaan, the land of their fathers' wanderings. In the traditional surroundings, in the thoroughly familiar habitat of the Patriarchs, they did not need new frameworks or novel economic methods.

The Rav spoke of Mizrahi, but we can read it as applying to him—the Torah genius who realized that "to render Abraham's heritage triumphant in alien surroundings," we would have to learn the language of the university and contemporary culture. With that approach, he established a vibrant traditional yet modern Orthodoxy in America. Like Yosef, he suffered for his dreams. Like Yosef, he saved his brothers from starvation.

Yet the Rav was enormously generous in how he judged people and was forgiving almost to a fault. He never held a grudge, even to people who tried to hurt him grievously. He was an instinctive *ba'al tsedaka,* and his munificence knew no ideological constraints.

Once, in *shiur,* the Rav was discussing the halakha that the *Sanhedrin*[4] sat as a semicircle around the *Nasi,* the head of the *Sanhedrin.* The Rav pointed out that the equivalent halakha is to be found in the laws of *Talmud* Torah[5]—students must sit before their teacher in a semicircle. For the Rav, this is a general law in the form of communication of Torah: it should be communicated in a fashion where the teacher and the student are visible to each other, so as to be able to engage in a dialogue.

To illustrate this point, the Rav recalled that when he was a youth in Chazlovitch, the secretary of the *Bet Din,* who was a very old man, recounted to the young Yosef Dov that he recalled as a boy seeing a very old cantor, who, when he was a child, was part of an itinerant choir that would go from town to town. The cantor had himself recalled that once, when this choir was in Vilna to perform, he saw a very imposing man, tall and handsome, walking in the street surrounded by his disciples in a semicircle. When he inquired who this imposing man was, he was told that he was the Hasid of Vilna. (In his lifetime, the Gaon of Vilna, because of his pious ways, was called the Hasid.) When he asked why his disciples surrounded him in a semicircle, he was told that it resembled the *Sanhedrin.*

This story made a powerful impression on me, for the Rav had met a man who had met another man who had seen the Gaon. I felt the link between the generations, the confluence of the mighty streams of the *mesora,* not only the immediacy but the intimacy of the relationship between the generations of the tradition, the dialogue that transcends time. The Rav was the Ramban of our generation. He walked with the *rishonim* and many of his students were fortunate enough to walk with him.

To Ramban, the fundamental theme of the Torah is the encounter with the *Shekhina* and Her dwelling place. He sees Torah as including the history of the encounter of man with the *Shekhina,* the Divine Presence.[6] Thus Ramban, in his introduction to the book of *Exodus,* the Book of Redemption, explains why the laws relating to the construction of the Tabernacle are included in the book of *Exodus,* answering the implicit question: would they not have been more appropriately placed as the introduction to *Leviticus,* which deals with the laws of the service in the Temple? Ramban's answer is that initially, God dwelled in the tents of the Patriarchs, and the redemption from Egypt was complete only when the *Shekhina* again dwelled amongst the Jews, when they were elevated to the prior exalted state of their forefathers. The divine presence manifested itself at Sinai—the first *mikdash*—and was transferred to the Tabernacle.

The Rav once commented that when engrossed in a difficult *sugya* in the Talmud, he could almost feel the *Shekhina*'s breath on his neck, as if she were looking over his shoulder, asking, "What do you say, Reb Yosha Ber, to resolve this problem?" Torah was the instrument for establishing that intimate, close relationship with God. Were it not for that concomitant association of Torah study with the *Shekhina,* that which goes beyond the intellectual gesture, the Rav said, he would have been crushed by the sense of loss and dislocation after the sequence of his triple *avelut* in 1967.

To see the Rav on *Yom Kippur* and appreciate the joy and trembling that it engendered in him, was to see him leap from the rigor of the halakha to the transcendent glory of Sinai. The joy of *Yom Kippur* stems, the Rav said, from our position of being *"lifnei* Hashem," before God. Whenever the Torah defines a mitsvah of *simha,* it is always attendant to the phrase *"lifnei* Hashem." Real joy can only come when we are before God, enveloped in His warm, caring embrace. *Yom Kippur* is inherently a day of closeness with God, and from that stance flows the obligation of joy. To see the Rav on *Yom Kippur* was to glimpse the majesty of the *Kohen Gadol* as he left the Holy of Holies whole and inspired.

We recite in the *Haggada* that, "Had He brought us to Mount Sinai and not given us the Torah, it would have sufficed, *dayeinu."* But to what purpose is it to come to Sinai and not receive the Torah? The Rav explained that even had we not received the Torah, the encounter with the *Shekhina,* as God descended on the Mount amidst thunder and lightning, would have left its impact on our souls forever.

It occurred to me that *Shavuot* is a celebration of that very notion, for ultimately, the Torah was not received on *Shavuot.* Upon descending Sinai, Moshe shattered the tablets at the foot of the mount; not until *Yom Kippur* was the Torah received by the Jewish people. Therefore, we may ask why celebrate *Shavuot* at all—after all, it represents only a failed attempt to deliver the Torah. The answer lies in the *Dayeinu*—we celebrate the encounter with *Shekhina* as an independently significant experience, isolated even from the giving of the law.

Ramban linked the logical and experiential aspects of Torah. The Rav, too had a dual goal. One was to teach Torah and communicate the halakhic methodology intellectually. The categories were elegant and, in a sense, so sound and compelling that, like science, there was almost an element of predictability about them. They all fit into a well-reasoned and coordinated system. But his other goal was to use halakha to sensitize the student to the Divine dimension which animates the halakha, to the link with generations past and to our great eschatological destiny. In this second challenge, he would bemoan the fact that he was less successful, as the path is less predictable and definable.

One summer, the Rav gave a few *shiurim* on *Likkutei Torah,* by Rav Shneur Zalman of Ladi, founder of Lubavitch Hasidism. He said it was important to study *Likkutei Torah* in order to properly appreciate the grandeur of *Rosh haShana.* When he sensed that some of us were resistant to learning the Hasidic work, the Rav related an apocryphal story, "Between Two Mountains," written by the classical Hebrew author, Y. L. Peretz.

The story describes the encounter of the Rav's great grandfather, Rabbi Yosef Dov Soloveitchik (the Beit haLevi, for whom the Rav was named), and the Bialyer Rebbi, a former *talmid* of his who had become a Hasidic Rebbe. The Bialyer Rebbe, filled with passion and religious fervor, had cajoled his master, the Beit haLevi, to come to visit at a gathering of the Rebbe's followers. As Peretz tells the story, the song and warmth of the Hasidim melted the outside snow and caused the trees to bloom and the birds to chirp. The cold Russian winter twilight had been transformed through the ecstasy of the Hasidim into a bright spring day. As sunset approached, the Beit haLevi—who had a profound and analytical mind and was devoid of undisciplined emotion—looked at his watch and interrupted the song to remind the assembly that it was getting late and it was time to *daven minha.* Suddenly, the glorious spring faded and reverted to the cold winter. The Rav then looked at me and said, "That's you." To the Rav, it was important to communicate both the logic and the passion of the Torah.

The Rav was very much a Jeffersonian. In the ancient tension between the individual and the State, the Rav came down on the side of the individual. For the Rav, this view had a theological root, for he believed that each individual was unique. This is the essential perspective which underlies the mitsvah of *avelut*—mourning—the belief that with each person's death, something precious and irreplaceable has been taken from the world. An individual's uniqueness and his ontological loneliness are reflective of God's uniqueness. Even more than man's intellect, it is that which defines his *tselem Elokim*. This idea of the importance of the individual, reflective of God similarly draped in mystery and loneliness, was an important theme in all of the Rav's writings.

The Torah records that Adam gave names to all the various animals. The Rav explained that by naming all the different animals of the creation, Adam was acting as a scientist, categorizing the animal kingdom into different species. We acquire knowledge by observation. If we had total observation, we would have complete definition of what we observe. When we look at a rock, if we know its density, its chemical composition, its place, etc.—all of these observations, when integrated, would define the rock. Similarly, when Adam looked at a horse, when he saw the different activities of the horse, its different dimensions and its various qualities, he integrated all these observations together into the definition of a horse. There is nothing beyond the observable data in terms of defining a horse. Adam was, therefore, capable of defining and giving a name to all the creatures, for they possess only a surface existence. However, a human has not only a surface existence, which is defined by his activities and is susceptible to observation, but is possessed of an inner world which can never be completely revealed. A human being cannot be understood simply by observation; he only becomes known to us, like God, through revelation. There is something about a person which remains always inherently unknown, an inner persona which can never be revealed.

The Rav commented that we have few biographies of Torah luminaries. We know almost nothing about the personal lives of even the giants in Jewish history, be they Biblical, Talmudic or post-Talmudic figures. Indeed, even the few biographies that were written never really revealed the person, because no one actually reveals his or her whole truth. Man is by nature a liar—*kol ha-adam kozev*—marked by posturing and hypocrisy, qualities that do not exist amongst the animals. The Rav commented that even Rousseau's confessions are a "pack of lies." Rousseau tries to impress us with his sinfulness, but a person never completely reveals himself.

It is this lonely dimension which makes us human. Our ability to form groups and communities is, in fact, a less human quality, found even in the herd mentality of animals. The Rav would say that he didn't like company. He was a recluse. "In a crowd I am lost, stripped of my dignity, that is why I don't attend meetings." He feared the crowd, where one's "individuality, originality, tenacity and stubborness are completely lost and his face is a mask of complete anonymity." This focus on the individual and his recognition of his rights, uniqueness and dignity resulted in the Rav's aversion to organizations. Though he recognized, on a utilitarian level, that organizations are necessary, the Rav was always concerned that the individual would be submerged in or suppressed by the multitude.

This distrust of organizations was a trait inherited from his grandfather, Reb Chaim. When someone mentioned to Reb Chaim the influence and effectiveness of a particular Jewish organization, Reb Chaim acknowledged its value, but he was concerned about the potential danger of relying on a single organization. His famous parable was that when the villages in Europe were first electrified, allowing people to read by the greater illumination of electric light, as opposed to the dim light of kerosene lamps, everyone was pleased. But when the generator in the central power station fails, all the lights in the city go out.

The pivotal role that the individual played in the Rav's philosophy resulted in strong emphasis on social justice. At a *Hag haSemikha,* he admonished his newly ordained *talmidim* to always concern themselves with the needs of the individual. "Don't be touched by megalomania, with dreams of empire," he warned. "Concern yourselves with the pain of the widow and the plight of the less fortunate." When you teach Torah, measure your success by the impact you have on a few individuals. Rabbi Akiva rebuilt Torah by teaching only five young students.[7]

Rav Meir Berlin told the Rav that he had asked three Torah

luminaries what was the primary job of a Rav. Rav Yechiel Epstein, the author of the *Arukh haShulhan,* responded that it was to answer "*shaylos,*" halachic queries. Rav Chaim Soloveitchik responded that the primary responsibility of a Rav is to do *hesed* and to protect the poor, the orphan, the widow, those who are bereft of comfort and security. When Rav Moshe Soloveichik became Rav in Rasayn, amongst the three things his father Rav Chaim reminded him was that the primary responsibility of the Rav is to "do *hesed,*" to be an example of loving-kindness to his flock.

After the death of Rav Isaac Herzog, *z.t.l.*, Religious Minister, the Mizrachi leader Moshe Chaim Shapiro came to America, and with the consent of Prime Minister David Ben Gurion, offered the Chief Rabbinate of Israel to Rav Soloveitchik. The Rav refused the offer. Minister Shapiro asked him why in 1935 the Rav had actively (though unsuccessfully) pursued his candidacy for the Chief Rabbinate of Tel Aviv, and now, when offered the Chief Rabbinate of all Israel, he was uninterested. The Rav responded that Tel Aviv is a city with *batei din,* butcher shops, shuls, *batei medrash,* people in need of pastoral tending. The Chief Rabbinate is a beauracracy.[8]

When the future Bet haLevi was a young child in *heder*, the *melamed* would favor the children from wealthy and prominent families over those who were poor. There was a little boy in his class, Dudele, who was a very poor orphan. Once, when there was a fracas in class, the teacher immediately blamed this poor boy, and even though he was completely innocent, the teacher hit him. The young Yosha Ber stood up and walked out of the class. He told his father, who was the Rav of the city, that he would never return to study with that teacher because the Torah says one must treat all people fairly and especially not bring pain to orphans. "I will not study under a teacher who doesn't observe the Torah," he exclaimed.

Shortly after this incident, the young Yosha Ber became deathly ill. He hovered for weeks between life and death, and was only semi-conscious. Finally, the crisis passed and the fever subsided.

After he recovered, he told his father that he had dreamt that the Angel of Death's hand, which was outstretched to grasp him, was stayed by Dudele's father, who interceded on his behalf because he stood up for his son.[9]

Reb Chaim's house in Brisk was a hovel. The so-called living room could be filled with itinerant disheveled beggars, counting their meager collections of the day. The lay people of Brisk thought that this unlimited access to the home of the Rav was inappropriate and undignified for their distinguished rabbi. Unbeknownst to Reb Chaim, they appointed a *shamash* to guard his door. Reb Chaim came down one day and saw that the living room was empty. When he discovered that the reason was that a gatekeeper had been apppointed to protect him, he immediately dismissed him. Reb Chaim insisted that a poor person has a right to go directly to whomever he pleases, including the rav. He quoted the *gemara* in *Bava Batra*[10] which, in discussing the laws related to construction and the zoning laws in the town, stipulates that one must have a gate that allows the poor to come in. Reb Chaim explained that all Jewish ethics is based on the principle of *imitatio Dei*. One of the principles of our faith, Reb Chaim said, is that when we pray, we pray not through any intermediaries, but directly to God. So too, a when a poor person wishes to approach a wealthy person, he has a right to communicate with him directly and not through any intermediaries.

It is because of his emphasis on the individual and his recognition that there is something always mysterious and unrevealed about each person that the Rav tolerated the most idiosyncractic of people.

The Rav also loved children. Once, when he was going though the halls of of his beloved Maimonides Yeshiva in Brookline, the Rav saw a little boy outside a room crying. When the Rav asked the boy why he was crying, the boy replied that he was unprepared for a test and because he was disruptive, the teacher threw him out of class. The Rav said, "Would you like me to study with you?" The boy looked up and said, "Are you sure you know the material?" The Rav said, "Let's take a chance," and he studied with him and later brought him back into the classroom. When the Rav's family was sitting *shiva*, this little boy—who had now grown up to be a young man—came to visit them and told them this story. Apparently, that one encounter with the Rav had changed his entire life. Before, he had lacked confidence and focus in his work. Subsequently, he became more serious about his studies, more disciplined, more focused.

The *Gemara* tells us in *Nida*[11] that when children are *in utero*, an oath is imposed on them. They must swear to be righteous and not iniquitous. The child is told: even if the entire world tells you that you are very righteous, in your own eyes you should be humble and see yourself as evil. You should know that God is holy, those who serve him are holy, and the soul that was put in you is holy. If you guard it with purity, that is well; but if not, it will be taken away from you.

The Rav explained that the oath reflects the fundamental belief that each child brought into the world, no matter how humble, has great potential; its *neshama* is pure, as all those who serve God are holy and pure. It also reflects that each person born into the world has a unique mission that no one else can fulfill. When Abraham commissioned Eliezer to find a wife for Yitshak, he made him swear an oath to fulfill his mission. So too, every child must affirm, so to speak, that he or she has a special, unique mission.

At the conclusion of the *Ne'ila amida*, we declare, "My God, before I was created, I was unworthy, and now that I have been created, it is as if I have not been created." The Rav, quoting Rav Kook, interpreted this enigmatic liturgical piece as meaning that had I been placed in a different generation, it would be for no purpose. Each person is born at a specific moment in history in order to fulfill his special mission. Had one been born either in an earlier or later period, that special, divinely endowed mission and purpose could not be realized. But now we lament that despite having been created at the proper time and place, we do not live up to the great potential that inheres in each of us. The sacred mission which we have been commissioned with even from before birth, remains unfulfilled.

This sense of mission engendered in the Rav a great humility. He felt privileged to carry on the traditions of the *bet ha-rav*, but he recognized that every person is significant, endowed with his own divine oath. He treated other people and other opinions with courtesy and deference.

He marvelled at the enigma of the human condition. He was ever sensitive to the lonely persona that was enveloped in mystery, a paradox unresolved. He was especially tantalized by the halakhic concepts of the *shtar*, the halakhic contract, because it testified to so much more that was stated or written in its text and was a concept much more expansive than the common-sense notion. Similarly, the human psyche is infinitely deeper and more profound than anything it reveals. Aware of the ambiguity in life, the public positions he took were subtle and nuanced.

He was always motivated by his individual sense of divine mission. With Joseph of old, he could say, "And now, be not distressed, nor reproach yourself for having sold me here, for it was to be a provider that God sent me ahead of you" (*Gen*. 45:5).

The Rav's majesty manifested itself not only in his magnificent intellect, his clarity of vision and decisive capacity for definition, but also in the saintly qualities of his spirit, his humility, integrity, generosity and always, always his sense of mission and purpose. I admired him and was awed by his genius, for the dazzling qualities of his mind. I loved him for the qualities of his spirit and the sanctity of his soul. It is the heroic dimension of his rich, glorious personality which will help sustain us and generations yet unborn.

But Joseph said to them, "Fear not, for am I instead of God? Although you intended me harm, God intended it for good; in order to accomplish—it is as clear as this day—that a vast people be kept alive. So now, fear not, I will sustain you and your young ones. Thus he comforted them, and spoke to their heart." (*Gen.* 50:19-21).

Notes

1. *Universal Jewish Encyclopedia.*
2. See Ramban, *Milhamot, R.H.* 12b (in pages of *Rif*): And learn that whoever departs from the words of the early generations, is as if he departs from life. And may the Lord double the reward of our toil that we have toiled to judge them meritoriously, and may He judge us favorably.
3. See the introductory quote to the Rav's *Ish haHalakha*. The Talmud (*Sota* 36b) relates that Joseph would have succumbed to the entreaties of Potifar's wife, but at that moment, "The image of his father (Jacob) appeared to him in the window."
4. *Yad, Hilkhot Sanhedrin* 1:3.
5. *Yad, Hilkhot Talmud Torah* 4:2.
6. The first Rashi in *Humash*, quoting Rav Yitshak, asks why the Torah begins with the story of creation. Surely, he asks, it would be more appropriate to begin with the first mitsvah commanded the Jewish people, the establishment of the lunar calendar. Rambam rejects the very premise of the question. How could the Torah ignore the story of creation and the history of the Patriarchs, which are so fundamental to understanding God's relationship to creation, and most specifically, the Jewish people.

   Rashi viewed the Torah as primarily a book of law, of halakha, encompassing the 613 *mitsvot*, and from that perspective, he asked why does it not begin from the first commandment. Rashi asserts the principle of "*Ein mukdam u-me-uhar baTorah.*" Since the Torah is a book of law, chronology is irrelevant. Ramban, however, who views the Torah also as a history, believes that the Torah follows a strict chronology, and only in limited cases, for specific reasons, is the chronology altered.
7. Talmud *Yevamot* 62b. See also the story of Rav Hiyya and the children he taught: *Bava Metsia* 85b.
8. Recounted to me by Chief Rabbi of Israel Yisroel Meir Lau.
9. *Rishon leShalshelet Brisk*, R. Chaim Karlinsky, p. 72.
10. Talmud *B.B.* 7b.
11. Talmud *Nida* 30b.

The Rav: Stranger in a Foreign Land

שר וגדול נפל היום בישראל—שר התורה וגדול ישראל

NORMAN LAMM

SURELY, SUCH A PRINCE AND SUCH A GIANT, who became a legend in his own lifetime, deserves an appropriate eulogy.

I therefore begin with a confession: I feel uncomfortable and totally inadequate in the role of a *maspid* for my rebbe, the Rav. Only one person could possibly have done justice to this task, and that is—the Rav himself; everyone and anyone else remains a מספיד שלא כהלכה. . . . Nevertheless, we owe it to him to try our best. And so I ask your—and his—forgiveness at the very outset.

The Rav was נפטר on the exact same day that, 17 years ago, we lost Dr. Samuel Belkin ז"ל, the late President of Yeshiva University, and the Rav eulogized him from this podium on the day that he himself would be interred, *erev* the last days of Pesach. He referred to him then as an *arami oved avi*, a "wandering Litvak," who as a

Dr. Norman Lamm, President of Yeshiva University, is Jakob and Erna Michael Professor of Jewish Philosophy and the founder of Tradition.

youngster was forced from his native town and took the wanderer's staff to these shores all by himself.

Unlike Dr. Belkin, the Rav was not an *arami oved,* he was not orphaned at an early age. On the contrary, he had the advantage of a stable, aristocratic home, of encouraging and even doting parents. He was heir, at birth, to a distinguished lineage—the *bet ha-Rav,* that of R. Moshe, R. Hayyim Brisker, back to R. Hayyim Volozhiner.

His genius was recognized while he was still in the crib. At age 6, his father had hired a *melamed* to come to the house to teach him. The tutor was a HaBaD Hasid who taught him *Tanya* without asking leave of his parents. He learned it so well, that his father was shocked and fired the *melamed.* . . . He then became a disciple of his own father—demanding, challenging, and critical, yet approving and proud.

At the age of 10 he presented his father with his written חדושי תורה. His father was so impressed that he showed it to his father, R. Chaim Brisker, who was so impressed that he sent it to his *dayyan,* R. Simcha Zelig. And, of course, he prophesied greatness for his precocious grandson.

The Rav's development continued unimpeded, and fulfilled and exceeded the hopes of father and grandfather.

The former Chief Rabbi of Israel, Rabbi Avaraham Shapira שליט"א, told me the following story to which he was a personal witness.

When the Rav came to visit Israel, the one and only time during his life, in 1935, it was the last year of the life of the elder Rav Kook. The Rav spoke in several places—as Mercaz Harav, at the Harry Fischel Institute, and several other yeshivot. At every *sheur* that he gave, Rav Kook's son, Reb Zvi Yehuda, attended and listened attentively.

When Rabbi Shapira asked R. Zvi Yehuda why he was doing so, he answered as follows: His father received Rabbi Soloveitchik and they "talked in learning." When Rabbi Soloveitchik left, the elder Rav Kook told his son that the experience of speaking with

Reb Yoshe Ber Soloveitchik reminded him of his earliest years when he was a student at the Yeshiva of Volozhin, during the time that Rabbi Soloveitchik's grandfather, Reb Hayyim Soloveitchik, first started to give *sheurim*. I believe, Rav Kook said, that the power of genius of the grandfather now resides with the grandson—and therefore, he said to his son, you should not miss a single *sheur* by Reb Yoshe Ber Soloveitchik.

But if, unlike Dr. Belkin, the Rav was not an ארמי אובד אבי then we may say of him that he embodied another passage in the Hagadah: ידע תדע כי גר יהיה זרעך בארץ לא להם, that Abraham's children will be strangers in another land. He was not a "wandering Aramean" but a "lonely Abrahamite," a Lonely Litvak, and this loneliness was one of the most painful and enduring characteristics of his inner life. This giant who was at home in every discipline, a master of an astounding variety of branches of wisdom, familiar with almost every significant area of human intellectual creativity—felt, ultimately, like a stranger dwelling in another's land. He somehow did not fit in into any of the conventional categories. His genius was such that the loneliness attendant upon it could not be avoided—a fact which caused him no end of emotional anguish, yet gave us the gift of his phenomenal, creative originality. He was both destined and condemned to greatness and its consequences.

This sense of loneliness, isolation, and differentness had a number of quite different sources, all of which reinforced each other. One of them was emotional and began quite early in his life. The Rav poignantly describes (in his *Uvikashtem Misham*) his early experiences of fear of the world, of social detachment, his feelings of being mocked and rejected and friendless. The only friend he had was—the Rambam and, as he grew older, all the other חכמי המסורה whom he encountered in his learning. The Rav identifies this as more than imagination and fantasy but as a profound experience—the experience of מסורת תושבע"פ. Yet, the sense of social loneliness and emotional solitude was not dissipated.

Indeed, that was the way he was brought up: he was taught to hide his emotions; he was never kissed by his father. He had no real friends in his childhood or youth—and no truly intimate comrades in his adulthood.

This sense of alienation was not only a psychological and social factor in the various roles the Rav played in life; it was also central to his whole conception of life. His most characteristic form of analysis in his philosophic essays and oral discourses was the setting up of typological conflicts, of theoretical antitheses: Adam I and Adam II; *Ish ha-Halakhah* and *Ish ha-Elohim*; the covenant of fate and the covenant of destiny; majesty and humility. . . . And, ultimately, conflict and dissonance make for alienation and loneliness.

This philosophical approach stems from two sources. One was his attempt, probably developed in his days in Berlin, to defend Judaism from the encroachments of a self-confident and aggressive natural science and equally arrogant then-modern philosophy. To counter them, he adopted the Neo-Kantian view in which there is a distinct chasm that separates the natural order of objectivity, quantification, order, and determinism (at least on a macro scale), from the internal human realm of the subjective, qualitative, and passionate where freedom reigns.

The second source is, I believe, the *hashkafah* of his Mitnagdic forbear, R. Hayyim Volozhiner, who saw the world and all existence as multi-layered and plural—as reflected in the Halakha with its multiple judgments, as in the Mishna of עשר קדושות, as against the Hasidic view of a monistic and unified world, one which blurred distinctions and sought to overcome contraries.

Thus, for instance, Rav Kook, strongly influenced by the Hasidic side of his lineage, saw underlying unity beyond all phenomena of fragmentation and opposition, while the Rav's view was anything but harmonistic. He saw not wholeness but conflict, chaos, and confrontation in the very warp and woof of life. Man was constantly beset by a torn soul and a shattered spirit, by painful paradoxes, bedeviled by dualities, and each day was forced to make choices, often fateful ones, in the confrontation of savage contraries, of the jarring clash of claims and counter-claims in both conception and conduct.

Both these sources—the neo-Kantian and the thought of R. Hayyim Volozhin—see fundamental disunity and a fractionization of experience in the world.

Such a vision of contradiction and incongruity leads inexorably to anxiety and tension and restlessness, to a denial of existential comfort and spiritual security. It results in loneliness—the Rav truly was "The Lonely Man of Faith"—and this philosophically articulated loneliness with its depth crises becomes enduring and especially poignant when superimposed on a natural tendency to solitude and feelings of כי גר יהיה זרעך בארץ לא להם.

Yet, paradoxically, in practice he made strenuous efforts to overcome these dichotomies, to heal the wounds of the sundering of experience and even of existence itself, to achieve the unity of man with himself, with nature, with society, and with the רשב"ע—even though he knew that such attempts were ultimately doomed to frustration. Hence, his efforts to bridge the worlds of emotion and reason, of Halakha and Agada, of חסידות and התנגדות. Perhaps the very attempt for אחדות and שלמות reflected his penchant for שלום—a goal he valued and cherished—although he knew that in reality disharmony and the pain of inexorable conflict and contradiction controlled.

Thus, for instance, in the area of *machshava,* where his fertile mind reigned supreme, he was a stranger amongst those who worked in Jewish philosophy. For he came to it from another world—one of *gadlut be'Torah* and mastery of Halakha as well as the classics of both general and Jewish philosophy; and his assumptions and aspirations and insights were derived from the Halakha, rather than seeing Halakha as irrelevant to Jewish philosophy. Thus, for instance, the Rav's reconciliation of the מחלוקת רמב"ם ורמב"ן לענין תפילה, אם מד"א או מד"ר, which became the source of his teaching on the "depth crisis" of everyday life. Amongst such

Jewish thinkers, he remained a *ger*, a stranger and alien. כי גר יהיה זרעך בארץ לא להם. The Rav was a lonely Litvak.

Similarly, he was a master *darshan* endowed with a richness of homiletic ingenuity combined with charismatic rhetorical prowess and stellar oratory— undoubtedly the גדול הדרשנים of our, or even several, generations. Yet he had no peer, no companion, no friend in this area too. The kind of *derush* that even the best of them practiced was not his home, not his way. He could be as ingenious—and more so—than the cleverest of them, with a sense of timing and drama that was astounding, but his uniqueness lay in his synthesis of both Halakha and *machshavah* rather than the conventional *derush*. Here too he was a *ger*, and the world of the other בעלי דרוש was for him ארץ לא להם. It was not his home.

Even in Halakha, where he was our generation's undisputed בעל בית, he still was a גר בארץ לא להם. Other גדולי הדור were also gifted thinkers capable of incisive insights, but he alone, in addition to his cognitive supremacy, his dazzling halakhic definitions and brilliant formulations, had a broader scope by virtue of his wider knowledge and his exposure to other modes of reasoning, which helped him in his halakhic creativity, so that he was singular amongst the giants of Halakha of our time. Thus, his quality as a "Lonely Litvak" expressed itself as well in his defiance of convention in dress and demeanor. He simply refused to conform to standards imposed from without, whether intellectually or in the form of stylistic niceties.

How did the Rav as a "lonely man of faith" overcome these bouts of loneliness, given his conception of dialectic and conflict as inscribed in human nature and existence itself?

First of all, his early emotional and social loneliness became bearable when he found fulfillment in his domestic life. Anyone who was privileged to visit with him and the late Rebbitzen in their home in Roxbury could tell immediately that for the Rav, his home was a haven—and a heaven. Do we not recall the bitter tears he shed at the *hesped* for her?

The second way, in response to his existential loneliness, was spiritual. This man whose goal was never mere peace or happiness but truth was able to assuage his feelings of גר יהיה זרעך by his deep and unshakeable *emunah*. The "lonely Abrahamite" knew not only the anguish of alienation inflicted upon Abraham's children, but he also knew the secret of our ancient forefather—that of ומצאת את לבבו נאמן לפניך, a faithful heart, a heart of *emunah*.

How does *emunah* overcome the loneliness of the stranger, the alien, the *ger*? Perhaps by understanding that none is more lonely, כביכול, than the כביכול Himself! Man's loneliness and Israel's loneliness as אם לבדד ישכון are both reflections of the divine loneliness. Even as He is אחד, the unsurpassably and ineffably One, so is He incomparably alone—אין עוד מלבדו; and does not such absolute and transcendent aloneness imply, from a human perspective, unparalleled and unimaginable loneliness?

The Almighty reaches out to His human creatures, seeking, as it were, the spiritual companionship of humans: the commandment of ואהבת את ה' אלקיך can be understood by the talmudic dictum that הקב"ה מתאוה לתפילתן של צדיקים ; and man eases his own pitiful terrestrial solitude by linking his loneliness to the majestic loneliness of the Divine. So does loneliness join loneliness, and out of this encounter is born the divine-human companionship, nourished by divine חסד and human אמונה. Bonds of friendship are created, as man gratefully acknowledges God as דודי, "my Beloved," and God regards the lonely Abrahamite as אברהם אוהבי, "Abraham My Friend."

Here did the Rav, in his most intimate and private moments, reveal the true dimensions of his spiritual *Gestalt* by dint of his profound faith. He was no longer a stranger, no longer an alien, no longer the Lonely Litvak.

Such exultation came to the Rav during תפילה. During these precious moments and hours, suffused with the purest אמונה, the Rav found both the truth and the peace to which he devoted his life, as his riven soul was healed and unified. Recall his moving description, in his article "Majesty and Humility" (in *Tradition*, p.33), of his experience of prayer when his late wife, ע"ה, lay dying in the hospital. Reread so many other of his famous essays where he bares his soul and reveals the depths and heights of his שהורה אמונה as expressed in תפילה and the companionship of the רשב"ע.

Finally, he was able to abolish or at least moderate both forms of his loneliness intellectually—and that, in a paradoxical manner: He found peace and tranquility—on the battlefield of Halakhah during his *sheurim* here at Yeshiva! Often, חז"ל speak of halakhic debate as משא ומתן של הלכה, the "give and take" of משא ומתן, the name for—business. It is a negotiation in the coin of ideas. But often they speak of a rougher kind of dialogue, as in עסק הלכה which refers not to a commercial analogy, but to strife, battles, as in כי התעשקו עמו in תולדות, referring to a struggle over the wells. That was the Rav's kind of *sheur*! That is what I think of when I recite daily לעסוק בדברי תורה. . . . Engaged in a war of wits with his own students, parrying ideas and interpretations, entering the fray between Rashi and Tosafot, between Rambam and Ramban—and Ramban with the בעה"מ—and trying to resolve their differences in a manner typical of the Brisker *derekh* which he inherited and then modified and perfected, he found his peace and his companionship.

Permit me to relate a story that I have told elsewhere as well. It was my second year in his *sheur*, and I was intimidated and in awe of him as was every other *talmid*—that is, almost every one else. There was one student, the youngest and one of the brightest, who was clearly the least frightened or awed. The Rav had been developing one line of thought for two or three weeks, when this *talmid* casually said, "But Rebbe, the חדושי הר"ן says such-and-such which contradicts your whole סברא." The Rav was stunned, held his head in his hands for three agonizingly long minutes while all of us were silent, then pulled out a sheet of papers from his breast pocket, crossed out page after page, said that we should forget everything he had said, and announced that the *sheur* was over and he would see us the next day.

I learned two things from this remarkable episode. First, we were overwhelmed by his astounding intellectual honesty. With his mind, he could easily have wormed out of the situation, manipulated a text here and a סברא there, maybe insulted a חוצפ׳דיק תלמיד, and rescued his theory and his ego. But the Rav did nothing of the sort! He taught by example the overarching goal of all ת"ת as the search for Truth. בקשת האמת was of the essence of his activity in Torah, and we witnessed it in action. He encouraged independent thinking by his pupils as a way to ensure his own search for the truth of Torah. The Rav was authoritative, but not authoritarian. No מוסר שמועס could have so successfully inculcated in us respect for the truth—at all costs.

The second lesson came with the anti-climax to the story. The very next day, it was a Wednesday, the Rav walked into class with a broad, happy grin on his face, held out his copy of the חדושי הר"ן, and said to the *talmid,* "Here—now read it correctly!" The Rav had been right all along.

What we learned was a secret of his greatness and success as a teacher, namely, his attention to preparation. I always thought that there was a vast difference between his formal דרשות and his *sheurim* in class. The former were finished, polished, conceptually and oratorically complete products, a joy to behold, each of them a marvel of architectonics. The *sheurim* he gave in class were of an altogether different genre. They were dynamic and stormy, as he formulated ideas, experimenting with a variety of סברות, testing, advocating and discarding, proving and disproving, as he brought us into his circle of creativity and forced us to think as he thinks, and thus learning his methodology in practice. A *sheur* by the Rav was always a no-holds-barred contest, a halakhic free-for-all, an open-ended process instead of a predetermined lecture.

Well, this incident proved otherwise. The Rav actually pulled out of his breast pocket his hand-written notes for this *sheur*! We were confounded: It was all prepared in advance! Yet his greatness was that, on the one hand, he prepared assiduously for every *sheur*, leaving as little as possible to chance. On the other hand, despite this thorough preparation, the *sheur* indeed was open-ended, because he listened carefully to any serious challenge by even the youngest of his students and was ready to concede an error. And all through this, so successful was he in engaging us in the act of creation, that we never realized that he had thought it all out ahead of time! Attending his class, I always felt, was like being present at the moment of creation, like witnessing the act of מעשה בראשית in all its raw and primordial drama, as conceptual galaxies emerged from the chaos of קושיות, as mountains collided and separated, עוקר הרים ושוחנן זה בזה as, finally, a clear and pellucid light shone upon us, bringing forth new and exciting worlds. He combined preparation and openness, determination and freedom, the fixed and the fluid. What a master pedagogue!

So awesome was his performance as both a thinker and a teacher, that emerging from an encounter with the Rav, whether publicly or privately, in a class or in an article, in Halakhah or in מחשבה, it was impossible to avoid feelings of grave inadequacy, a vast inferiority. Each of us would think: How could I ever attain such depths, such heights—of content or style, of thought or of language? In students, that usually resulted in hero-worship; in colleagues and contemporaries—it often eventuated in envy and even enmity.

It is a measure of the Rav's character that he was not spoiled by our adulation, and he ignored the slurs against him; never, publicly or privately, did he mention them. Giants pay no attention to mosquitoes.

Whenever I think back to the Rav as a מגיד שעור I recall the fascinating tale recorded in Pirkei de'R. Eliezer (chap.2): R. Eliezer comes to Jerusalem where he meets his rebbe, R. Yohanan b. Zakkai. The latter invites his pupil to "say Torah," and he declines, explaining that he has derived all his Torah from R. Yohanan b. Zakkai and therefore has nothing to tell him. But, replies R. Yohanan b. Zakkai, you can do so; indeed, אתה יכול לומר דברי תורה יותר ממה

שקבלו מסיני. Sensitive to the fact that R. Eliezer is shy about displaying originality in the presence of his teacher, R. Yohanan b. Zakkai stands outside the *Bet ha-midrash*:

> והיה ר"א יושב ודורש ופניו מאירות כאור החמה קרנותיו יוצאות כקרנות של משה, ואין אדם יודע אם יום ואם לילה. בא ר' יוחנן מאחוריו ונשקו על ראשו; אמר לו: אשריכם אברהם יצחק ויעקב שיצא זה מחלציכם אמר הורקנוס: . . . לא כך היה לו לומר, אלא אשרי אני שיצא זה מחלצי

Indeed so! The Rav's Torah was a revelation of Torah in its own right. There was something radiant about him, his vigor, his dynamism, as the original analyses and pursuit of truth and creative gestures poured forth from him in such triumphant excitement. More over, as a rebbe or teacher, he was simply unsurpassed. His gift for explanation, for elucidating a difficult concept or controversy or text, was that of sheer genius; who could compare to him? Happy are the אבות of our people, happy are his father and grandfather זכרונם לברכה—and happiest of all are we, we who had the זכות to study under him. How sad I am for our younger תלמידים who did not and will never be so privileged; at best they can get only a reflection of his greatness כלי שני.

What kind of person was the Rav?

Despite his no-nonsense attitude while teaching, he was a man of sensitivity and graciousness. It would not be a mistake to say that he was, in the best sense of the word, a gentleman. He might be a terror in the classroom, but he was attentive and polite and accepting and warm outside the *sheur.* Above all, he possessed great חסד and he was a בעל צדקה.

He also very vigorous. In the days of his strength, his *yemei ha'aliyah,* he never walked; he ran. It is almost as if his body was rushing to keep up with the flow of his ideas. Vigor, dynamism, vibrancy dominated his being, from his *lomdus* to his gait.

Above all, the Rav was a man of independence. He was a true heir of his great-great-grandfather, R. Hayyim Volozhiner, who held that in ת"ת one must pursue the truth no matter who stands in your way; respect no person and accept no authority but your own healthy reason. So, the Rav was his own man, and often went against the grain of accepted truths and conventional opinion. Once, after a particular original *sheur,* a stranger who was not used to such unusual independent creativity, asked him, "But Rabbi Soloveitchik, what is your source?" He answered, "a clear and logical mind". . . .

He was an independent thinker not only in his Halakha and his philosophy but also in his communal leadership. He had great respect for some of his peers—eminent Rabbanim and Rashei Yeshivot of the generation—but he did not allow that respect to intimidate him. He rejected קנאות as well as קטנות המוחין, even as he deplored קטני אמנה. He was not afraid to be in the minority, and refused to be cowed by pressure of the majority. He was horrified by extremism and overzealousness as well as superficiality and phoniness in communal policy-making almost as much as he contemptuously dismissed them in "learning." And if he sometimes seemed to waver in setting policy or rendering a decision in communal matters, it was because he saw all sides of an argument and was loath to offend or hurt even ideological opponents.

Thus, for instance, almost alone amongst contemporary גדולי תורה, he viewed the emergence of the State of Israel as a divine חסד; he saw its appearance as opening a new chapter in Jewish history, one in which we enter the world stage once again. He was not afraid—despite the opinions of the majority of Roshei Yeshiva and his own distinguished family members—to identify with the goals and aspirations of religious Zionism.

Perhaps the most significant area where he diverged from other גדולים and followed an independent way was with regard to למודי חול, to Torah Umadda. The Rav was an intellectual Colossus astride the various continents of human intellectual achievement and all forms of Jewish thought. Culturally and psychologically as well as intellectually, this made him a loner amongst the halakhic authorities of this century. How many גדולים in the world, after all, have read Greek philosophy in Greek, and German philosophy in German and the Vatican's document on the Jews in Latin? A Ph.D. from the University of Berlin in mathematics and especially philosophy, he took these disciplines seriously, not as an inconsequential academic flirtation or a superficial cultural ornamentation, or as a way of impressing benighted and naive American Jewish students who did not know better. There is no doubt where his priorities lay—obviously, in Torah—but he did not regard Madda as a בדיעבד or a de facto compromise. The Rav believed that the great thinkers of mankind had truths to teach to all of us, truths which were not necessarily invalid or unimportant because they derived from non-sacred sources. Moreover, the language of philosophy was for him the way that the ideas and ideals of Torah can best be communicated to cultured people, it is Torah expressed universally; and he held as well that his philosophic studies helped him enormously in the formulation of halakhic ideas.

The Rav had no use for the currently popular transcendent parochialism that considers whole areas of human knowledge and creativity as outside the pale. We must guard, therefore, against any revisionism, any attempts to misinterpret the Rav's work in both worlds—akin to the distortion that has been perpetrated on the ideas of R. Samson Raphael Hirsch. The Rav was not a למדן who happened to have and use a smattering of general culture, and he was certainly not a philosopher who happened to be a ת"ח. He was who he was, and he was not a simple man. We must accept him on his terms, as a highly complicated, profound, and broad-minded personality, and we must be thankful for him. Certain burgeoning revisionisms may well attempt to disguise and distort the Rav's uniqueness by trivializing one or the other aspect of his rich personality and work, but they must be confronted at once. When R. Yehezkel Abramski eulogized R. Hayyim Brisker, he quoted the Talmudic *hesped,* "אם בארזים נפלה שלהבת מה יעשו אזובי הקיר."—and interpreted that as: after the giants have been taken from us, who knows what the dwarfs who follow them will do to their teachings. . . .

The Rav was exceedingly loyal to our Yeshiva. Thus, when some 14–15 years ago we faced the threat of bankruptcy, I asked him to help rescue the yeshiva, and he immediately accepted. At a meeting in the late Herbert Tenzer's office in 1978 he appeared at a critical meeting of our leaders and read to them his confession of gratitude to YU. He spoke of how much Yeshiva meant to him, how it afforded him a platform, how critical it was in whatever he had attained in his life, how much it meant to his family.

It was he who gave סמיכה to some 2000 רבנים and thus influenced hundreds of thousands of Jews throughout the world. And he graciously allowed us to name the סמיכה program the Rabbi Joseph B. Soloveitchik Center for Rabbinic Studies, because he knew it would help the Yeshiva. He was, indeed, the *ruah hayyim* of the Yeshiva.

Additionally, the Rav refused to isolate himself in an ivory tower. He sought contact with ordinary Jews—whom he never disdained. This practical turn of mind and interest served him well. Thus, the Rav functioned not only as a Rosh Yeshiva but also as a *rav,* as a Rabbi for ordinary Boston *baalebatim.* As such, he was in contact with the realities of American Jewish life, and as a result his halakhic decisions and communal policies were leavened by an intimate awareness of their lives and loves, their needs and limitations and aspirations, their strengths and their weaknesses. His *rabbanut* in Boston was the perfect counterpoint for his life as rosh yeshiva in Manhattan, and protected him from making decisions that were appropriate, perhaps, for the high ideals of a yeshiva but not for *amkha.* He dominated the ivory tower; it did not dominate him.

The Rav was deeply devoted to his family. Just as his father was his teacher, so did he teach his three children—and he treated his daughters the same as his son. He was fortunate to have brilliant children, and he was זוכה to brilliant and famed sons-in-law and gifted grandchildren; all are involved, in one way or another, in the world of Torah, many of them educated at Yeshiva and some teaching here.

But most important to us—his students and their students and the thousands who came under his or his students' influence—is what he meant to us as our Rebbe.

Despite the austere majesty and the irrepressible dynamism of his *sheurim*, and despite the fear of coming to a class of the Rav unprepared, we intuitively knew that we had a friend—a father, an older brother—in him. We invited him to our weddings, and later to our children's weddings; and he came. We consulted him on our personal as well as rabbinic problems; and he listened and advised. We presented our שאלות and he taught us את הדרך אשר ילכו בם.

He exerted a powerful emotional pull on his students: I know so many, each of whom secretly (and sometimes not so secretly) knows that he was the Rav's favorite disciple! Who knows?—perhaps all were and, then again, perhaps none were. He so profoundly affected the lives of so many of us—in the thousands—and yet remains somewhat remote, because hardly a one fully encompasses all of his diverse areas of expertise, let alone the acuity of his intellect. Those who were his *talmidim* in Halakha generally were not fully informed or sensitive to his מחשבה, and those who considered themselves his disciples in philosophy hardly appreciated his גאונות in Halakha. So, he had many students, and no students... But cannot the same be said of the Rambam—some of whose students followed his Halakha, and some his philosophy, and very few, if any at all, both?

The Rav never blurred the distinctions between the roles of Rosh Yeshiva and Hasidic Rebbe. He aspired to have *talmidim*, not *hasidim*—challenging, questioning, independent-minded disciples, not fawning, accepting, unquestioning acolytes. That is why at the same time that he forced us into systematic thinking and molded our *derekh*, our methodology, he also gave us "space," insisted that we think and decide certain halakhic questions on our own. He lived his interpretation of the injunction in פרקי אבות that העמידו תלמידים הרבה—as, "make a great effort to have your students stand on their own" and not be permanently tied to your apron-strings. But so great was his personal charisma that many of us ended up as both תלמידים and חסידים. . . .

In II Kings 1 we read of the last moments in the life of Elijah as he is accompanied by his disciple Elisha. Elijah has been told that he must prepare to be taken to Heaven in a whirlwind, and so he wishes to take leave of his *talmid*. But three times Elisha refuses to leave his רבי. Elijah casually splits the waters of the Jordan, and teacher and pupil cross the river. Elijah and Elisha continue their conversation—an important one, but not relevant to my point—and then we read: ויהי המה הולכים הלוך ודבר. והנה רכב אש וסוסי אש ויפרידו בין שניהם ויעל אליהו בסערה השמים. "And it came to pass as they were walking, walking and talking, that there appeared a chariot of fire and horses of fire which separated the two men, whereupon Elijah was swept up by a whirlwind to heaven."

I have often wondered about that last, fateful, conversation as the two walked, each to his own destiny, הלוך ודבר. What did they talk about, that Rebbe and his *talmid*, during that fateful but very brief period of time? How I would have wanted to over-hear that incredible conversation! Further, I was always troubled by the peripatetic nature of that conversation, הלוך ודבר; why a walking discussion, why not seated or standing?

In response, I put myself in Elisha's position vis-a-vis my own Rebbe, and wonder: if I were granted but 10 minutes with the Rav, both of us certain that this was the last chance to talk before the winds bore him away, what words would pass between us? I would not presume to suggest what he would say to me; but what would I say to him? What last message, last impression, would I want to leave with him?

Two things: First, I would walk with him rather than sit or stand because when walking you do not look at each other; I would be too embarrassed to do that. For I would say to him:

Rebbe, forgive us for taking you for granted. You were so much a part of our lives, so permanent a fixture of our intellectual and spiritual experience, that we failed too often to tell you how much you meant to us—as children often neglect to let their parents know how much they love them. We were so engrossed in our own growth that we ignored your feelings. I leave you with a feeling of shame.

Second, we thank you. Our hearts overflow with gratitude to you, our master in Torah and in life itself.

There is not one of us who does not owe you an undying debt of gratitude. You inspired us; we bathed in admiration of your genius, fought to be accepted as *talmidim* in your *sheur,* and were actually proud when you took note of us—even to be singled out for rebuke for a קרומער סברא, for our intellectual sloth or slovenliness. You were our ideal, our role model, even though we all knew that our natural limitations prevented us from ever reaching your level. We thrilled at the sheer virtuosity of your creativity and the brilliance of your originality in your *sheurim* in which you forced us to join you in bold experiments to dissect a סוגיא, understand a מחלוקת ראשונים, propose a solution to a שווערער רמב"ם or a puzzling Ramban—and, to be critical of you! You gave shape and direction to our lives. We knew we were in the presence of greatness, that our Rebbe was a unique historical phenomenon. And deep down we were secretly frightened at the prospect that some day we would no longer have you with us.

What consolation can make up for our enormous loss? For now that greatness is gone, hijacked from us by history. No more for us the exquisite intellectual delight of his incomparable *sheurim,* the esthetic pleasure of discerning the artistic architectonics of his masterful *Yahrzeit derashot,* the edification of his *hespedim,* the wise counsel we sought from him on matters private or public.

The years of his decline have drained us of most of our tears. But with the finality of his *petirah,* we utter a collective sigh *ad lev ha-shamayim,* a composite sigh composed of one part of disconsate *avelut*, of an endless and bottomless sadness; one part of pity for the world, *rachmones* for a world now denied the privilege of presence of the *sar ha-torah* of this generation; and one part of a promise to him that neither he nor his *derekh* nor his *hashkafah* will leave our midst or ever be forgot. And that is why I would walk with him, הלוך ודבר, because sitting or standing imply an end, no future, stagnation, whereas walking implies something unfinished, a destination still beckoning, a sense of continuity. Our loyalty to the Rav and his teachings will live as long as we do, as long as our *talmidim* do, as long as this yeshiva exists; it will go on and on. Here, in this Yeshiva where he presided as Rosh ha-Yeshiva for half a century, his presence will always be palpable, his teachings will endure, and זכר מורנו הגאון הרי"ד הלוי לא יסוף ממנו ומזרענו עד עולם; and finally, one part of love. Yes—to this scion of Litvaks for generations, those of emotional restraint who abjured any display of affection as unbecoming ostentation, to this commanding and self-disciplined intellect, we express openly and unabashedly our affection and our love. And so I would conclude my הלוך ודבר session with him by saying, "We loved you, Rebbe, and if we felt inhibited and embarrassed to say it to your face, we profess it to you now. We feared you, we admired you, and we loved you as well."

How appropriate it would have been for the Rav, that living dynamo, to leave this world as Elijah did—ויעל אליהו בסערה השמים. . . . But alas, that was not granted to him.

When R. Avraham Shapira came here a few years ago to give a *sheur* and he met the Rav for the first time, he kissed him publicly, and whispered to me, as an aside, "it's a mitzvah to kiss a *sefer Torah*."

Now, nothing lasts forever. Even a ספר תורה does not endure forever. Sometimes, we know of a ס"ת שנשרף, such as the one consumed together with רבי חנינא בן תרדיון. At other times, a ס"ת does not have the fortune of such a dramatic end whereupon גויל נשרף ואותיות פורחות באויר; instead, it is a ס"ת שבלה, it suffers, withering away slowly, as letter by letter is wrenched away from it painfully, until it is no more. That, בעוה"ר, was the bitter end to the life of our very own ס"ת. It was the very thing he feared most, and it happened to him. In the words of Job, את אשר יגורתי יבוא לי. Alas!

But we know that even if the ס"ת is gone, the תורה of the Rav will always live on with us. I recently heard of something that happened at the Brisker Yeshiva in Jerusalem, led by Rabbi Dovid Soloveitchik, son of R. Velvele Soloveitchik זצ"ל. The details may be fuzzy, but the essential story, I am told, is true.

A very, very old, bent-over man wandered into the Yeshiva one day, and sat down and began to learn by himself. Reb Dovid came over and greeted him. The old man said, "is this the Hebron Yeshiva?" No, answered Reb Dovid, this is the Brisker Yeshiva. At which the old man opened his eyes wide and, in disbelief, asked, ר' חיים לעבט נאך, "is then Reb Hayyim still alive?"

It transpired that the old man had studied in Brisk when Reb Hayyim was still alive, and left in 1913. Caught up in the Russian Communist Revolution, he was exiled to a remote area in Georgia, completely cut off from any contact with fellow Jews, especially those from Lithuania. He continued his studies for some 75 years all by himself until the great Soviet emigration to Israel. He had just arrived, and that is why, upon encountering the Brisker Yeshiva, he thought that Reb Hayyim was still alive. . . .

And, indeed, ר' חיים לעבט נאך, Reb Hayyim still lives. . . .

And we are here to testify and promise that מו"ר הגרי"ד still lives, and always will, in our midst. . . .

I read someplace that the Gaon of Vilna said that in the עולם האמת they await the coming of a ת"ח, who is accompanied to the ישיבה של מעלה in גן עדן, so that he can deliver a *sheur* and expound his best *hiddushim*. He is given 180 days to prepare this public *derashah*.

Farewell, Rebbe. You always prepared for us, well and meticulously, and you no doubt will do the same now. And when you give your שעור, your דרשה, before the ב"ד של מעלה with all the great גדולי תורה of the ages in attendance, those who were your closest companions and comrades during the years of your lonely sojourn, remember us—your family and your *talmidim*—even as we shall always remember you; and may your זכות and the זכות of your תורה and your חדושים protect us and grant health of body and mind and soul, שלום—שלום above all—in every way, and אהבת ה׳ הבריות ואהבת תורה ואהבת ישראל ואהבת, to all of us—your family, your *talmidim* and their *talmidim*, and all of this Yeshiva to which you came half a century ago, which you graced with your greatness of mind and heart, and which was your home and our home together—and in which your presence will always be palpable and from which your memory will never fade.

For you were a blessing to us in your lifetime. And זכר צדיקים לברכה, your memory will be a blessing to us forever, עד ביאת הגואל במהרה בימינו אמן.

The Rav as Communal Leader

BERNARD ROSENSWEIG

THERE IS A PROVIDENTIAL PRINCIPLE IN JEWISH HISTORY.[1] As religious Jews, we believe that God never abandons the Jewish People and that in a time of crisis, He always provides us with new hope and new leadership. This has been true throughout Jewish history, and the American experience is no exception. When the Rav, Rabbi Joseph B. Soloveitchik, came to the United States in 1932, the Torah community was at a terrifying crossroads. To read the literature of the twenties, thirties and forties is to wade through countless eulogies over the impending demise of the Orthodox community. We were consigned to the limbo of obsolescence, and we were assured that a Torah-true Jewish life could not strike roots in the pragmatic soil of America.

There were good grounds for these assessments and predictions; everything pointed in that direction. Only a guiding, providential hand could change the course of history; only a towering spiritual and intellectual figure could, by dint of his teachings and his personality, reverse the process of religious self-destruction and open a new era of Jewish creativity on the American continent. That man was the Rav.

The Rav was the architect of our approach to Torah Judaism. He was not the creator of what some now call Modern or Centrist Orthodoxy; that preceded his coming to the shores of America. Men like Rabbi Dr. Bernard Revel were the original visionaries of

Dr. Rosensweig is rabbi of Kew Gardens Adath Jeshurun Synagogue, and professor of Jewish History at Yeshiva University.

Torah uMadda, but it was the Rav who was destined to give it direction, substance and meaning. Through his *shiurim,* lectures and essays, his *weltanschauung* was impressed on the minds and hearts of two generations. Thousands hung on his every word, and his comments and statements became guides for action.

The status of the Rabbinical Council of America as an authentic Orthodox rabbinic body was legitimated by the presence of the Rav in our midst. His universally recognized Talmudic erudition, coupled with his vast secular knowledge, made him the undisputed guide and teacher for the Modern Orthodox rabbinate and its lay constituency. And given his identification with the RCA, the Agudas haRabbanim could no longer trifle with the RCA and its decisions.

The Rav, in his capacity as the Chairman of the RCA Halakha Commission, revealed another aspect of his prodigious personality: the Rav as *posek,* as halakhic decisor. The Jewish world revered the Rav as creative teacher, as halakhist par excellence and as the seminal Jewish thinker. Few had the opportunity to experience him as a first-class authority in practical areas of Jewish Law and the author of responsa on religious and social issues, which reflected his masterful scholarship, his brilliant insight into the American Jewish community and his ability to communicate his decisions in a manner which made them binding on broad sections of the community.[2]

It was in this capacity as *posek* that the Rav took his stand, for example, against mixed pews. In the forties and fifties, the problem of mixed pews became a very serious matter for the Orthodox rabbinate. Orthodox synagogue after Orthodox synagogue was falling to the Conservative movement over this issue. Finally, the struggle was joined in the secular courts when two famous cases were brought, one involving a synagogue in New Orleans and the other a congregation in Mt. Clemens in Michigan. In this struggle, the RCA and the Union of Orthodox Jewish Congregations of America, which played a key role in this legal confrontation, were buttressed by the strong position which the Rav enunciated and which was used in these cases.

In unusually strong terms, the Rav denounced those Orthodox rabbis who were lax, timid or indifferent to the principle of separation—reflecting the depth of his feeling on this issue. In clear and decisive language, he declared that a "synagogue with mixed seating arrangements forfeits its sanctity . . . and is unfit for prayer. . . ."[3] It was in keeping with this unequivocal opposition to mixed pews that he directed a young man who lived in a neighborhood where the only synagogue was a mixed-pew congregation, to remain at home on *Rosh haShana* and not hear the blowing of the *shofar* "rather than to enter a synagogue whose sanctity has been profaned."[4]

The Rav rejected any attempt to justify mixed pews on the basis that it was being practiced by increasing numbers of congregations. In his view, it was completely irrelevant whether five percent or fifty percent of the pulpits of Orthodox rabbis were mixed. The violation of a religious or ethical principle does not affect its validity and cogency even when a large segment of the community is guilty of that violation. Dramatically, the Rav posed the rhetorical question: "Was the commandment against murder declared null and void while Nazi hordes were practicing genocide?"[5]

The Rav's statement here, as well as in other areas, had a powerful impact. The number of mixed pew positions serviced by Orthodox rabbis has been sharply reduced and has become a rare phenomenon. The Rav's decision fortified the Orthodox rabbinate not only because of its substance, but also because of the manner in which the Rav succeeded in intellectualizing the traditional opposition to innovations in the synagogue. He not only spelled out the halakha in a language which educated American laymen could understand; he advanced a cogent rationale for the halakha which could not be readily dismissed by those who sought to impose reason rather than religious authority as the arbiter of religious law in the synagogue.

RCA involved itself in an internal struggle over relationships with non-Orthodox rabbinic bodies and non-Jewish religious groups. The Rav's role in determining these directions was crucial and definitive.

The RCA, as a rabbinic body, had maintained ongoing relationships with the Conservative and the Reform—and we did so on the basis of ground rules which our halakhic authority had set down for us. For many years, the RCA and the UOJCA were members of the Synagogue Council of America, which housed representatives of the Conservative and Reform movements as well as our own.

In 1956, our relationship to non-Orthodox bodies was challenged when eleven *rashei yeshiva* signed an *issur* prohibiting Orthodox rabbis from belonging to the Synagogue Council of America. The RCA then turned to its Halakha Commission for direction. The truth is that a definitive decision was never handed down. The Commission and its chairman, our beloved Rav, were criticized for equivocation and for not taking a stand. But the Rav's approach was the only wise course to take. The Rav felt that the atmosphere was too highly charged emotionally for a public response. He had not been consulted by the signers; indeed, they had asked him to join in the *issur* only after the fact—and one can easily speculate as to the reasons. Nonetheless, they were colleagues in the larger sense and men of scholarly distinction. The Halakha Commission would not disagree publicly now that they had ruled, and neither the Rav nor the RCA were prepared to sever all relationships with these eminent men and their world. In such a circumstance, "no decision was also a decision."

The Rav set down for us his famous guidelines of *kelapei huts* and *kelapei penim*.[6] In an interview with a Yiddish newspaper, he made this historic distinction (which he had previously made at an earlier RCA conference). Underlying his approach was the unity of the Jewish people. When the representation of Jews and

The Rav's relationships and influence moved across a wide spectrum and embraced the greater part of American and world Jewry. The people who related to him and sought his guidance and advice covered the gamut of the Jewish community, including the late giants of the previous generation. Rav Moshe Feinstein was his cousin and his friend; his relationship to Rav Hutner went back to their days in Berlin, as did his relationship with the Lubavitcher Rebbe. I remember accompanying the Rav to three meetings with Rav Aharon Kotler in 1949. Witnessing the mutual respect and the genuine friendship which flowed between these two spiritual giants is an experience which remains indelibly imprinted on my mind.

Thirty years later, in 1979, I accompanied the Rav to a meeting with the leadership of the Joint Distribution Committee. The Va'ad haYeshivos had asked the Rav and me (in my capacity as president of the Rabbinical Council of America) to intercede on their behalf for a much-needed grant for their institutions. When we walked into the conference room, the top leadership of the Joint was present. Not one of them was an Orthodox Jew, but when the Rav walked in, instinctively, they stood up as a sign of their respect for a great man.

The Rav spoke to them for thirty minutes—and they were mesmerized. He developed the concept of *hakarat ha-tov,* of gratitude, and he thanked them for what the Joint had done for his family in the aftermath of the First World War. I can still see that wonderful smile which lit up his face as he told them that he could still feel the taste of the chocolate in his mouth. He then proceeded to apply this principle to the need to support Torah and Torah institutions. When he was through, the president of the Joint responded that because the Rav had appeared before them and had spoken to them, the grant would be forthcoming.

The Rav provided Orthodoxy with respect, dignity and stature by articulating its basic philosophical premises. It was within the framework of the Rav's thinking and approach that the

Jewish interests vis-a-vis the non-Jewish world—*kelapei huts*—are involved, all groups and movements must be united. There can be no divisiveness in this area, for any division in the Jewish camp can endanger its entirety. "In the crematoria, the ashes of Hasidim and *anshei ma'ase* (pious Jews) were mixed with the ashes of radicals and freethinkers. We must fight against an enemy who does not recognize the difference between one who worships and one who does not." However, in internal matters—*kelapei penim*—such as education, synagogues, rabbinic organizations and halakhic decisions, "when unity must be manifested in a spiritual-ideological meaning as a Torah community, it seems to me that the Orthodox cannot and should not join with other such groups that deny the foundations of our *weltanschauung*."

Within this framework, the Rav strongly opposed joint religious services with the Conservative and Reform movements; he also urged the RCA never to sign proclamations with other national rabbinic bodies, "particularly if it should manifest a religious character." These guidelines enabled the RCA to cooperate with other groups in external matters without compromising or blurring the lines which separate the Torah community from those who do not have a similar halakhic commitment.[7]

In a similar vein, the Rav provided direction for the Torah community on how to address non-Jewish religious manifestations. In *Confrontation*, the first essay of the Rav's to appear in English,[8] the Rav developed the ground rules for that very delicate and potentially dangerous relationship. We need not re-articulate those positions here, but it was in keeping with those principles that the Rav took a strong stand on Vatican II. In 1960, at the time of Vatican II, the Jewish community was asked to send representatives to the Council as observers. Then, like today, there was a strong inclination in certain circles not just to go to the Vatican, but to run. The Rav was unalterably opposed to sending Jewish observers to participate in Vatican II, which was, in his view, strictly a Christian matter. Indeed, no official observers were sent.

The minute the Rav opposed it, Dr. Nachum Goldman, who was anxious to participate, withdrew rather than oppose the Rav and jeopardize the unity of the Jewish community.[9]

In 1962, the Rav had a secret meeting with Cardinal Willebrands, a Church liberal who was very friendly to Jews and very active on Vatican II, at Willebrands' request. The purpose was to discuss the possibility of a religious dialogue between Jews and Christians. The Rav rejected this notion totally, using the basic arguments which he had developed in *Confrontation*. He understood the missionary character of Christianity and its commitment to both demonstrate its truth and persuade individuals and groups to accept salvation through a Christian affirmation of faith.[10]

The RCA remained loyal to the guidelines which the Rav had set down and distinguished between theological discussions and ethical-secular concerns, which have universal validity. Every program involving either Catholic or Protestant churches in which we participated was carefully scrutinized and analyzed—we literally would go over it with a fine-toothed comb. Every topic which had possible theological nuances or implications was vetoed, and only when the Rav pronounced it to be satisfactory did we proceed to the dialogue.

Few people realize the kind of influence the Rav wielded in Israeli affairs. When I was President of the RCA, I received a call from the then-Prime Minister Begin's office asking me to receive his personal advisor on Russian affairs, who was coming to America with a special mission in which we could play a key role. The emissary arrived, and he, I, and Rabbi Israel Klavan met in the offices of the RCA. At that meeting, the emissary laid out the Israeli concern on Russian Jewish emigration, in which approximately 90% of the immigrants were opting for America. The Israelis felt that only those Jews who agreed to go directly to Israel should be allowed to emigrate, and all others should be actively discouraged. He asked us to intervene with the Rav and solicit from him a statement supporting that position. He felt that with the Rav's religious and moral authority, they would be able to sell their position to world Jewry.

I had personal reservations, but I agreed to speak to the Rav. I flew up to Boston and met with him in his study. He rejected the notion out of hand and related to me that his father, Rav Moshe, had told him during the 20's and 30's that to get a Jew out of Russia was in the category of *pidyon shevuyim* (redeeming captives) and should be undertaken at all costs. At that point, the Israeli government dropped its plan, only to revive it a number of years later.

During the Lebanon War, the Rav was terribly agitated by the situation. He felt that the Israelis had gone too far, particularly in the last phase of their operation, which involved the Christian invasion of the Palestinian camps of Sabra and Shatilla. When the question of a special commission to investigate what had happened in Sabra and Shatilla was brought before the Israeli cabinet at that time, the swing votes were in the hands of the National Religious Party; it was the Rav's insistence that the Commission be established which played a major role in the decision of the Mafdal to opt for the creation of a Commission and the results which then followed.

The Rav's position on the future of Judea and Samaria was solicited by spiritual and political leaders of every shade and description. It is true that the Rav consistently rejected the notion that the obligation to hold on to Judea and Samaria at any cost is a religious or halakhic imperative; at the same time, the Rav never said that Israel should give back all of Judea and Samaria. He insisted that the future of the territories should be determined by those who are its properly constituted authorities, in terms of the best long-term interests of the Jewish people, with the least danger to human life. Only those who are politically and militarily informed, and whose lives depend upon that decision, have the right to make that decision.

The Rav clearly had a great love for the land of Israel and a great affection for the State of Israel. He saw the State as a means to an end, as meaningful only insofar as it helps fulfill the historic destiny of what he called "the covenant of the committed." The State of Israel, dedicated to God, aware of its unique historical and political position, is an indispensable instrument of national religious fulfillment.

The Rav, in one of his addresses to the Mizrachi, said:

> You may ask, what is the attitude of Orthodoxy to the State of Israel? Certainly our attitude is positive, can it possibly be otherwise? Which faithful Jew can be against Israel? . . . But the State is but one bank of the river. . . . We admire the State with all our heart, we pray for her welfare, we send her our sons and stand united to defend her. But it is not the highest good. Our highest ideal is our faith; the basic foundation of our existence is that which is "beyond the river," which symbolizes the people in confrontation with God and its unique way of life. . . . If the question is put to us, what do you choose, a secular State of Israel . . . or the God of Israel? then it must be clearly understood that all of us, with one voice, will choose the God of Israel.[11]

The Rav himself was a card-carrying member of Agudath Israel. In 1935, he travelled to Israel, for the first and only time in his life, to try out for the position of Chief Rabbi of Tel Aviv. He made a brilliant impression with his *shiurim* and lectures, but he was not elected. The reason that was given was that he was too young. The real reason was that his great-uncle, Rav Meir Berlin, vetoed him because of his Aguda credentials.

The Rav was the star of Aguda conventions, and people flocked to hear him. For example, when Rav Chaim Ozer Grodzensky died, it was the Rav who delivered a masterful eulogy over Rav Chaim Ozer at the Aguda convention. At that time, no one questioned the Rav's credentials, and his Berlin doctorate was not a detriment to his honored position in the Agudath Israel hierarchy. However, in the forties, the Rav underwent a slow transformation, and by the fifties, he was a committed Religious Zionist. The Rav admits that his "links with Mizrachi grew gradually," that he had his "doubts and reservations about the validity of the Mizrachi approach," and that his decision ran counter to his family tradition.[12] But the Rav made his decision firmly on behalf of Mizrachi. He was impressed by its achievements. He was convinced that "from the point of view of history, Religious Zionism had saved the honor of religious Jews." It had created "a network of schools in which *Bnei Akiva Yeshivot* and *Hesder Yeshivot* are the crown; it has insured the unity of the Jewish people by making matters of personal status answerable to the Rabbinate and excluding civil marriage." The Rav recognized this and affirmed that without the pioneering efforts of Mizrachi, the "yeshiva world" could not have transplanted itself to the land of Israel in the aftermath of the Holocaust.[13]

> However, to our great sorrow, while the Tribes of God thousands of years ago finally admitted Joseph's righteousness and begged his forgiveness . . . today, a segment of our brethren still lack the capacity to see reality as it is and the courage to admit their error. Even today, after Treblenka and Auschwitz—as assimilation putrefies a great portion of Diaspora Jewry and the State of Israel is occupied in protecting the Jewish settlement from the Arab Amalek—they hold fast against their brother Joseph (Religious Zionists) "and they viewed him from a distance."

It goes without saying that the Rav did not always agree with positions and actions taken by the Mafdal;[14] nor was he above levelling his criticisms when they were warranted, in his opinion. Nonetheless, the Rav supported Religious Zionism with great consistency, re-affirmed his faith in its historical validity, hailed its enduring achievements on behalf of religious Jewry and, to the end, never wavered in his commitment to the movement.

The Rav's multifaceted personality, unfortunately, lends itself to distortion and revisionism. The process has already begun, and many of those who presume to speak in his name sometimes do him a great disservice. The Rav was, throughout his lifetime, the teacher of Torah par excellence, and all of his involvements were simply reflections of that commitment. At the same time, he was, like other *gedolei Yisrael,* no recluse, and his impact was felt in many directions. To picture him in any other light is to distort reality. Never, then, has it been more important to place the Rav, his life and his contributions in historical perspective. This is a humble, but sincere attempt in that direction.

Notes

1. Cf. *Midrash Rabbah, Kohelet,* I,5.
2. Cf. L. Bernstein, *Challenge and Mission,* pp. 51-64.
3. Cf. B. Litvin, *The Sanctity of the Synagogue,* p. 110.
4. *Ibid.,* p.115.
5. *Ibid.,* p.141.
6. *The Jewish Day,* November 19, 1954.
7. Cf. Bernstein, *Challenge and Mission,* p.56, where Bernstein quotes a letter from the Rav to Rabbi Theodore Adams, *z"l,* on August 11, 1953.
8. *Tradition,* vol. VI, pp.5-29.
9. Cf. Bernstein, *Challenge and Mission,* p.206, for the background.
10. Based on an article written by Dr. Hillel Seidman, in the *Morning Journal* at the time.
11. *The Rav Speaks,* pp.116-117.
12. *Ibid.,* pp.34-36.
13. *Ibid.,* p.32.
14. *Ibid.,* pp.9 and 185-186.

Rabbi Joseph B. Soloveitchik: The Early Years

AARON RAKEFFET-ROTHKOFF

RABBI JOSEPH DOV HALEVI SOLOVEITCHIK was born in Pruzhan, Poland on 12 Adar, 5663 (1903). His father, Rabbi Moshe Soloveichik (1878-1941), was the scion of a preeminent Lithuanian rabbinical family which traced itself back to Reb Chaim Volozhin (1749-1821), the leading disciple of the Vilna Gaon. Reb Chaim Volozhin organized the Ets Hayyim Yeshiva in Volozhin in 1802. This school achieved renown as the leading Talmudic academy of the nineteenth century until its forced closure by the Russian government in 1892. Rabbi Joseph Soloveitchik's paternal grandfather was Reb Chaim Soloveitchik (1853-1918), who was widely known as "Reb Chaim Brisker" since he served as the rabbi of Brisk (Brest-Litovsk). Previously, Reb Chaim Soloveitchik had been on the faculty of the Volozhin Yeshiva, where his wife's grandfather, Rabbi Naftali Tsevi Yehuda Berlin (1817-1893) was the *rosh haYeshiva*. Reb Chaim had radically changed talmudic study with his introduction of what became known as the "*Brisker* Method." This approach was characterized by its insistence on incisive analysis, exact classification, critical independence, and emphasis on Maimonides' *Mishne Torah* as the focal point of rabbinic research.[1]

Rabbi Rakeffet-Rothkoff is Professor of Responsa Literature at the Yeshiva University Gruss Institute in Jerusalem.

Rabbi Joseph Soloveitchik's mother was Pesia Feinstein (1880-1967), the daughter of Rabbi Elijah Feinstein (1842-1929), the spiritual leader of Pruzhan and author of *Halikhot Eliyahu*. "Reb Elya Pruzhaner," as he was popularly known, was also the uncle of Reb Moshe Feinstein (1895-1986), who later became the leading *posek* of American Jewry.[2] In conformity with the conventions of Torah society in those days, Reb Moshe Soloveichik was supported by his father-in-law during the initial years following his marriage. The young couple resided in the Feinstein home in Pruzhan, where Reb Moshe immersed himself in study. This period was described decades later by his son:

> Maimonides was a constant guest in our home. During the days when my father was a newlywed, supported by my grandfather, the pious *ga'on* Rabbi Elijah Feinstein of Pruzhan, father studied Torah day and night. A small group of outstanding young scholars gathered around him and eagerly absorbed his teachings. My father studied with his disciples in the salon where my bed was located. My wont was to sit on my bed and listen to my father's words. He constantly quoted Maimonides. His method was to first open the Talmud and analyze the text under discussion and the relevant commentaries. He would generally say: "These are the explanations of Rabbi Isaac of Dampierre and the other authors of *Tosafot*. Now, let us analyze the explanations of Maimonides."[3]

At the age of thirty-one, Reb Moshe was elected to succeed the late Rabbi Alexander Moses Lapidot (1819-1906) as the spiritual leader of Rossiyeny, Lithuania. Rabbi Lapidot, a student of Rabbi Israel Salanter (1810-1883), was renowned both for his scholarship and his public activities on behalf of the nascent Zionist movement. In Rossiyeny, Reb Moshe also organized a yeshiva in which he was aided by Rabbi Nathan Zvi Finkel (1849-1927), the founder and guiding spirit of the Slobodka Yeshiva. The latter sent some of his best students to Reb Moshe with the expectation that they would master the Volozhin-Brisk method of Talmudic exposition under his tutelage.

Reb Moshe became the rabbi of Chaslovitz, White Russia, in 1913. The local Jewish community consisted of a large number of Lubavitcher Hasidim, many of whom also became devotees of Reb Moshe. He was to remain there until 1921, and in this city he endured the tribulations of World War One. Reb Moshe remained with his community and was a constant source of support during these difficult years.

The young Joseph Soloveitchik spent his formative years in Chaslovitz. Here, at the local *heder*, he came under the influence of a *melamed*, Reb Baruch Reisberg, who was a Lubavitcher Hasid. That year, the young Soloveitchik learned more about the *Tanya*, the focal classic of *Habad* Hasidic literature, than about the Talmud. The influence of this gifted teacher and the study of the *Tanya* were to remain with the Rav (as Rabbi Joseph Soloveitchik became popularly known) for decades to come. It introduced the youngster to the disciplines of Hasidic thought, philosophy and theology. This period in his life was thus described by his son-in-law, Rabbi Aharon Lichtenstein:

> For the better part of a year, young Soloveitchik's Talmudic progress was impeded while the study of *Tanya* accompanied by enthralling stories of Hasidic lore proceeded merrily apace. While Rav Moshe was somewhat slow to detect the true state of affairs, his wife—herself the learned daughter of an outstanding rabbinic scholar—was more perceptive. Detecting the slow rate of growth in her son's Talmudic knowledge, she prodded Rav Moshe to remedy the situation. Failing to obtain proper satisfaction, she finally complained to Rav Haym and upon the family's next visit to Brisk, the budding scholar was duly examined and found wanting. The result was that Rav Haym recommended that Rav Moshe henceforth take personal charge of his son's Talmudic education, and it was from that day that the period of rigorous mutual study dated.[4]

With his father, the young Soloveitchik studied the following Talmudic tractates: *Bava Kama, Bava Metsia, Bava Batra, Sanhedrin, Shevuot, Makkot, Gittin, Kidushin, Nedarim, Nazir, Sota, Zevahim, Menahot, Me'ila, Bekhorot, Temura, Kelim, Oholot, Yadayim, Berakhot, Pe'a, Terumot, Ma'aser Sheni,* and *Bikkurim.*[5] During these studies, the youngster developed innovative approaches and novellae to explain difficult Talmudic and Maimonidean passages. Reb Moshe later sent a notebook of these insights to his father, Reb Chaim. The latter was overwhelmed with his grandson's precocious abilities and predicted that he would be a major source of Torah illumination for the next generation.[6]

The well known Rabbi of Kovno and the author of the *Devar Avraham*, Reb Avraham Dovber Kahana-Shapiro (1870-1943), was later to write:

> The spirit of his illustrious grandfather, the leading rabbi of his time, Rabbi Chaim Soloveitchik, rests upon Rabbi Joseph Dov Soloveitchik. Just like his grandfather, he also is a master of the entire range of Talmudic literature. . . . Happy is the country that will be privileged to be the home of this great sage. The sages have ordained him to be the true interpreter of all religious problems, and the halakha shall always be in accordance with his rulings.[7]

During this span of time, the young Soloveitchik did not engage in formal secular studies. However, he acquired a life-long taste for literature from his mother, who led him from fairy tales to the works of Aleksandr Pushkin (1799-1837), Mikhail Lermontov (1814-1841), Henrik Johan Ibsen (1828-1906), and Chaim Nachman Bialik (1873-1934). In his late teens, the Rav acquired the equivalent of a gymnasium education from a series of tutors.[8] While still in his parents' home in Warsaw, the Rav entered the local Free Polish University in 1924. Here he spent three terms studying political science. For the first time, the Rav was exposed to the serious study of secular disciplines.

In 1926, at the age of twenty-three, the Rav commenced his studies at the University of Berlin. Here he majored in philosophy and was attracted to the neo-Kantian school. The Rav formally received his doctorate in 1932 after the acceptance of his dissertation on Hermann Cohen's epistemology and metaphysics.[9] The latter was a German Jewish philosopher (1842-1918) who taught at the University of Marburg. Cohen brought about a new interpretation of Kant's philosophy which came to be known as the "Marburg School of Neo-Kantianism." Cohen stressed the supremacy of the mathematical and scientific (especially the physical) interpretation of reality. The Rav retained an interest in mathematics and physics during the ensuing decades and utilized this approach in many of his philosophical lectures and writings. The Rav's dissertation was entitled: "*Das reine Denken und die Seinskonstituierung bei Hermann Cohen*" ("The source of pure knowledge and the foundations of reality [in the philosophical system] of Hermann Cohen").

Originally, the topic that the Rav wished to write his doctoral dissertation on was "Maimonides and Plato." Its thesis was to have been that general Maimonidean scholarship had erred in seeing Maimonides as a confirmed Aristotelian. However, since there was no one in the University's department of philosophy qualified to supervise such a thesis, it never went beyond the planning stage.[10]

In Berlin, the young Soloveitchik sought out other devotees and interpreters of Torah Judaism. Among his contemporaries at the University was Rabbi Menachem Mendel Schneersohn (1902-1994), who was to succeed his late father-in-law as the Lubavitcher Rebbe in 1950. Decades later, in 1980, the Rav was to attend the public hasidic gathering (*Farbrengen*) in honor of the Rebbe's thirtieth anniversary as the head of Lubavitch. During the 1926-1927 academic year, the Rav also attended classes at the Berlin Rabbinical Seminary for the training of Orthodox rabbis, which was founded by Rabbi Azriel Hildesheimer (1820-1899) in 1873.[11] Here he gained insights into German Orthodoxy, which had inscribed "Torah and *Derekh Erets*" or "Torah and Civilization" on its banner. The most profound intellectual relationship that the Rav forged in Berlin was with Rabbi Chaim Heller (1878-1960). The latter was a unique Torah scholar who combined vast erudition of the traditional type in rabbinic literature with a thorough competence in modern methods of textual research. Rabbi Heller established an advanced yeshiva, the *Bet haMedrash ha-Elyon,* in Berlin. The goal of this institution was to combine intensive study of classic rabbinic literature with a modern scientific approach towards research in Bible and Talmud. Although the Rav was never a formal student in Rabbi Heller's school, the young man became a disciple of Rabbi Heller and their relationship developed into a paternal bond. Decades later, the Rav's hesped of Reb Chaim Heller was to be widely acclaimed as one of his most seminal and creative expositions in the disciplines of homiletics and theology.[12]

A contemporary thus described his memories of a frequent Berlin street scene during this period:

> In those years one could frequently encounter three men walking along the streets of Berlin who stood out even amongst Berlin's Jewry, which was certainly not short of eminent personalities. The three men were Joseph Dov Soloveitchik with Professor [Eugen] Mittwoch (1876-1942), an Orthodox Jew and a distinguished Orientalist, and with Rabbi Chaim Heller, one of the great scholars of his time; sometimes accompanied by Rabbi Dr. [Yehiel Jacob] Weinberg (1885-1966), rector of the Hildesheimer Rabbinical Seminary.[13]

While in Berlin, the Rav also displayed sensitivity towards manuscripts and the establishment of proper texts. While the Vilna Gaon (1720-1797) made this science one of the touchstones of his method of study, it was generally neglected in the yeshiva method of study. The Rav was cited four times in the *Avodat ha-Melekh* for having checked ancient manuscripts in the Berlin libraries for their variant textual readings. The Rav's uncle, Rabbi Menachem Karakowski (d. 1929), authored the *Avodat haMelekh* on Maimonides' *Mishne Torah.* This volume was unique in rabbinic circles, since it combined the traditional yeshiva approach with a keen appreciation for correct textual structure.[14]

Rabbi Soloveitchik married Tonya Lewit (1904-1967) in 1931. Her backround was similar to that of her husband in that she was raised in Vilna and sought higher education in Western Europe. She was the recipient of a Ph.D. in education from Jena University and was to ably assist her husband in all his endeavors until her death. In 1932, the young couple, together with their first-born child, emigrated to the United States. The Rav's family had already arrived in the United States, where his father, Reb Moshe Soloveichik, had headed the Talmudic faculty of the Rabbi Isaac Elchanan Theological Seminary in the Washington Heights section of Manhattan since 1929. (This school was popularly known as the "Yeshiva" and was to evolve into Yeshiva University in 1945.)

The Immigration Act of 1924 provided for any person who had been a "minister of any religious denomination, or professor of a college, academy, seminary, or university" to enter the United States "solely for the purpose of continuing this vocation."[15] In accordance with these guidelines, the Hebrew Theological College of Chicago, at the request of the Union of Orthodox Rabbis, enabled the emigration of the Rav and his immediate family. However, due to the financial difficulties engendered by the Depression, the school could not afford to engage the Rav. Rabbi Oscar Z. Fasman, later the president of the Hebrew Theological College (1946-1964), described this march of events:

> Indeed, to preserve an interesting note in history, I record that Rabbi Joseph Dov Soloveitchik, who is considered the leading international Orthodox authority, was brought to this country with immigration papers issued by the Hebrew Theological College; upon his arrival at Ellis Island in 1932, however, my alma mater sent word to the Union of Orthodox Rabbis that it

was unable to pay his salary, and a position on the East Coast should be found for him.[16]

A few months after his arrival, the younger Soloveitchik was invited to become rabbi of the *Va'ad ha'Ir* of Boston, Massachusetts. This fellowship, which united many of the Orthodox Boston synagogues, was dedicated to sustaining Torah study and observance on the communal scene. The *Va'ad ha'Ir* (later succeeded by the *Chevra Shas* of Boston) engaged the Rav and brought him to Boston, which was to remain his home throughout the rest of his life. The Rav's main responsibilities were to provide spiritual leadership for the community and to deliver discourses in the various synagogues at the appropriate occasions. He was installed in his new position on December 11, 1932 by Rabbi Eliezer Silver (1881-1968), the president of the Union of Orthodox Rabbis.[17]

The Rav was soon caught up in the vexations and burdensome quests of the American Orthodox rabbinate of that period. Boston had long experienced controversy among its rabbis in the area of kashrut supervision.[18] The new rabbi not only endured these difficulties, but also encountered the resentment of some of the elder rabbis in the greater Boston area because of his attempts to establish higher kashrut standards and more humane working conditions for the *shohatim*. There was also opposition to the Rav's upgrading of the kashrut standards by the proprietors of the kosher meat and poultry industries, who resented the extra costs incurred by implementing Rabbi Soloveitchik's regulations. This simmering resentment later became a source of acute pain and distress for the Rav. In 1939, the Rav acceded to the requests of the representatives of the poultry *shohatim* that he reorganize their association. The *shohatim* were being exploited by meager wages and long hours. Some worked twenty-four hours at a stretch, and under these conditions, their slaughter rituals could not be executed properly.

As part of his reform of the *shehita* process in Boston, the Rav insisted on the use of kosher bands or rings on the poultry slaughtered by the reorganized *shohatim* under his supervision. These bands not only indicated that the poultry was kosher, but also minimized the possibility of fabrications. The expense of these bands (one cent per foul) was to be borne by the proprietors and not the consumers. In 1941, accusations were made against the Rav that he was personally reaping monetary gain from this system at the expense of the Jewish community. In addition, the Rav was accused of tax evasion in hiding this income. These charges were brought to the attention of the Attorney-General of the Commonwealth of Massachusetts, Robert T. Bushnell. At his behest, Judge Abraham K. Cohen was requested to serve as the investigator into these charges. After a fourteen–month meticulous investigation and examination of the entire kosher poultry industry, the Judge totally cleared the Rav. With a sense of deep indignation, Judge Cohen declared that the charges against Rabbi Soloveitchik were totally untrue and "sheer fabrications." Cohen declared that "those who originated [the charges] knew that they were unfounded. The evil rumors were spread with malice and the Rabbi was dreadfully abused and baselessly accused." The Judge declared that the general kashrut situation in Boston was a "disgrace to its Jewish community." The Judge cited a letter from Swift and Company which declared that during the nine years that Rabbi Soloveitchik supervised their kosher production, it was carried out with "scrupulous integrity, unquestioned probity and rare efficiency."

In a letter to Rabbi Herbert S. Goldstein (1890-1970), a prominent New York rabbi, Judge Cohen summarized his conclusions by declaring:

> I feel, however, that it is not improper for me to say to you that the report embodying the results of the investigation very specifically clears Rabbi Soloveitchik of the charges thus made and, on the contrary, commends him for his honesty of purpose

> and the order which he brought out of the chaos which existed when he undertook the supervison of the slaughter of kosher poultry and the marketing thereof. He did not have the supervision of the slaughtering of kosher cattle except in a very small extent. He did not participate in any "racket" and, on the contrary, served the community in connection with the slaughter of poultry without any compensation to him whatsoever.[19]

On November 3, 1943, Judge A. K. Cohen addressed the Greater Boston Rabbinical Asociation regarding the local kashrut situation. His address was thus summarized by the Boston Jewish Advocate:

> 1. The Judge, with a sense of deep indignation, stated that the charges against Rabbi Soloveitchik were utterly untrue; that, morever, his accusers knew that they were unfounded and made them in malice with the intent to harm his reputation.
>
> 2. That there are some individuals without scholarship and even less character who assume wrongfully the title of Rabbi. Such persons acquire a small organization, call it a Synagogue and obtain for themselves official status. Being untrained, undisciplined and irresponsible, they are in no way prepared to serve the needs of the community.
>
> 3. Before Rabbi Soloveitchik assumed the supervision of the slaughtering of kosher poultry, the Shochtim were definitely exploited. The hours were unduly long (some toiling 24 hours a stretch), their salaries minimal. Rabbi Soloveitchik was then invited to put order into the chaos. The Rabbi agreed to do so provided that kosher bands were used, since the Rabbi, as well as others in our community, knew that an enormous amount of misrepresentation was practiced. After Rabbi Soloveitchik undertook this task, the living conditions of the Shochtim were considerably improved and the standard of Kashruth raised. They began to receive a living wage and began to work decent hours.

> 4. The expense of the bands (one cent per fowl) was borne by the proprietors of the slaughterhouses and not by the consumers. All monies obtained from the sale of these bands, approximately $15,000 a year, were spent on the purchase of the bands, Mashgichim (ritual supervisors), on aiding Orthodox rabbis who were in need, sick benefits, etc. Rabbi Soloveitchik did not obtain even one cent from these monies. The financial statement published by the Shochtim in the "Jewish Advocate" in May 1941 was correct in all details.

Despite his total vindication by the Judge's report, the personal strain engendered by the false accusations and the lengthy investigation greatly influenced the Rav's public posture during the ensuing decades. At times he instinctively shied away from public controversy and unnecessary pronouncements which could provoke dissent.[20] Following these events, the Rav made the study and teaching of Torah the focal point of his life and minimized his involvement with kashrut supervision. He would often cite this change in his priorities as the blessing that resulted from these tribulations. He declared that this investigation taught him that kashrut supervision was not the area to which he should devote his main energies. It was rather with the study and teaching of Torah that he should preoccupy himself.[21]

In Boston, the Rav was also introduced to the ignorance of the American Jewish community. Coming from Europe, his initial encounters with the Jewish illiteracy of the average American Jew were at times shocking for him. Reminiscing years later, he would regale audiences with his description of the first wedding he officiated at in Boston. The groom did not know whether he was a *Cohen, Levi,* or *Yisrael*. At other times, the Rav would describe the synagogue president who would unfold a newspaper and study the latest financial information while *Megilat Ester* was being read in the synagogue on the night of *Purim*.[22]

Rabbi Soloveitchik's main achievements in Boston were in the area of Torah education. In 1937 he founded the Maimonides

School, which was the first Jewish day school in the greater New England area. It began with six students, and its first real location was at the Young Israel of Roxbury. There was much opposition to the new school by the great majority of Boston Jewry, who considered it "a return to the ghetto!"[23] The early years of the new school were also filled with daily difficulties. At times, the initial class continued its studies in the Soloveitchik home. Rabbi William Millen, a member of the first class, later recalled that the heating system of the Young Israel of Roxbury routinely broke down. When this happened, the students marched through the New England chill to the warmth of the nearby Soloveitchik home. The Rav and his wife "opened their door and their hearts to the pupils. The children huddled on the living room sofa, and learning resumed. Nothing seemed different," Rabbi Millen declared. "The kids smiled and Rabbi Bernstein continued with his lesson. We couldn't fully appreciate the Herculean task that the Rav undertook with the kind of love that he gave to it."[24]

During the initial years of Maimonides, it was only the indomitable spirit and vision of the Rav and his wife that enabled the school to take root. Dr. Atarah Soloveitchik Twersky later recalled that her father "appreciated those people who gave money, but he was much more appreciative of those who sent their children to the school. To send a child to an unknown and unproven school was an act of faith. One stood to lose more than money. Here you were risking the education of a child."

The Rav emerged as a visible force in the fund-raising arena for Maimonides. Mr. Joseph Abelow recalled how his father, Rabbi Leo Abelow (who was a committee member of the *Va'ad ha'Ir* which brought the Rav to Boston and was later the President of the *Chevra Shas*), joined the Rav in fund-raising missions for the school. "I was always waiting for my father to come home from going with the Rav collecting money. When a major gift came in, there was much glee. It was like a Yom Tov festival."

Mrs. Dorothy Greenwald, a Maimonides parent, recalled how

Mrs. Tonya Soloveitchik also fought tenaciously to collect funds for the school. "She solicited a contribution from someone who four or five times had refused. Asked why she would go back, she responded: 'I didn't do it for myself, I did it for the school!' That person finally contributed large sums."

Dr. Twersky explained that what appeared to be fund-raising savvy was actually hard work for her parents. "They were not natural-born fund-raisers. They had to go beyond their natural proclivities in doing this." It became a labor of love.

Assisted by his adherents, the Rav forged ahead and the Maimonides student body increased. The school accommodated the influx of new students by relocating from the Young Israel of Roxbury to the Adams Estate at the corner of Washington Street and Columbia Road in Dorchester, which was purchased in the early 1940's. The school now had six grades. In 1947, Maimonides moved ahead with the addition of the seventh and eight grades. In 1950, the High School division opened. By now the Adams Estate was too small, and after its sale, the school was housed in two buildings in Roxbury: The former Menorah Hebrew School on Elm Hill Avenue and the dilapidated Otisfield Street Hebrew School a few blocks away. In 1959, Maimonides purchased its four-acre campus on Philbrick Road in Brookline. The staggered relocation to the modern new facility was completed in 1964, when the elementary wing also reopened there.

Not only was the Rav the guiding force of the religious studies curriculum, but he also instituted modifications in the daily functioning of Maimonides. To ensure that the pupils learned to pray properly, he insisted that the school day begin with the morning *Shaharit* prayers, rather than save time by having the children pray at home. The Rav instituted formal classes on *Hol haMoed Sukkot* to provide an opportunity for children from non-observant homes to eat in a *sukka* and fulfill the mitsvah of *lulav* and *etrog*. Yearly, on *Erev Yom Kippur*, the Rav addressed the High School students on the subject of *teshuva* (repentance) and then *davened* the special *Erev Yom Kippur Minha* prayer with them. The Rav also pioneered in the Torah education of women and included the study of Talmud in their curriculum. For many years, the Rav would devote Friday mornings to classroom visits at Maimonides. Thus, during the decades, the guiding hand of the Rav shaped Maimonides as it expanded its activities and influence. The school gradually became the focal institution for Orthodox Judaism in the greater Boston area.

At the urging of his father, Reb Moshe Soloveichik, the Rav also organized an advanced institution called Heichal Rabenu Haym Halevi and Yeshivath Torath Israel in 1939 to accommodate the influx of erudite European yeshiva students who were reaching American shores. The Rav delivered advanced Talmudic lectures to these select students and also arranged for the new immigrants to be tutored in the English language. Rabbi Bernard Revel (1885-1940), the president of the Yeshiva, sent a group of the leading arrivals to Boston to study under the tutelage of Rabbi Soloveitchik. Agreement was reached between Rabbis Revel and Soloveitchik for the Heichal to function as a branch of the Rabbi Isaac Elchanan Theological Seminary. In a subsequent letter to Revel, the Rav thus described the study schedule at the Heichal:

> At 7:30 a.m. morning prayers are held; between 9 to 10:30 a.m. the English language is studied; from 11 a.m. to 2 p.m. the first Talmud study period is held; and from 3 p.m. to 7 p.m., the second Talmud study session takes place.
>
> My lectures are delivered to the students twice a week, on Mondays and Thursdays.

The Heichal might well have developed into a postgraduate Boston branch of the New York Yeshiva. However, upon the deaths of Rabbis Revel and Moshe Soloveichik and Rabbi Joseph Soloveitchik's subsequent appointment to succeed his father as the Yeshiva's senior *rosh yeshiva,* the Boston branch was soon terminated.[25] An attempt was later made by Rabbi Yehiel Michal Feinstein to continue an advanced Torah postgraduate school in Boston. The latter, who was the nephew of Rabbi Moshe Feinstein, later became the son-in-law of the Rav's uncle, Rabbi Yitschak Zev Soloveitchik (1886-1960). This Boston institution functioned for a limited period, until Reb Yehiel Michal joined his uncle at Mesivtha Tifereth Jerusalem in New York.[26]

The Rav journeyed to Palestine in 1935, where he was a candidate for the position of Ashkenazic Chief Rabbi of Tel Aviv. During his visit, he delivered Talmudic lectures and philosophical discourses at many of the advanced Torah and educational institutions which then existed in the *yishuv*. The Rav was yet able to meet the Ashkenazic Chief Rabbi of Palestine, Avraham Yitshak haCohen Kook (1865-1935), who died later that year. The Rav's discourse in Jerusalem's Yeshivat Mercaz haRav, which Rabbi Kook had established, was thus described by Rabbi Moshe Tsevi Neria, then a student in the school:

> The Torah community of Jerusalem was privileged to a day of spiritual contentment and joy. One's heart skipped a beat upon seeing the announcements that Rabbi Yosef Dov haLevi Soloveitchik would deliver a lecture in Yeshivat Mercaz haRav. Immediately, the memory of Volozhin came to mind in all its glory and renown. As the years pass, the reputation of Volozhin only intensifies and we are awed by the achievements of this exalted Torah institution.
>
> This chain of tradition now continues. It has passed from the Bet haLevi, the first Reb Yosef Baer, to his son, Reb Chaim of Brisk. It has continued with Reb Moshe Soloveichik, and now we are greeting his son, our distinguished guest, the young *gaon*, Reb Yosef Baer.
>
> The day of the lecture, many assembled at Mercaz haRav. Among them were the elder scholars, who saw the Volozhin

> Yeshiva in its glory. With them were the younger generation from the old Etz Chaim Yeshiva and the new Hebron Yeshiva. These are students of students of the Netsiv [Rabbi Naphtali Tsevi Yehuda Berlin] of Volozhin. All wanted to ascertain whether the Brisker grandson was truly the heir to this intellectual dynasty. . . .
>
> The Rosh Yeshiva, Rabbi Yaakov Moshe Charlop (1883-1951), a native Jerusalemite, entered the auditorium. Following him was a tall young man with a large forehead, a black beard and dark eyes. One could sense that he was engrossed in his own deep thoughts.
>
> The Rosh Yeshiva delivered a few words of introduction and then the guest began his discourse. To the august audience he declared that "I am not here on my own merits, but because of the merits of my distinguished ancestry." The discourse then began with questions on the Talmudic text and the Maimonidean codification. The terminology was that of Reb Chaim and the audience was totally caught up in this intellectual exposition. About one of his elucidations, the lecturer remarked: "I believe that I heard this concept from my grandfather." Yes, we also felt that we were hearing Reb Chaim lecture that day. After the lecturer's questions came a brilliant, logical and clear analysis. New concepts and explanations were introduced and gradually all the questions were resolved.
>
> The lecturer held the audience spellbound for over an hour and a half. In truth, the "House of Levi" (Bet haLevi) did not disappoint our greatest expectations that memorable day![27]

Some of the activists in the Tel Aviv community considered the Rav too young at the time. His father attempted to alleviate these fears in a letter he wrote to Rabbi Yaakov Bauminger, the secretary of the Religious Council of Tel Aviv. Reb Moshe declared:

> I have heard that it is said that my son is too young. First, this is not true. He is between thirty and forty years. In the previous generations, those possessing outstanding abilities were already appointed to the most illustrious and influential rabbinical positions at such an age. They soon became the leading rabbis of their times. The elder rabbis coexisted with their younger colleagues in love and brotherhood and they honored one the other.[28]

Nevertheless, it was Rabbi Moshe Avigdor Amiel (1883-1946) who was chosen. Then in his prime, Rabbi Amiel was a prominent Mizrachi ideologist and the rabbi of Antwerp, Belgium.[29]

This 1935 journey was to be the Rav's only visit to the Holy Land. Following his return to Boston, the Rav intensified his local rabbinical activities. He also became more active in the Union of Orthodox Rabbis of the United States and Canada. As an honorary officer of the organization, he aided in adjucating rabbinical disputes in both the United Sates and in Canada. Together with Rabbis Eliezer Silver of Cincinnati and Bernard Levinthal (1865-1952) of Philadelphia, the Rav formed a committee which investigated an ongoing kashrut dispute in New York City. On April 26, 1939, the rabbis issued guidelines for good relations between the local rabbis in the areas of poultry and meat supervision.[30] In 1940, the Rav joined with Rabbis Israel Rosenberg (1875-1956) and Silver, members of the presidium of the Union of Orthodox Rabbis, in visiting Toronto. There they stressed the urgency for the Toronto rabbis to form a local unified rabbinic group. This body was to have sole jurisdiction over all the *gittin* administered within Toronto. They were also to attempt to regulate the local marriage ceremonies so that only qualified personnel would perform them. The visiting rabbis also issued detailed guidelines for enhanced kashrut supervision in the greater Toronto community.[31]

In the midst of these activities, the Rav's father, Rabbi Moshe Soloveichik, died, on January 31, 1941. The Rav was soon to succeed his father as the senior faculty member of the Rabbi Isaac Elchanan Theological Seminary of Yeshiva University in New York. With this appointment, a new epoch was to begin for the Rav and for Torah Judaism in the Western Hemisphere.

Notes

The author wishes to thank Joseph Epstein for his extensive editorial assistance in preparing this manuscript for publication.

1. For the background of the Soloveitchik family, see Shmuel Kalman Mirsky, "Yeshivat Volozhin," *Mosedot Torah beIropa* (New York: Histadrut Ivrit of America, 1956), pp. 1-86, and Eliezer Leoni, *"Toledot Yeshivat Etz Hayyim beVolozhin veRosheha,"* (Tel Aviv: Irgunim Shel Benei Volozhin, 1970), pp. 77-187.

   For the biography of Rabbi Moshe Soloveichik, see Aharon Ben-Zion Shurin, *Keshet Giborim* (Jerusalem: Mossad Harav Kook, 1964), pp. 200-206.

   For the biography of Rabbi Joseph Soloveitchik, see Aharon Lichtenstein, "Rabbi Joseph Soloveitchik," in *Great Jewish Thinkers of the Twentieth Century*, ed. Simon Noveck (Clinton, Mass.: Bnai Brith Department of Adult Jewish Education, 1963), pp. 281-297; and Hillel Goldberg, Between Berlin and Slobodka (Hoboken, N.J.: KTAV Publishing House, 1989), pp. 89-113.

   Rabbi Soloveitchik was also called Joseph Baer since "Baer" was the Yiddish version of the Hebrew "Dov." Many Yeshiva University press releases referred to him as Rabbi Joseph B. Soloveitchik. While he spelled his last name with a "t" in the middle, his father Reb Moshe omitted the "t."

   For an analysis of Reb Chaim Soloveitchik's "Brisker Method," see Shelomo Yosef Zevin, *Ishim veShitot* (Tel Aviv: Bitan haSefer, 1952), pp. 43-70.
2. Shimon Finkelman and Nosson Scherman, *Reb Moshe* (New York: Artscroll History Series, 1986), pp. 28-29.
3. Joseph Dov haLevi Soloveitchik, *Ish haHalakha: Galuy veNistar* (Jerusalem: The Department for Torah Education and Culture in the Diaspora of the World Zionist Organization, 1979), pp. 230-231.
4. "R. Joseph Soloveitchik," in *Great Jewish Thinkers of the Twentieth Century*, pp. 282-283.
5. This list was detailed by the Rav in his *Yahrtseit* lecture in memory of his father which was delivered on January 11, 1970 at Yeshiva University. In

the published version of this lecture, this list is omitted. See *Shiurim leZekher Abba Mari Zal* (Jerusalem, 1985), Vol. 2, p. 15.

6. *HaPardes, Tishrei* (October) 1932, p. 2, cited in *Mesora* (A Torah Journal published by the Kashruth Division of the Orthodox Jewish Congregations of America), No. 9 (February-*Adar*, 1994), pp. 5-6.
7. *Ibid.*, p. 7. Also see Aaron Rothkoff, *Bernard Revel: Builder of American Jewish Orthodoxy* (Philadelphia: The Jewish Publication Society of America, 1972), p. 128.
8. "R. Joseph Soloveitchik," in *Great Jewish Thinkers of the Twentieth Century*, p. 283.

   Dr. Manfred Lehman obtained a copy of a *curriculum vitae* prepared by the Rav for the University of Berlin and published it in the Bnai Brith Messenger, November 11, 1994, p. 16. In this document, the Rav states: "In 1922, I graduated from the Liberal Arts gymnasium of Dubno." After consultation with members of the Rav's family, the author has concluded that the government certification for the equivalent of a high school diploma was arranged through the Dubno school. However, the Rav did not actually attend the gymnasium. Dubno became part of Poland in 1921, the year that the Soloveichik family moved to Warsaw.

   The author was aided in coming to this conclusion by Mrs. Shulamit Meiselman of Boston, the Rav's sister, who was interviewed by Dr. Samuel Dershowitz on February 26, 1995 and by Rabbi Ahron Soloveichik of Chicago, the Rav's brother, who was interviewed by Dr. David Applebaum on February 13, 1995.

   The information regarding the Rav's attending the Free Polish University was also contained in his *curriculum vitae.* These details were confirmed by Mrs. Shulamit Meiselman and Rabbi Ahron Soloveichik.

   The Rav also asserts in his *curriculum vitae* that 1926 was the year that he came to Berlin and entered the University.
9. The title page of the dissertation reads that the degree was awarded on December 10, 1932.
10. "R. Joseph Soloveitchik," in *Great Jewish Thinkers of the Twentieth Century*, p. 285.
11. Interview with Dr. Esriel Hildesheimer, April 21, 1994. Dr. Hildesheimer was a great-grandson of the founder of the Seminary and studied there from 1931-1933. He heard about Rabbi Soloveitchik's participation from other students who studied at the Seminary at the same time.

    This information was confirmed by Dov Genachowski on April 22, 1994. His late father, Elijah Moshe Genachowski, also audited classes at the Berlin Seminary that year. When in Berlin, he roomed with the Rav, who was his companion since the time that Elijah Moshe came to Warsaw to study with Reb Moshe Soloveichik. Elijah Moshe Genachowski later was elected to the Israeli Knesset, representing the Mizrachi National Religious Party.

12. The *hesped,* entitled *"Peleitat Sofereihem,"* was published in Joseph Dov ha-Levi Soloveitchik, *Divrei Hagut veHa'arakha* (Jerusalem: The Department for Torah Education and Culture in the Diaspora of the World Zionist Organization, 1981), pp. 137-162.
13. Werner Silberstein, *My Way From Berlin to Jerusalem* (Jerusalem: Special Family Edition Published in Honor of the Author's 95th Birthday, 1994), pp. 26-27. For some reminisences of the Rav during the Berlin period, see pp. 24-26, 52-53.
14. The Rav is cited on pp. 8A, 8B, 18B, and 77B. The Rav gave Aaron Rakeffet these details in what was to be their final conversation on February 2, 1983, at Yeshiva University.

    Rabbi Karakowski was married to Badana Feinstein, a sister of the Rav's mother. He served as a member of the Vilna rabbinate and devoted his scholarship to researching the sources for the *Mishne Torah.* Only one volume of the *Avodat haMelekh* appeared. The rest of the manuscript was destroyed during the Holocaust, in which his widow perished.
15. For full details of the immigration laws, see: *Bernard Revel,* p. 210.
16. "An Orthodox Communal Leader Reminisces," in *American Jewish History,* ed. Henry L. Feingold, Vol. 69, No. 2 (December 1979), p. 160.
17. Aaron Rakeffet-Rothkoff, The *Silver Era: Rabbi Eliezer Silver and His Generation* (Jerusalem: Feldheim Publishers, 1981), p. 130.
18. Harold P. Gastwirt, *Fraud, Corruption and Holiness* (Port Washington, N.Y.: Kennikat Press, 1974), pp. 92-94; and *The Silver Era,* pp. 124-154.
19. The details of the charges and investigation of this episode in the Rav's life and the report of Judge A. K. Cohen were detailed in the English article entitled, "Judge A. K. Cohen Reports on Kashruth in Boston," published by Rabbi Joseph S. Shubow in the rabbinical journal *HaPardes,* Vol. 17, No. 10 (January 1944), pp. 23-27. See also: *The Forwards* (Yiddish daily newspaper published in New York), November 6, 1943, p. 9, and undated clippings from the *Commentator* (undergraduate newspaper of Yeshiva College) and the *Boston Jewish Advocate.* These sources were in the archives of the late Rabbi Sidney A. Gordon of Winthrop, Mass. His son, Rabbi Macy Gordon, shared them with the author. Rabbi Meir Lichtenstein, a grandson of the Rav, also made documents on this topic available to the author.

    While all the documents refer to the investigating judge as A.K. Cohen, the author was informed by Joseph Abelow of Brookline, Mass., in an interview on December 10, 1994, that the Judge's first name was

Abraham. Abelow obtained this information from the Massachusetts Judiciary.

For the biography of Rabbi Herbert S. Goldstein, see Aaron I. Reichel, *The Maverick Rabbi* (Norfolk/Virginia Beach: Donning, 1986). The letter to Rabbi Goldstein is cited in *HaPardes* (January 1944), pp. 26-27.

20. During his student days at Yeshiva University in the 1950's, the author often heard speculation by the faculty and administration in this vein to analyze the Rav's public posture. A similar thesis was proposed by Rabbi Menachem Genack in an October 29, 1994 interview with the author.

21. Interview with Dr. Tovah Soloveitchik Lichtenstein, November 10, 1994. *Cf.* The Rav's talk delivered at the Yeshiva University Rabbinic Alumni Conference on March 1, 1956. The talk was entitled, "*Kavod-Kaved*: Why I Identify with Yeshiva University."

22. *E.g.*, the story of the groom was detailed during the Tonya Soloveitchik Memorial Lecture on May 22, 1979, at Yeshiva University, and the story of the synagogue president, at the *Purim Shiur* in memory of HaRabbanit Tonya Soloveitchik, which was delivered on her *Yahrtseit*, February 24, 1983, at Yeshiva University.

23. *Legacy: Rabbi Dr. Joseph Soloveitchik and Maimonides School* (Brookline, Mass.: Maimonides School, October 1993), p. 4. All subsequent quotations and information about Maimonides School are from *Legacy*.

24. *Legacy*, p. 4. Also stressed in an interview with Dr. Meyer Weiner of Boston-Jerusalem on May 27, 1994. See also his "Letter to the Editor" in the *Jerusalem Post* on May 20, 1993.

25. For details of the Heichal, see *Bernard Revel*, pp. 213-214. The above–cited letter is dated June 1, 1940. Information about the Heichal was also conveyed by Rabbi Israel Shurin of Efrat, Israel, to Aaron Rakeffet in an interview on August 8, 1994. The former was a student in the Boston Heichal.

26. Letter from the late Rabbi Benjamin Bak of Baltimore to Aaron Rothkoff, May 20, 1965. The former was a student in the Boston Heichal.

For the Rav's analysis of the relationship between his uncle and his daughter and son-in-law during their subsequent American sojourn, see *Divrei Hagut veHa'arakha*, p. 92.

27. Written by Rabbi Moshe Tsevi Neria in 1935 and published in *HaTsofe* on April 16, 1993, p. 6.

28. Rabbi Moshe Soloveichik's letter was published at the conclusion of *Sefer haYovel liKhvod Moreinu haGaon Rav Yosef Dov Soloveitchik* (Jerusalem: Mossad Harav Kook, 1984), Vol. 1, p. 620.

29. Interview with Reb Nahum Genachowski of Tel Aviv, January 25, 1994. He related that Rabbi Meyer Berlin (Bar-Ilan; 1880-1949), the president of the World Mizrachi movement and the uncle of Reb Chaim Soloveitchik,

declared about the three leading candidates: "Rabbi Soloveitchik is the greatest scholar. Rabbi [Isaac] Herzog is the most saintly. However, Rabbi Amiel is the most suitable for the Tel Aviv community!"

30. For details of the New York dispute, see *HaPardes*, June 1939, pp. 4-5; *The Silver Era*, pp. 150-151; and *Fraud, Corruption and Holiness*, pp. 184-85.
31. For the background and details of the Toronto visit, see *HaPardes*, May 1940, pp. 6-7, and *The Silver Era*, pp. 137-139